A Prologue
to
National
Development
Planning

A PROLOGUE TO NATIONAL DEVELOPMENT PLANNING

Jamshid Gharajedaghi

IN COLLABORATION WITH
Russell L. Ackoff

Contributions in Economics and Economic
History, Number 70

Greenwood Press
New York · Westport, Connecticut · London

338.9
G411p

Library of Congress Cataloging-in-Publication Data

Gharajedaghi, Jamshid.
   A prologue to national development planning.

   (Contributions in economics and economic history,
ISSN 0084–9235 ; no. 70)
   Bibliography: p.
   Includes index.
   1. Economic policy.   2. Economic development.
I. Ackoff, Russell Lincoln, 1919–   II. Title.
III. Series.
HD87.5.G45   1986   338.9   86–9921
ISBN 0–313–25285–8 (lib. bdg. : alk. paper)

Library of Congress Catalog Card Number: 86–9921
ISBN: 0–313–25285–8
ISSN: 0084–9235

First published in 1986

Greenwood Press, Inc.
88 Post Road West
Westport, Connecticut 06881

Printed in the United States of America

The paper used in this book complies with the
Permanent Paper Standard issued by the National
Information Standards Organization (Z39.48–1984).

10 9 8 7 6 5 4 3 2 1

Contents

Tables

Figures

Preface

We have participated in so-called national development planning in a number of mostly less developed countries. None of these efforts has been successful. We were unable to bring about those changes in the governments' concepts of nation, development, and planning that we thought were necessary for success. On the other hand, we have successfully engaged in development planning with parts of governments: ministries, secretariats, agencies, and departments. We have been even more successful working in private enterprises. This book is an effort to translate what we have learned from both our successes and failures into a proposal for what we believe would be effective national development planning.

This book deals with what we think national development planning ought to be, not what it is. It focuses on philosophical, methodological, and conceptual aspects of such planning. It is not a how-to-do-it book. It tries to explain rather than instruct. Its intended output is understanding rather than know-how. It is for this reason that we call this work a prologue. We have taken this approach because we believe that most national development planning fails for lack of understanding, not knowledge. Moreover, we believe that even the most developed countries are not as developed as they might be, and this gap is also due to lack of understanding.

We have not encountered any government that has a clear and precise conception of development. Most confuse it with growth. Growth, as we will try to show, is neither necessary nor sufficient for development. Nor is development either necessary or sufficient for growth. The most developed countries seem to be unaware of this. For this reason, we believe their development has not been as much the consequence of deliberate actions as of fortuitous circumstances.

Most governments, it seems to us, have a misconception of the nature and location of the principal obstructions to development. Like Don Quixote, they attack windmills thinking they are giants. The principal obstructions to a country's development are usually taken to lie in its environment, in conditions or other countries that it cannot control. We believe to the contrary: these obstructions lie within countries and are subject to their governments' control. This is not to say that there are no external obstructions, but that they are not nearly as obstructive as those that are internal. We believe that the development of any nation depends more on what it does and does not do than on what is done to it.

It seems to us that most governments lack the will and courage required to identify and attack internal obstructions to their nations' development—for example, corruption. Attacking such obstructions is often risky political business, and most governments are risk-aversive.

Most of those governments that have produced national development plans have implemented only an insignificant portion of them. They do not hold themselves responsible for this lack of implementation but blame others. We believe these failures are due to the way they carried out their planning. Moreover, many of the governments who engage in national development planning seem to be aware that it is unlikely to have any significant effects, but they cynically engage in it because they believe it to be politically expedient.

These and other deficiencies in national development planning are addressed in this book. In Part I we attempt to remove deficiencies that arise from misconceptions of nation, development, and planning. In Part II we develop our conception of planning in detail. Finally, in Part III we identify what we believe are the principal obstructions to development and try to show how they can be converted into opportunities for development.

We do not believe that we or any other planners can plan effectively for the development of any country. Such planning can only be done participatively by those who will be directly affected by it. Professional planners should be used only to encourage and facilitate planning by those so affected.

Nor do we believe that any country can serve as an effective development model for another. Even the most developed countries appear to us to be making serious errors that should be avoided by less developed countries sincerely seeking development. They cannot afford the luxury of these errors; they must learn from them even if those who make them don't.

We are grateful to the many students who have thought through this work with us. We are also grateful for the suggestions and criticism received from our colleagues Thomas A. Cowan, Aron Katsenelinboigen, and Wladimir Sachs.

Final preparation of this manuscript was made possible by the valuable assistance of our associates and colleagues in the Busch Center, including Jack Meszaros, Ali Geranmayeh, Omid Nodoushani, Pat Brandt, and especially Joan Lonetti. They all gave their help generously and with affection. We owe them our thanks and affection in return.

Russell L. Ackoff   Jamshid Gharajedaghi

SPECIAL NOTE

This book has been a work-in-progress since 1975. It was begun when Professor Ackoff and I undertook a joint project to develop a new approach to national development planning in Iran. The first version was a project report that drew heavily upon Ackoff's previous work with the government of Mexico and his writings on systems thinking.

During the course of this project I had the opportunity to use and test the basic ideas presented in this book, particularly in the areas of rural development, health, and education in local communities in Iran. The results were very encouraging. The revolution of 1979 ended these experiments. I joined Ackoff in the Busch Center of the Wharton School and welcomed his invitation to expand and rewrite the report into a book on national development planning.

The next two versions of this work were written with Ackoff as their co-author. Many useful contributions by our colleagues in the Busch Center, especially our mentor Thomas A. Cowan, enriched the original ideas. The final version was to be co-authored by Ackoff and myself. However, due to exploding demands on his time and other personal considerations, Russ asked me to assume the responsibility for the completion of this work. I have attempted to do this with utmost care to remain loyal to the original concepts. However, there have been modifications, additions, and deletions that have not benefitted from his critical review. Therefore, I accept authorship with sole responsibility for any limitations that appear in this work.

Jamshid Gharajedaghi

Part I

Basic Concepts

The content and process of national development planning obviously depend on how the planners conceptualize nation, development, and planning. Not so obvious are the different ways these terms are conceptualized and the effects of these differences on the content and process of planning. In Chapter 1 we deal with the different ways of conceptualizing a nation; in Chapter 2, development; and in Chapter 3, planning.

1

On the Nature of Nations

Nation, of course, is a very familiar concept. However, its connotations and denotations are not always clear or shared. For example, are Puerto Rico, Granada, Singapore, and Monte Carlo nations? Because the term is not free of ambiguity we would like to make explicit the connotations and denotations we attribute to it.

Even when the meaning of nation is precisely formulated, nations as things may be conceptualized in different ways. They are commonly conceptualized either as mechanisms or organisms. There is an alternative: to conceptualize them as social systems. We will argue that there is considerable advantage to conceptualizing them in this way.

THE MEANING OF NATION

A nation is an entity that is usually very easy to identify but very difficult to define. This is reflected in the very large number of different definitions that appear in the literature. We need not dwell on these differences; for our purposes, it is sufficient to state how we use the term here:

> A nation is an autonomous social system that occupies a defined territory
> and controls or influences (a) the occupants and use of that territory and (b)
> its members, whether they occupy that territory or not.

Some of the occupants of a nation's territory may not be members of it, for example, visitors. Others, such as immigrants, may have limited membership in the system. On the other hand, not all the members of a nation need be occupants of its territory; some may be living or visiting abroad. But all its members, wherever they may be, and all its occupants, nationals or not, are subject to its control and influence.

To clarify the definition further, the meanings of *autonomy, control, influence*, and *social system* need to be made explicit.

Autonomy, Control, and Influence

To say that a nation is autonomous is to say it is self-determining or self-governing, that is, not subject to external control. However, this does not imply complete independence from other nations. A country that is not subject to external control may be subject to considerable external influence. It may depend on other nations for raw materials, capital goods, technology, markets for its products, financial aid, and even defense. Moreover, a nation may voluntarily give up some of its autonomy by joining a supranational organization such as the European Economic Community.

> One entity (A) controls the behavior, properties, or states of another (B) if the behavior of the first (A) causes (is necessary and sufficient for) the behavior, properties, or states of the other (B).

Therefore, one party controls another if the behavior of the first determines the behavior, properties, or states of the other. Since the first and second parties may be the same entity, an entity can be self-controlling. To the extent that it is, it is autonomous.

Control has a number of widely accepted properties that, nevertheless, we would like to make explicit. One party may control only part of another's behavior, and one obviously may be subject to control by a number of others. One who is subject to some control by another may exercise some control over that other. For example, the government and citizens of a democratic nation have some control over each other.

The controller and the controlled need not be persons or groups; they may be mechanisms (for example, a thermostat and a heating system), a mechanism and a purposeful entity (for example, a driver and his automobile), or two purposeful entities (for example, a parent and child).

A thermostat controls a heating system, the heating system controls room temperature, and the people who set the thermostat control both. These people exercise intentional control because they choose to do so. Control can be unintentional, for example, as when a person who takes the last reservation on an airplane prevents another from taking the same plane. A thermostat's control of a heating system is nonintentional because it cannot display choice.

The amount of control that one entity (A) has over another (B) or itself depends on the range of behavior, properties, or states of the second (B) that the first (A) can control, and the range of environments of B in which A can control them. For example, a parent may control what a child eats when he or she is at home but not when the child is visiting others. Different nations obviously have different amounts of control over their occupants and members.

To be controlled is to react to the actions of others or oneself. To be influenced is to respond to the behavior of another or oneself. In the case of control, the one controlled displays no choice; in the case of influence, the one influenced does display some. For example, a parent may control the location of an infant but only influence the location of an adult offspring.

> One entity (A) influences another (B) if the behavior of the first (A) produces (is necessary but not sufficient for) the behavior of the second (B).

One who exercises *influence* over another does not determine the behavior of the other, but increases the likelihood of that behavior. For example, what one reads may influence one's behavior, but it seldom controls it.

The amount of influence that one entity (A) has over another (B) depends on the range of behavior of the second (B) that the first (A) can influence and the range of environments in which the second can be influenced by the first. The degree of influence that one party has over another in a particular environment is the probability that the first party's behavior will produce the behavior of the second in that environment.

Influence is often exercised by promising rewards or punishment. Therefore, those who can either give others something they want or take from them something they want to retain can usually exert more influence than those who lack these capabilities. This is as true of nations as it is of individuals.

Control is often exercised by the use of force, for example, by the police or an army. To force someone to do something is to deprive them of choice.

It can now be seen that autonomy is not an absolute but a relative concept. The amount of control and influence nations exercise over each other and their respective nationals varies considerably. Nations in the Soviet bloc are less autonomous than those in the European Economic Community. Externally controlled countries may have so little autonomy that they are treated as colonies or provinces of the nation that controls them.

In essence, then, a nation consists of those things over which it can legitimately and unilaterally exercise some control. This excludes both those countries external to its territory that it controls by force and voluntary associations of nations to which it may belong. Nations do not give up any autonomy when they voluntarily associate with others even if the association can exercise some control over them. Because the association is voluntary, each member has the ability to withdraw from it at will.

Those things external to a nation that it does not control but that affect it constitute its environment. That part of its environment over which it exercises some influence is called transactional; that over which it has no influence is called contextual.

What is part of a nation or its environment may, of course, change over time because its control and influence over others, and the extent to which it controls and influences others, may increase or decrease. The nature and content of a nation and its environment are dynamic. How dynamic they are depends on both that nation's choices and those of other nations. The choices that nations make depend on how they conceptualize themselves.

ALTERNATIVE CONCEPTS OF NATIONS

How one plans for a nation depends on how one conceptualizes it. An explicitly formulated representation of a concept is a model of what is conceptualized. In planning, concepts and models of nations—not nations themselves—are manipulated. Models of nations are simplified and selectively represented in that they include only those properties and relationships that we consider relevant at the time they are formulated. What we consider to be relevant depends on our purposes. For example, a model of a nation used in transportation planning is usually quite different from one used in planning its agriculture.

Those who govern, their staffs, and those who are governed seldom explicitly formulate their concepts of a nation. Therefore, they are usually unaware of the effects of their concepts on their thinking about their nation. Their concepts may differ both in detail and in fundamental characteristics. We will argue that use of the wrong type of concept is a principal source of deficiencies in national development planning.

Although most of those who think about a nation think of it as a system, few know precisely what a system is, what different types of systems there are, and what these differences imply for system planning and management. It is to these matters that we now turn.

A *system* is an entity that consists of two or more parts that satisfy the following three conditions.

> 1. The behavior, properties, or state of each part can affect the functioning of the whole.

For example, an automobile is a system. Its engine, transmission, and distributor are among its parts. They can and often do affect the automobile's ability to perform as intended. On the other hand, a book lying on an automobile's seat does not affect its functioning and hence is not part of that automobile.

Human bodies are organisms, biological systems. Each organ can affect their health. The appendix, which is not known to have any role in the body's functioning, is so named because of this. It is added or attached to the body. If it should be found to have a function, its name would have to be changed.

The essential parts of a system are those that, when removed, preclude the system's functioning as intended. Those parts without which a system can function, but with loss of efficiency, are nonessential. For example, an automobile's engine and transmission are essential to it, but its emergency brake is not. Government is an essential part of a nation; athletic associations, however desirable, are not.

Those parts of a system whose removal increases the efficiency or the effectiveness of a system are obstructions, for example, sludge in a car's engine, a tumor in a person, and corrupt officials in a nation.

> 2. The effect of the behavior, properties, or state of each part of a system on that system depends on the behavior, properties, or state of at least one other part of that system.

Put another way, no part of a system has an independent effect on the whole; every part interacts with some of the others. For example, the way the heart affects a body depends on how the lungs are functioning. Government departments have interdependent effects on a nation. Therefore, the behavior of a system is never the sum of the actions of its parts; it is the product of their interactions.

> 3. Every possible subset of two or more parts of a system that form a subsystem can have an effect on the functioning of the system, and the behavior of each is affected by at least one other subsystem.

Therefore, subsystems interact as parts do, for example, the fuel and electrical subsystems of an automobile and the circulatory and metabolic system of human bodies. The same holds true for government departments.

In summary, a system is a whole that cannot be divided into independent parts. Three very important additional properties of systems derive from those already identified.

> A. The essential properties of a system are properties that none of its parts have.

For example, taken alone, neither an automobile's engine nor its transmission can transport us. Legs cannot walk, tongues cannot talk, and eyes cannot read. This is apparent when these parts of a body are removed from it. Similarly, no department of a government can function when separated from that government. Therefore, if a system is taken apart it loses its essential properties. A disassembled automobile cannot transport us. A disassembled body cannot live. A disassembled government cannot govern.

> B. The essential properties of each part of a system are properties that derive from its interactions with other parts. Therefore, these properties are lost when a part is separated from the system of which it is a part.

For example, a detached steering wheel steers nothing. A detached hand cannot write. A detached government—for example, one in exile—cannot govern,

C. When each part of a system, taken separately, is made to operate as efficiently as possible, the system as a whole will seldom, if ever, operate as effectively as possible.

For example, if we try to assemble the best of each part required for an automobile, regardless of make, we would not even get an automobile. The parts would not fit together. If they were forced together, they would not work well separately or collectively. Similarly, if each part of an organization, including a government, is taken separately and made to operate as efficiently as possible, the organization as a whole will not operate as effectively as possible. Nevertheless, this is just what most government officials and public administrators try to do.

Because of these properties of systems, coordination of the behavior of their parts is essential for their efficient and effective operation. The reason that the United Nations operates so poorly is that it cannot coordinate the behavior of its member nations. A system whose parts are autonomous and resist coordination is disorganized. Coordination is essential to organization.

A concept of any system, including a nation, incorporates a set of assumptions about the way its parts interact. Incorrect assumptions of this type are major obstructions to effective government. Therefore, the increasing number and seriousness of problems and crises faced by nations should make us suspect that something is fundamentally wrong with the way the interactions of their parts are modeled. The way these interactions are conceptualized depends on the type of system a society is assumed to be.

TYPES OF SYSTEMS

There are three fundamental types of systems: *mindless* (or mechanistic), *uniminded* (or organismic), and *multiminded* (or social). The failure to distinguish among these types of systems is a major source of development problems.

Mind is the ability to behave purposefully, to choose means and ends. Mindless systems are exemplified by machines. A machine's behavior is determined by external forces and its internal structure. It can display no choice, hence it is mindless. However, although it has no purpose of its own, it can serve the purposes of other systems, as an automobile serves the purposes of its driver.

The parts of a machine are also mindless, purposeless, and choiceless. Their behavior, like the machine of which they are part, is determined by external forces and their internal structure.

Uniminded systems are exemplified by such organisms as human beings. They have one mind each, hence have purposes of their own, but their parts do not. Hearts, lungs, stomachs, and so on have no purposes of their own. Uniminded systems are at least partially self-determining but are affected by, responsive to, and dependent on their environment. For this reason, they are said to be open systems, in contrast to some machines that operate with relative independence of their environment—for example, hermetically sealed clocks.

Multiminded systems are exemplified by social systems. They have purposes of their own, they contain parts that have purposes of their own, and they are generally parts of larger (containing) systems that have purposes of their own. A nation is such a system. It has purposes of its own, its parts do, and it is usually a part of a "family" of nations that also has purposes of its own.

Structural Differences among System Types

By "structure of a system" we mean the way the tasks of the whole are functionally divided among its parts and the way their behavior is coordinated to assure satisfactory task performance. The division of labor is reflected in social systems in the allocation of responsibility, and coordination, by the allocation of authority.

The structures of mechanical and organismic systems are "given," designed into them. Mechanical systems generally have no ability to restructure themselves; the functioning of their parts is not subject to change from within. They function reactively. Organismic systems have more, but limited, ability to restructure themselves. Some of their parts can assume some of the functions of other parts. Social systems can restructure themselves with virtually no constraints.

Machines are controlled from without, as an automobile is controlled by its driver. This is even true of "self-controlling" machines, for example, self-guiding missiles that are programmed by an external mind. Although an airplane may be controlled by an automatic pilot, that pilot is always controlled by a purposeful individual.

In contrast, an organism can be self-controlling and it may have virtually exclusive control over the functioning of its parts as, for example, the brain does in human beings. In social systems, both the whole and its parts are capable of self-control, and control of the whole can be assumed by one or more of its parts. It is the most difficult type of system to control from without because of the pervasive freedom of choice among its parts.

In a mechanical system, parts interact by the transmission of energy from one to another. For example, the engine of an automobile applies a force to the driving wheels through a transmission and axle. In a social system, parts interact by the transmission of information. In an organism, parts interact by transmitting either energy or information to each other.

Organisms need not be conceptualized as uniminded systems. They can be conceptualized as mechanical systems and were through much of the history of biology. Similarly, social systems can be, and commonly are, conceptualized as either mechanical or organismic systems. Such mismatches of type of system and type of conceptualization can have very serious consequences. When nations, which are social systems, are conceptualized as mechanical or organismic systems, major obstructions to their effective government and development are created.

In the discussion that follows we do not mean to imply that those who conceptualize a nation as a machine or organism mistake it for either, nor that they consciously think of it as one or the other, although they may. What we do mean to imply is that they treat it as though it were a machine or organism.

Nations Conceptualized Mechanistically

The universe was conceptualized by Newton as a machine created by God to do His work. A nation that is conceptualized similarly is conceived to have a power external to it that it is intended to serve. It has no purpose of its own; it is an instrument of its god. That god is usually a ruler who is above and untouched by the laws that apply to all those who are part of the nation. Absolute rulers, like Khomeni of the Islamic Republic, have these properties.

Those who have claimed absolute power have often justified it by also claiming some special relationship with either an all-powerful god; destiny, a determining force; or a secular god (e.g., Karl Marx) and an associated secular religion, an ideology. Ideologies are doctrines that specify both ends and means, leaving practically nothing to choice. They mechanize societies that pursue them.

Because a machine is completely subject to the will of its external controller, consent is not required of it. The driver of an automobile can run it into a wall if he so desires. For this reason, mechanical systems are the easiest to control. Therefore, those who want to maximize their power over a nation tend to treat it as a machine and try to make it behave in as machine-like ways as possible. They do this by measures such as the following.

1. By analysis they reduce the things to be done by the nation to a set of simple tasks that can be done either by machines or people who behave like machines. These tasks are designed so as to require little or no judgment. Moreover, by imposing standards, rules, and regulations on those people who perform these tasks, the amount of judgment required to perform them is even further reduced. People are then required to fit themselves to their assigned tasks, often with the aid of training. Education is equated with training, instruction. Management is equated with command. Discipline is rigorous. Individuals who do not perform well are treated as replaceable machine parts. By these means, human behavior is made to approximate conditioned responses to external stimuli.

2. Coordination and control are also reduced to simple tasks that require as little judgment as possible. Power is allocated by the one(s) with absolute power to those who require it, but they receive no more than the minimum deemed necessary for their tasks.

3. All persons except the one at the top are provided with only the information required to perform their assigned task. This information and associated instructions are passed down from above. Reasons for instructions are seldom given. The recipients are expected to follow them to the letter—"theirs is not to question why; theirs is but to do or die."

4. Horizontal communication and other forms of interaction among peers are prohibited or discouraged. This makes difficult the formulation of coalitions that oppose higher authority. All coordinating is done from above. Executive and administrative responsibilities are restricted to control and coordination of subordinates.

5. Resources other than information are also concentrated at the top and dispensed downward. The use to which allocated resources are to be put is almost always prescribed. Few if any resources are made available for discretionary use.

These measures generally induce machine-like behavior in people if any of the following conditions pertain: (1) people are educationally deprived, hence have low levels of aspiration, and are economically insecure; (2) they are persuaded that machine-like behavior is necessary to obtain personal or social objectives; and (3) they are subject to severe punishment for noncompliance with instructions from above.

Because mechanistically conceptualized social systems are inflexible, they can operate effectively only if they have a static environment or are unaffected by what goes on around them. Few contemporary nations operate under either of these conditions. Therefore, as interactions with external entities increase, and as the rates of change in their environments also increase, they are not able to maintain their effectiveness. Their rigidity precludes learning and adaptation. With decreasing effectiveness they usually retreat to an even stricter adherence to rules and regulations, thereby accelerating their deterioration.

It is apparent that many colonized and conquered nations were once treated mechanistically. Some still are. Their governments are said to be puppets. Such nations are treated as machines for either producing raw materials or products required by the dominating nation, or providing a defensive buffer against potential invaders.

Wherever and whenever human rights and freedom are curtailed, conformity is imposed and individuals are treated as expendable, the society involved is almost certain to have been or to be conceptualized mechanistically.

Nations Conceptualized as Organismic Systems

A nation conceptualized as an organism takes survival, growth, and "health," to be its principal objectives. Growth, like health, is considered to be necessary for survival. Contraction is thought to imply deterioration and eventual death. Such a nation is seen as both dependent on its environment for essential resources and subject to harm from it. If that environment changes, then an organismically conceived nation must be capable of changing itself, of learning and adapting, if it is to survive. A mechanistically conceived nation attempts to immunize itself against change rather than adapt to it.

Organismically conceived nations believe that growth is necessary but not sufficient for survival. Nothing is sufficient to avoid death, but continuity through reproduction keeps death from being "terminal." Therefore, such nations try to reproduce themselves either by creating colonies in their own image (as England did in America and Australia) or by absorbing old countries (as England did in India and Africa). Growth and reproduction were also seen as ways of bringing at least part of a nation's environment under control.

Preoccupation with growth and reproduction by one nation often exacts a cost from others. One nation's growth and expansion often occurs at the expense of others and its environment. An increasing rate of growth, sought by many nations, cannot be sustained indefinitely. Moreover, for each type of system there seems to be an optimal size beyond which a decline in efficiency and effectiveness is experienced (Boulding, 1970). History reveals that empires have become too large to govern efficiently and effectively.

Territorial control and influence over those in other territories are as much preoccupations of organismically conceived nations as they are in some organisms. Such nations tend to form packs or herds (coalitions or alliances) to facilitate their defense and, in some cases, their acts of aggression.

Unlike mechanistically conceived nations that seek a static equilibrium in changing environments, nations conceptualized as organismic systems seek a dynamic equilibrium. They operate homeostatically, adjusting the behavior and properties of their parts to maintain the state of the whole within acceptable limits.

In organismically conceived nations, such institutions as government, industry, and the military are thought of as organs, each of which has a responsibility for one or more functions necessary for national survival or growth. People are regarded as cells that replace themselves periodically and whose principal function is to serve the national body of which they are part. Since the functioning of cells is generally more complex than that of machine parts, more knowledge and skills are expected of members of an organismically conceived nation than of the members of one that is mechanistically conceived. The health and safety of their members are more critical because they cannot be replaced or repaired as easily as machine parts.

Government is thought of as an organismically conceived nation's brain (Beer, 1982). It is linked to the rest of the nation by a communication network (a nervous system) through which it receives information about what is going on internally and externally from its sensing organs (e.g., its diplomatic corps, intelligence services, census bureaus, and the press). Continuous surveillance of its environment and its parts enables it to perceive existing and potential threats and opportunities. In response to such perceptions, it commands appropriate actions by its parts. Many of its parts, however, are expected to sense and respond directly to external threats, if not opportunities. Some parts can communicate with each other directly (horizontally). Therefore, organismically conceived nations have an informal as well as a formal structure.

Organismically conceived nations are organized hierarchically but, since some of their parts can respond to stimuli without intervention of their "brains," they are not as centralized as mechanistically conceived nations. Not only do they allow more horizontal communication, but they also encourage more upward communication. Conformity and obedience of parts are not essential as long as they perform well. Therefore, the parts are managed by controlling their outputs, not their inputs as in mechanistically conceived systems.

Although organismic systems are capable of self-control, they are subject to influence and control by other systems. Force is often required to make an organism do something it does not want to do. For example, a horse, unlike an automobile, cannot be run into a wall without compulsion. Influence over organisms is exercised through communication, particularly through threats of punishment and promises of rewards.

To treat a social system like a nation as an organism is to ignore essential differences between these types of systems. An organism has very limited control over its internal structure; such control by a social system is virtually unlimited. This is particularly important because restructuring is often the most effective way of responding to environmental change.

In addition, an organism and its parts are related very differently from an organization and its parts. One's heart cannot decide for itself that it does not want to pump blood or that it wants to do so for someone else. The parts of a social system can do both; they have purposes of their own. Therefore, an effective social system requires agreement and consent from its parts.

Nations Conceptualized as Social Systems

A social system, like an organismic system, is purposeful, but its parts, unlike those of an organism, are also purposeful. Both the parts and the whole can display choice of ends and means. Unlike mechanical and organismic systems, social systems have unlimited ability to organize and reorganize themselves, and they can do so as either mechanistic, organismic, or social systems. To organize a social system as a social system is to accept its principal function as service to its parts and the larger systems of which it is part. It is an instrument of its parts and its containing systems, enabling them to obtain objectives otherwise unobtainable. The principal purposes of an organismic system is self-service, survival; its parts are expected to serve it but not as a matter of choice. Although a mechanistic system can serve an external purposeful system, it too does not do so as a matter of choice.

The principal way a social system serves its parts and containing systems is to encourage and facilitate their development. In this respect, it differs significantly from nations as mechanisms to which encouragement and facilitation are foreign concepts and from nations as organisms that mistakenly identify growth as development and focus on their own, not that of its parts or its containing wholes.

The structure of a nation conceptualized as a social system is determined by its parts. The parts organize the whole; the whole does not organize the parts. Therefore, consensus is essential to the creation and effective operation of such a system. Whatever power the whole has over its parts is given to it voluntarily by those parts. Therefore, the government of a nation conceived as a social system is a servant of the governed, not their master or brain. Such governments tend to be decentralized, dispersed, and largely in the hands of the governed.

The parts of a social system are held together not by coercion but by one or more common objectives and collectively acceptable ways of pursuing them. The governed share values that are embedded in their folkways and mores. They also have shared concepts of the system of which they are part and its containing systems. In other words, they have a shared view of the world.

Folkways, mores, and a shared view of the world constitute a social system's culture (Boulding, 1956). Culture, not coercion, is the cement that integrates the parts of a nation conceptualized as a social system. A society is a social system whose members share a common culture.

Membership in a nation conceived as a social system is voluntary. Individuals are free to disassociate themselves from it, to emigrate. They generally do so only when the system fails to serve their purposes well. On the other hand, such a nation can expel, isolate, or constrain individuals who try to deprive others of their freedom of choice. A major objective of what centralized control there is in a nation as social system is protection of this freedom. The system and its parts control each other.

A nation conceptualized as a social system is taken to be related to its containing systems in the same way its parts are related to it. Containing systems (e.g., alliances) are also conceptualized as social systems that have the same obligation to their members as nations have to theirs.

ON THE STRUCTURE, BEHAVIOR, AND FUNCTIONS OF SYSTEMS

To understand a system of any type, its structure, behavior, and functions have to be known and understood. A system's structure, as we have already observed, is the way the tasks of the whole are divided among its parts and how the behavior of the parts is coordinated. Its behavior and functions are other matters.

To grasp the meaning of behavior we must first understand the difference between the cause-effect and producer-product relationships. A cause is both necessary and sufficient for its effect; a producer is only necessary, not sufficient, for its product. For example, when a typewriter is in normal working condition, striking the space bar is both necessary and sufficient for skipping a space; hence, striking the bar is the cause of a skipped space, its effect. On the other hand, an acorn planted in a garden is only necessary, not sufficient, for obtaining an oak tree. The proper amount of water, temperature, soil conditions, and other environmental conditions are also necessary. Therefore, an acorn is the producer of an oak, not its cause; and an oak is a product of an acorn, not its effect. A cause determines its effect; a producer does not determine its product.

The importance of the distinction between cause-effect and producer-product becomes apparent when we consider the nature of behavior and functions.

The behavior of an individual or system is a change of one or more of its properties. For example, persons display behavior when they move from one place to another because their locations are changed. When a light is turned on it displays behavior.

The structure of a mechanical system determines its behavior in any particular environment. The system has no choice. Nevertheless, it can have a function. Although the behavior of a machine is determined by its structure, the behavior of those who use the machine is not so determined and therefore is a matter of choice. One person may use an electric drill to drill holes, another to tighten screws. Therefore, such user behavior as drilling a hole and tightening a screw is a product, not an effect, of the machine; it is co-produced by the machine and its user. On the other hand, mechanical devices with different structures (e.g., spring watches, electronic clocks, hour glasses, and sun dials) may produce the same behavior in people (e.g., telling time). Production of this response, then, is a function of these structurally different devices. A function is a property of production shared by structurally different objects or behavior.

Such a function as telling time is said to be extrinsic because it is attributed to members of a class of structurally different objects all of which can produce the same type of response.

An organism, unlike a machine, can display choice, hence, can produce structurally different behavior in the same environment. If each of these behaviors produces the same type of outcome—for example, striking a match, flicking a lighter, and rubbing two pieces of wood together—then the organism that produces them can be said to have an intrinsic function. An intrinsic function is one that can be attributed to an individual or system by virtue of its own behavior.

Now we can distinguish three types of system behavior: *reactions, responses,* and *actions*.

A reaction of a system is behavior of that system that is caused (determined) by something external to it. Reflexes in human beings are reactions and so is the lighting of a lamp when its switch is turned on.

A response of a system is behavior of that system that is produced (but is not determined) by something external to it. The external producer is called a stimulus. The system itself is also a co-producer of a response because it could have responded differently to it. A person's switching on a lamp is a typical response to increasing darkness in a room, but the light's going on is a reaction to the change in the switch's position. The person could have gone to a lighter room in response to the darkness. The lamp had no choice.

An act of a system is behavior of that system for which no external event is either necessary or sufficient and that could have been different in the same environment. Therefore, acts are self-determined choices, autonomous behavior. Our decision to write this book was an act.

Nations conceptualized as machines are predominantly reactive, nations conceptualized as organisms are predominantly responsive, and nations conceptualized as social systems are predominantly active.

Reaction, response, and action form a hierarchy. Systems that can act can also respond and react, but systems that can respond cannot necessarily act, and systems that can react cannot necessarily respond. Purposeful systems are necessarily active. They can produce the same outcome in different ways in the same environment, and they can produce different outcomes in the same and different environments. Therefore, they can choose both ends and means under constant as well as changing conditions. This capability exemplifies free will.

Reactive systems can neither learn nor adapt; responsive systems can. But only active systems can create as well as learn and adapt.

CONCLUSION

Mechanistically conceptualized nations are designed and governed so as to react to change in a prescribed way. Organismically conceptualized nations are designed and governed so as to respond, rather than react, to change. They can choose their behavior. Nations conceptualized as social systems are designed and governed so as to restrict reactions to emergencies when there is not enough time for choice. They can respond to change but prefer to act on it, to control it. Through efforts to control it they try to create their futures.

Many of the implications of the social-systemic concept of nations are explored in the rest of this book. We obviously advocate this type of conceptualization. We believe it is by far the most conducive to national development.

2

On the Nature of Development

This chapter begins with a discussion of some commonly held beliefs about development. Among these is the assumption that growth and development are closely related. Then we present our definition of development, in which the concept *competence* plays a critical role. From this concept, we derive the societal functions that are necessary to promote national development: scientific and technological, economic, ethical and moral, aesthetic, and political. Because the aesthetic function is generally not well understood, we explore it in depth and argue that the increasing concern with quality of life derives from aesthetic considerations.

SOME COMMON BELIEFS ABOUT DEVELOPMENT

It is very difficult, if at all possible, to find an explicitly formulated operational definition of development. The meaning of development and the relevance of commonly used indicators of it are usually taken to be obvious or self-evident. To demonstrate the relevance of such indicators of development as gross national product, real per capita income, and life expectancy, one must show them to be highly correlated with a measure of development. But an operational definition of development is required for construction of an appropriate measure of it. Since none is available, the indicators currently in use are based exclusively on subjective judgments. Since there is no consensus among those who make these judgments, there is no generally accepted set of indicators. Even if there were, this would not constitute evidence of their suitability.

Some argue that there is no need for either precise definition or accurate measurement of development because we can easily distinguish between more and less developed countries. A country in pursuit of development only has to select a more developed country as its model and imitate it. There is no agreement, of course, on which nation to choose for this purpose. The choice is generally influenced more by political and economic ideology than by a concept of what development is. A choice made in this way leaves open such questions as: Which aspects of the country used as a model should be imitated and which should not? Is something done by one country at one time and place appropriate for another country at a different time and place? Additional questions are raised by the frequent crises and dilemmas faced by well developed countries.

Imitation could lead to now-different countries becoming more and more alike. Some argue that this is inevitable and even desirable. To the extent that different countries become more alike, their roles in the world system also become more alike. But wholes whose parts all perform the same functions cannot operate as systems. Systems require their labor to be functionally divided among their parts. Furthermore, countries with the same roles are more likely to compete and conflict than cooperate.

A plurality of functions and structures is essential for effective interactions. The world can operate as a system only if nations are functionally differentiated, but such differentiation must be of the "right kind": it must serve both the world as a whole and its national parts. It must be based on cooperation and constructive competition, not exploitation and destructive competition.

Each nation should select a path to development that takes into account its current condition and all of its unique characteristics. Ivan Illich (1973) put it well:

It is evident that only one man in a thousand in Latin America can afford a Cadillac, a heart operation or a Ph.D. This restriction on the goals of development does not make us despair of the fate of the Third World, and the reason is simple. We have not yet come to conceive of a Cadillac as necessary for good transportation, or a heart operation as normal health care, or of a Ph.D. as the prerequisite of an acceptable education [p. 357].

Countries starting from different points of origin cannot take the same route to development; but this does not mean that their routes must be completely different.

DEVELOPMENT VERSUS GROWTH

In our opinion, the most serious consequences of the lack of definition of development derive from mistaking *growth* for *development*. They are not the same thing. Neither is necessary for the other, and either can take place without the other. Rubbish heaps can grow without developing, and people can develop without growing.

Growth, strictly speaking, is an increase in size or number. Therefore, a national economy grows when its product increases. Confusion arises when "growth" is used to imply development—for example, when we use "grown up" to mean mature—and "development" to imply growth.

In organisms, growth usually occurs without choice; not so in a social system.

We have a concept of excessive growth in organisms; not so in social systems. For example, continuous growth of a nation's economy is generally considered to be desirable if not necessary for continuous national development. We will try to show that this is not the case. If economic growth were necessary for a nation's survival, one could understand the preoccupation with it. But not even the authors of *The Limits to Growth* (Meadows et al., 1972) claim that this is the case. The relationship between growth and development can only be understood when the nature of development is understood.

DEVELOPMENT DEFINED

First we consider development of a person, then development of a nation. Development of a person, contrary to what many believe, is not a condition or a state defined by the amount of wealth a person has. For example, poor people who win a lottery and become wealthy do not suddenly become more developed. Rich people who suddenly lose their wealth do not thereby become less developed. Development has less to do with how much people have than with how much they can do with whatever they have. For this reason, Robinson Crusoe is a better model of development than J. Paul Getty.

What we have said about the relationship between wealth (standard of living) and development (quality of life) does not imply that wealth is irrelevant to either development or quality of life. How much people can improve their quality of life depends on the resources available to them as well as on their development. Whatever their level of development, people can obviously do more with resources than without them. However, those who are more developed can often improve their quality of life more with few resources than those who are less developed can with unlimited resources.

Resources are more often taken than given; they are created by what people do with what nature provides. What nature provides does not become a resource until people transform it or learn how to use it. Therefore, the more developed people are, the more capable they are of finding or creating resources.

Because quality of life is the joint product of development and resources, a lack of resources can limit or constrain improvement of the quality of life but not development. Development is a potentiality for improving the quality of life, not the quality of life or standard of living actually attained.

A limit is a boundary that a variable cannot exceed; for example, nothing can move faster than the speed of light. The maximum speed at which an automobile can move is also a limit. But we use "limit" differently when we speak of "speed limits" that obviously can be exceeded. They are better referred to as constraints or restrictions.

The maximum speed of an automobile need not limit those who use it; they can take an airplane if they want to travel faster. The effects that limits can have on us can be evaded either by changing what we want or by using better technology. A limited resource limits us only if we want to do something that requires more of the resource than is available and there is no suitable substitute for that resource. Put another way: A limited resource becomes less limiting when either our need for it decreases or we learn how to use it more effectively, that is, when we develop.

Now we propose the following definition of development:

> Development is the process in which people increase their abilities and desires to satisfy their own needs and legitimate desires and those of others.

This definition requires clarification of the distinction between *needs* and *desires* and the meaning of *legitimate*.

By needs we mean those things that are necessary for survival; for example, food and oxygen. What is needed may or may not be desired; for example, persons who are not aware of their need for calcium may not desire it. On the other hand, persons may desire things they do not need, for example, caviar and diamonds.

By a legitimate desire, we mean one that the pursuit or fulfillment of which does not reduce the likelihood of fulfillment of the needs and (legitimate) desires of others. Therefore, an increase in the ability or desire to harm others is not development, but an increase in the ability or desire to help them is. This implies that efforts to prevent illegitimate acts are themselves legitimate.

DEVELOPMENT AND COMPETENCE

An unlimited ability to satisfy one's own needs and desires and those of others can be called *omnicompetence*. The connotation of this term differs significantly from that of omnipotence. Omnipotence implies power or control over others; omnicompetence implies power to and self-cntrol.

The American philosopher E. A. Singer, Jr. (1936) pointed out that whatever people want, they must want the ability to obtain it, and this is competence. Nevertheless, the desire for omnicompetence is not universal. In some cultures, the largest obstruction to development is the belief that magic or prayer can be used to satisfy needs and desires and, therefore, competence need not be sought.

The belief in magic is reflected in such stories as those of Aladdin's lamp and Suleyman's flying carpet. Nevertheless, the desire for omnicompetence was also present in ancient cultures. This is reflected in the Persian story of Simorg. In this story, birds were told that a bird named Simorg, which lived at the top of the highest mountain, had the ability to make all their wishes come true. Thousands of birds set out to find Simorg. Only thirty birds survived the trip. When they arrived they discovered that they were Simorg. (In the Persian language "Simorg" also means thirty birds.)

Omnicompetence is the ability to satisfy every need and desire. This ability can never be attained but it can be approached continuously. Therefore, it is an ideal but a special kind of ideal: Its attainment would be sufficient for the attainment of any other ideal. It is both an ultimate end and an ultimate means. For this reason, we call it a *meta-ideal*. To make progress toward this meta-ideal is to develop.

There is no limit to how closely an ideal can be approached, but it can never be attained. For example, although perpetual motion can never be attained, it can be approached continually by increasing the efficiency with which energy is used.

Something considered to be an ideal, hence unattainable, at one time may be found to be attainable at another. As our knowledge increases, some ends once considered to be unattainable in principle become attainable in practice. For example, Bishop Berkeley (1897) believed that measurement of less than 1/1,000 of an inch was impossible. Today we measure as little as 1/10,000,000 of an inch.

Ideals motivate human behavior. The Spanish philosopher Jose Ortega y Gasset (1966) knew this:

Man has been able to grow enthusiastic over his vision of . . . unconvincing enterprises. . . . Beyond all doubt it is one of the vital sources of man's power, to be . . . able to kindle enthusiasm from the mere glimmer of something improbable, difficult, remote [p. 1].

Nations can also be moved by ideals. They must be if they are to develop continuously.

DEVELOPMENT OF A NATION

Unlike organisms, nations are social systems that have parts that have purposes of their own and are parts of larger purposeful systems. Recall that when a nation is conceptualized as an organism, its parts and environment are treated as purposeless instruments that enable it to survive. But a nation conceptualized as a social system is treated as a purposeful instrument of its members and the larger system(s) of which it is part. Its purpose is to serve them. This no more deprives a nation of purposes of its own than saying that the purpose of teachers to instruct students deprives teachers of purposes of their own.

The principal objective of a nation, we believe, should be to encourage and facilitate the development of all its members and the larger systems of which it is part. Therefore, a nation can be said to develop when it increases its ability and desire to encourage and facilitate the development of all its members and the multinational system(s) of which it is part.

Because the development of individuals and nations requires their learning how to serve themselves and others more effectively, they can neither develop others nor be developed by them. One can neither learn for others nor be learned for by them. Therefore, self-development is only one kind of development. To encourage and facilitate the development of others one must induce appropriate learning and desire, not dictate it.

National development is not so much a matter of what governments do as it is of what they enable the governed to do. Development of the governed also requires an increase in their desire to help each other, in a reduction of conflict among them. Although a conflict-free society is an ideal that can never be attained, it can be continuously approached. Such progress requires that the governed share a vision of a desirable national future. Creation of such a vision should be a major objective of national development planning. This objective is not likely to be obtained unless there is widespread participation in the planning.

Requirements of Development

What must a nation do to encourage and facilitate the development of its members? The answer to this question lies in identifying those ideals the pursuit of which is necessary for development. These ideals are identified in the writings of ancient Greek philosophers. They are truth, plenty, good, and beauty.

A nation's pursuit of these ideals requires a functional division of societal labor. Such a division of labor gives rise to what we call social institutions. This becomes apparent when we examine each of the ideals in detail.

Truth. The pursuit of truth is the function of science. Its objective is to produce the information, knowledge, and understanding that enable people to develop and use increasingly efficient means to their ends. Research is science's production process. Conversion of the output of research into useful instruments and behavior is the function of technology. Dissemination of the outputs of research and technology is a function of education. Each of these activities is imbedded in a variety of social institutions.

Plenty. The pursuit of plenty is the function of economic institutions. Their objective is to provide each person with the resources that are required to obtain and use the most efficient means and instruments available. This requires production and distribution of goods and services—protection of people and their possessions from harm or theft by (a) others in the same society, a function of the system of justice; (b) other societies, a function of the military; and (c) nature and accidents, a function of fire protection, building inspection, and health departments, and insurance; and preservation and conservation of resources, functions of maintenance and repair services, and environmental protection agencies.

Good. The pursuit of this ideal is the function of the ethical-moral institutions of society. These institutions have two principal objectives. The first is to eliminate conflict within individuals, to produce peace of mind. This has traditionally been the responsibility of religious institutions but is increasingly shared with mental-health institutions. The second objective is to eliminate conflict between individuals, to produce peace on earth. This function is shared by diplomatic, legal, and educational institutions as well as the family.

Unless conflict within individuals is removed, they will have some objectives that they cannot obtain. Unless conflict between individuals is removed, there will always be some people who cannot obtain at least some of what they need or want.

The reduction of conflict between individuals, the function of morality, is necessary but not sufficient for continuous progress toward omnicompetence. There are many needs and desires that people have that cannot be satisfied without the help of others. Therefore, the production of cooperation, a function of ethics, is also necessary. Morality operates proscriptively: "Thou shalt not. . . ." Ethics operates prescriptively: "Thou shalt. . . ."

Beauty. The pursuit of beauty is an aesthetic function. Its objective is to encourage and sustain pursuit of ideals.

The pursuit of beauty requires special attention, which it receives below, because it is the least understood aspect of development. The underdevelopment of aesthetics is reflected in the fact that few philosophers have incorporated it into their philosophical systems. Most of those who have, have treated it as an appendage rather than as an integral part of their systems. On the other hand, most of those who have contributed to our understanding of aesthetics have made no contribution to our understanding of science, economics, or ethics-morality. Historically, aesthetics has been the "odd function out."

The Function of Aesthetics

People may be the only animals that can formulate and pursue ideals, ends that can never be attained but can be continuously approached. If people are to pursue any ideal continuously, they must never settle for any ends less than ideals. They must never be either permanently discouraged in their pursuit of ideals or completely satisfied with the ends they have obtained. Therefore, whenever they fulfill a need or desire, they must have other yet-to-be-satisfied desires whose fulfillment will bring them closer to their ideals. This requires that people always have visions of states more desirable than the ones they are in.

The American philosopher E. A. Singer, Jr. (1948) argued that the function of beauty is to inspire, to stimulate the creation of visions of better states than we are in, and to provide us with the courage to try to realize them. Inspiration elevates aspiration, and this is necessary for continuous pursuit of ideals.

In the *Republic*, Plato depicted art as a potentially dangerous stimulant because it could threaten his utopia's, his ideal state's, stability. This concern derived from his conception of utopia as static. Art would be disruptive in a static state, but an ideal state need not be static; it can be a state in which ideals are continuously pursued. If people had all they wanted, they would be bored stiff. This is hardly ideal. There is at least as much satisfaction to be derived from the pursuit of ideals as from obtaining them. Such pursuit should not be excluded from our conception of the ideal state. Moreover, since ideals, whether static or dynamic, cannot be obtained, their continuous pursuit requires the type of stimulation Plato wanted to abolish from his Republic.

Aristotle, in contrast to Plato, saw art as cathartic, as a palliative for dissatisfaction, a producer of stability and contentment. For Aristotle, art produces satisfaction with the "here and now"; it is recreative rather than the creative force Plato believed it to be.

The difference between Plato's and Aristotle's views of art is apparent but not real. They were concerned with different aspects of the same thing, like two sides of the same coin. Art is both creative and recreative, inspiring and cathartic. Recreation is the extraction of satisfaction from what we do, rather than what we obtain. It provides "the pause that refreshes"; it re-creates the creator. People cannot sustain continuous pursuit of ideals without rewards along the way. Art as recreation provides this. Art is also inspiring, stimulating visions of something better and commitment to its creation. A single work of art may do both. Little wonder that both those who entertain us and those who inspire us are called "artists." Now let us approach aesthetics from a very different direction.

The psychology of aesthetics. Decision making is a major activity of purposeful individuals and systems. It involves selecting a course of actions or means to a desired outcome, an end. The efficiency of a means for an end is the likelihood that it will produce that end. The more efficient a means, the more valuable it is. This value is instrumental or extrinsic because it lies in what the means leads to. On the other hand, ends are valued because of the satisfaction their attainment brings. This satisfaction is an intrinsic value.

Means have intrinsic as well as extrinsic value, and ends have extrinsic as well as intrinsic value. We often prefer one means to another even though both have the same likelihood of producing the same outcome. For example, most people prefer shoes of one color to shoes of another even though they are identical in all other respects. Yet their color has no effect on their efficiencies. This preference is based on the satisfaction that color brings, its intrinsic value. We simply like some colors more than others.

Preferences that are independent of efficiency constitute what psychologists call a person's style. Individuality lies as much in style as it does in the efficiency with which ends are pursued. Stylistic preferences are based on the satisfaction we derive from what we do independently of what we do it for, on its recreational value. Put another way: every means is also an end in itself. Means and ends are relative concepts, not absolute.

Every end is also a means and therefore has extrinsic, efficiency-related, value. Ends are desired outcomes. All outcomes have consequences, other outcomes that follow their attainment. To the extent we desire such consequences, they are ends for which our immediate end is a means. For example, we may nail wood together (a means) to build a bookcase (an end). But building a bookcase (now a means) is intended to enable us to store books (a more ultimate end). Storing books is itself a means to reading more, and so on and on. Attainable ends are potentially means of moving closer to an ideal, to making progress.

The intrinsic value of means and the extrinsic value of ends are aesthetic values. Art consists of works that create these values; beauty is the property through which it does so. But there is an aesthetic aspect to every decision since every decision involves stylistic considerations and has a potential impact on progress toward ideals. This is what quality of life is all about.

Most people believe that mankind has made significant scientific and economic progress during its recorded history. Whether ethical-moral progress has been made is still being debated. But few argue that aesthetic progress has been made, that we can either produce greater works of art or appreciate beauty more than our predecessors. Some would even argue that mankind has retrogressed in this regard. However, we believe that a growing awareness of the lack of aesthetic progress is responsible for the currently increasing concern with quality of life.

The meaning of quality of life is far from clear, but it seems clear that it has less to do with how much material goods one has than with the condition under which these goods are acquired and used. Quality of life is more a matter of process than products. It has to do with the satisfaction or dissatisfaction we derive from what we do, not from what we have. This, as we will try to show, is a matter of aesthetics. Before we do, there is one other aspect of national development that requires attention, politics.

Politics

National development depends on a coordinated pursuit of truth, plenty, the good, and beauty. This, in turn, requires coordination of the social institutions responsible for these pursuits. Such coordination is a function of management, and management of a nation is the function of its government. Management, hence government, involves the application and allocation of authority. Authority is the power over, the ability to control others. On the other hand, the objective of national development is to increase each of its member's competence, and competence is the power to do so. Some people's efforts to obtain power over others often conflict with the others' pursuit of power to satisfy their needs and desires. The management of such conflict is the subject of politics.

Quality of Life

Those who argue that the quality of life is deteriorating generally base their argument on two observations. They assert that we derive less satisfaction than we once did from the ordinary things we do, for example, taking a Sunday walk or drive, reading or listening to the news, watching a movie, attending school, or working. These activities, they argue, are losing their recreational value; they are deteriorating aesthetically.

In addition, the argument goes, the quality of life is decreasing because of the growing belief that we are "getting nowhere," making no progress. We do not seem to be approaching such ideals as peace of mind, peace on earth, equal opportunity, and the elimination of poverty and hunger. A sense of progress toward such ideals gives meaning to life. It raises life from mere existence by lending significance to our decisions. If people feel that what they do makes little difference to themselves and others, life loses meaning. (See Ellul, 1967, and Wald, 1969.) They come to regard choice as illusory rather than real, to accept fatalism and resign themselves to a future that is believed to be determined. This degrades the quality of life. One might ask: By how much?

Measurement of the quality of life is very difficult, to say the least. Perhaps the principal source of difficulty is the fact that quality of life involves stylistic preferences, or what psychologists refer to as "traits"; and 17,953 of these have been identified (Allport and Odbert, 1936). Imagine trying to measure the extent to which individuals are able to satisfy each of these stylistic objectives. Of course, not all of them are affected by every decision, but imagine the difficulty of determining which ones are for each decision.

Because of this and other difficulties, simple-to-use social indicators are used instead of measures of quality of life, for example, life expectancy, the number of people living in poverty, and average educational level attained. However, the use of indicators leaves much to be desired methodologically. The appropriateness of an indicator depends on how well it correlates with the measure for which it substitutes. But since we do not have measures of quality of life with which to compare the indicators, we cannot carry out the correlation analyses required to evaluate them. Their use is "justified" solely by the subjective judgments of those who uses them. Whose subjective judgment ought to be used for this purpose? How can we determine whose judgment is best without a measure of quality of life to compare them to?

Nevertheless, since it appears to be easy to distinguish between a low and a high quality of life, why aren't subjective judgments good enough? Good enough for what? Are they good enough to enable governments to allocate effectively their limited resources to the unlimited demands for them? Such allocation requires comparative cost-benefit analyses of all projects intended to improve quality of life, and such analyses require accurate and reliable measurements of this quality. There is no evidence that the subjective judgments of those who govern or their advisors are good enough for this purpose.

Then must we wait until we can measure quality of life before governments can plan effectively for its improvement? No; there is a good alternative: use of participative national development planning. How can this help?

Those who suffer from a poor quality of life are usually not able to do much to improve it. For this reason, those who govern and their planners try to do something for and to those so deprived. But doing this efficiently, let alone effectively, requires the type of measurement they cannot make. However, if those who have a poor quality of life were given the opportunity to improve it, they would learn by trying to do so, and are very likely to enjoy the effort. By learning they would develop, and by deriving satisfaction from the effort, if not from its results, they would improve the quality of their lives. Therefore, those who govern and their planners should not try to improve the quality of life of the governed, but should try to encourage and enable them to improve their own quality of life. This requires involving the governed, particularly those with a poor quality of life, in planning for their own and national development. Participants in such planning cannot avoid injecting their stylistic preferences and ideals into the plans they help prepare. Others need not do this for them.

What we have said about the difficulty of measuring quality of life can also be said about the difficulty of measuring individual and national development. Participative development planning makes it possible to escape the dilemmas created by the inability to measure quality of life and development.

In subsequent chapters we provide a design of participative national planning that we believe effectively promotes development and improvement of quality of life.

SUMMARY

We have defined development as an increase in people's ability and desire to satisfy their own needs and legitimate desires, and those of others. Because development, defined in this way, is as much a matter of motivation and learning as of wealth, it can take place with or without resources. Therefore, shortages of resources that limit growth need not limit development, but they can limit what can be accomplished. The quality of life that can be realized at any stage of development depends on the kind and amount of resources available. Nevertheless, the effect of development on resources is at least as great as the effect of resources on development. The more developed people are, the more effectively they can find, create, and use resources to improve their quality of life as well as their standard of living.

Development requires increases in competence. Omnicompetence is the ability to attain any attainable end or to make unlimited progress toward any ideal. It is a meta-ideal because its attainment would enable one to attain any other ideal. Progress toward this meta-ideal is necessary for development.

A proper role of government, we argued, is to encourage and facilitate the development of the governed. This requires a government to lead a nation toward truth, plenty, good, and beauty. These pursuits are the scientific, economic, ethical-moral, and aesthetic functions of society.

Coordination of the four essential pursuits, a responsibility of government, involves the exercise and use of power, authority. There are two kinds of power, power over and power to, and these often come into conflict. Resolution of such conflict is the function of politics.

Quality of life is a matter of aesthetics and aesthetics is the least understood of the four essential ideal-pursuits. It involves the intrinsic value of the means we employ, the satisfaction derived from what we do independently of what we do it for. Such satisfaction is recreative. Quality of life also involves satisfaction derived from the extrinsic value of the end we obtain, from making progress toward ideals. Such satisfaction is creative. Measurement of these two types of satisfaction is at best very difficult. Without such measurement we cannot develop effective indicators of quality of life. Subjective estimates of this quality by those who govern and their planners are not good enough to make cost-effective allocations of resources among the many things that might be done to improve quality of life. We argued that this difficulty could be overcome by enabling those who are governed to participate in planning for improvement of their quality of life and their own development.

The key to development and improved quality of life does not lie in evaluating the quality of life of others and planning for their development, but in enabling them to evaluate and plan for themselves. This is reflected in the very appropriate motto of a self-development group in Mantua, one of Philadelphia's black ghettos: Plan or be planned for. To enable people to design and plan for their own individual and collective futures is to enable them to make an art of living.

3

On the Nature of Planning

It is difficult to find two individuals, groups, or governments that plan in exactly the same way, but few of the differences are fundamental. Three basic approaches that derive from planners' attitudes toward time predominate in most organizations. These approaches are:

1. *Reactive*, the objective of which is to restore the past;

2. *Inactive*, the objective of which is to preserve the present; and

3. *Preactive*, the objective of which is to accelerate the future.

Each of these approaches to planning consists of ways of coping with change. All share the assumption that change is largely out of anyone's control but some of its important effects can be controlled. Recently, however, a new approach to planning has emerged that denies this assumption.

4. *Interactive planning*, the objective of which is to create the future.

This approach to planning is based on the assumption that change itself is subject to some control. It is called interactive for two reasons. First, it is synthetic rather than analytic; it involves putting things together rather than taking them apart. It deals with organizations holistically by focussing on interactions among their parts. Second, it is participative.

The four basic approaches to planning are, in a sense, like primary colors. Pure primary colors seldom appear; we usually see mixtures. Nevertheless, in many of these mixtures we can identify the primary color that dominates. Similarly, in most organizations, including governments, mixtures can be found of the basic approaches to planning, but one approach usually dominates which may change over time.

THE REACTIVE APPROACH

Reactivists try to re-create a previous state of the system they control by unmaking changes that have converted that state into one that they find less desirable.

Reactivists generally view change unfavorably and blame technology for most of it. In the war of two cultures described by C. P. Snow (1964), reactivists are aligned with humanists against technocrats. History offers many examples of reactivism in action. In the early years of the Industrial Revolution in England the Luddites organized to destroy the new factories being built. These, they argued, were destroying the quality of life. They wanted to return to manual craft production. At about the time of the French Revolution, Jean-Jacques Rousseau led an anti-technological "back to nature" movement. In the 1960s numerous young people abandoned technological societies and returned to the land and primitive farming. This movement was greatly stimulated by the literary attack made on technology by Jacques Ellul (1967).

Reactively managed governments and organizations tend to use the oldest form of organization, that of the paternalistic family. They favor highly centralized hierarchical structures. Status in such organizations is strongly correlated with age because they take experience to be the best teacher and "the school of hard knocks" the best place to acquire it. Reactive organizations try to emulate "a great big happy family." They value loyalty and obedience to "the old man" above all other virtues.

Reactivists search for corrective actions that are good enough, that *satisfice*. These are seldom the best possible. In their search they rely heavily on experience, qualitative judgment, and common sense. Their solutions to problems tend to be traditional, "tried and true."

Reactive planning begins at the bottom of reactive organizations and works its way up. It involves the following steps:

1. Current deficiencies are identified;
2. A project is designed to identify and remove or suppress the cause of each deficiency;
3. The expected costs and benefits of each project are estimated;
4. The net value of each project is then estimated as a function of its expected cost and benefit;
5. Priorities are assigned to projects based on their estimated values;
6. Using an estimate of the amount of resources that will be made available to the unit, the highest priority projects requiring less than this amount are selected; and
7. The projects selected are "packaged" as the unit's plan and sent up to the next level.

At each successive level of the organization, projects from lower levels are modified, aggregated, and supplemented with projects generated at that level. This process continues until the final plan is assembled at the top. This plan consists of projects separately formulated at each level of the organization. Finally, resources are allocated by the top to the second level, by the second level to the third, and so on until the lowest level is reached once again.

Reactive planning has two major deficiencies. The first derives from the fact that when we get rid of what we do not want, we may not get what we do want. We may get something much worse, as Iranian revolutionaries found out with Khomeni. Removal or suppression of a cause in our present state does not guarantee a return to a previous state, as the prohibitionists in the United States discovered. When alcoholism became a serious social problem in the United States earlier in this century, alcohol was identified as the cause. Therefore, its production, importation, sale, and use were prohibited by law. Prohibition did not succeed but in its wake left an even greater problem: organized crime.

The second deficiency in reactive planning derives from the fact that solutions to problems are treated independently of each other, as though they did not interact. They do. Action taken to resolve one problem may render ineffective or harmful the actions taken to resolve another. For example, the combination of two drugs, each prescribed independently for different ailments, may be very harmful, even deadly. Because the treatments of problems interact, the focus of planning should be on their interactions, not just on their separate reactions.

THE INACTIVE APPROACH

Inactive administrators and managers try to conserve the present by preventing change. They advise: "Don't rock the boat." The world may not be perfect, but it is good enough.

Inactivists believe that meddling with the natural course of events creates most of our problems, but even these problems would pass or fade away if left alone. Most change is thought to be either illusory, transitory, or superficial. The fundamentals do not change; they are "external verities."

Inactivists respond to serious threats, by engaging in what has come to be known as "crisis management." They act when necessary for survival or stability, but do no more than is required to "turn off the heat." Crisis management focuses on suppressing symptoms rather than on curing ailments.

Preventing change, however, does not mean literally not acting. Inactivism actually requires a great deal of effort. A large number of people must be kept busy without actually accomplishing anything or they must be busy keeping others from doing something. For this, inactivists have an ingenious design. They use study groups, committees, task forces, and commissions without the power to decide or act, only to investigate and recommend. Committees consume large amounts of time without effect. If they do come up with recommendations, these are often sent to another committee for evaluation and review. This process can often be extended long enough that the initial problem will have so changed as to make the committee's work irrelevant. If timely recommendations are unexpectedly produced they will be assigned inadequate resources, assuring their failure. Little wonder that inactive governments are wrapped in bureaucracy and tied with red tape.

Because inactivists try to prevent change, they are concerned about errors of commission, doing something that should not be done. They are little concerned about errors of omission, missing opportunities, not doing something that should be done.

The behavior of inactivists is conventional because convention protects the status quo. They equate manners and morality. Connections are more important than competence; who one knows is more important than what one knows. This follows from the importance inactivists place on knowing what is going on. Gathering facts is necessary for determining where and when interventions are required to prevent change. It is also an activity that can fully occupy many and accomplish nothing.

THE PREACTIVE APPROACH

Preactive managers and administrators try to accelerate movement into the future; they encourage change. For them, the future is filled with opportunity, and change is virtually synonymous with progress. They approach the future by predicting and preparing. Prediction is the more critical of the two because, if it is incorrect, then the preparation, no matter how good, is either ineffective or harmful. On the other hand, even if preparations for a correctly predicted future are less than perfect, one is likely to be better off with them than without them. Therefore, the focus of the preactive methodology is on efforts to foresee the future. To preactivists, futurology is a basic science. The Oracle of Delphi is the paradigm of consultants.

In contrast to inactivists, preactivists try harder to avoid missing opportunities (errors of omission) than doing something wrong (errors of commission), because "opportunity knocks only once" and errors of commission can usually be corrected before they become serious. In general, nothing is worse than doing nothing, inactivity.

Growth is the ultimate objective of preactivists: to become the largest, wealthiest, strongest, and so on. They tend to be fiercely competitive. Because of this they value entrepreneurship more than administrative skills. They focus on standard of living rather than quality of life because they believe that it is only through increases in wealth that quality of life can be improved.

Like reactivists, preactivists view technology as the principal agent of change; but unlike reactivists, they view change, hence technology, as good. They believe that with enough time and money there are few problems that research and development cannot solve. They employ or support highly trained scientists, engineers, and other types of technologically based professionals. Computers, telecommunications, word processors, operations research, program budgeting, cost-effectiveness analyses, and so on permeate these organizations.

Preactivists are not satisfied with things as they are, as are inactivists, or with merely doing better or well enough, as reactivists are; they want to do as well as possible, to optimize. Therefore, they try to solve (i.e., to optimize) rather than resolve (i.e., to compromise) problems, relying heavily on quantitative methods and scientifically based research. They look for solutions in experimentation rather than resolutions in experience. In this view, experience is a poor teacher because, in a rapidly changing world, what worked in the past is not likely to work in the future. Experience in driving an automobile, for example, is not relevant to piloting a space vehicle. Therefore, competence and the ability to learn are more important than familiarity with the past. Today's and tomorrow's problems need new solutions. Technological obsolescence is the greatest threat to survival and growth. Preactivists are drawn away from tradition and convention to the new and novel.

To get the best out of them, competent professionals must be given a good deal of freedom. They require little supervision and control. Therefore, preactive organizations tend to be decentralized and managed permissively. They rely more on informal than formal structure. This, they believe, facilitates rapid detection of and adaptation to changes in the environment. Preactivists favor overlapping chains of command (e.g., matrix organizations), and horizontal communications.

Recall that the "great big happy family" is a favored metaphor of reactive organizations, and the "well-oiled machine" is that of inactive organizations. Preactive organizations prefer either the "winning team" on which each player has a different but essential role and good teamwork is the secret of success or the "healthy organism," each part of which is a vital organ. The chief executive is referred to as the "head," and management as "the brain" (Beer, 1982). The military is a preactive government's "muscle," its intelligence system is its "eyes and ears," and its ordinary workers are the "guts" of the organization. With such organismic thinking, it is not surprising that growth is the preactive planner's dominant objective.

Preactive planning, prediction and preparation, is the dominant mode of planning in more developed countries. Unlike reactive bottom-up planning, preactive planning is top-down. It begins at the top where, with the assistance of a professional staff of planners, the future to be planned for is predicted and a statement of long-range objectives and associated strategies is prepared. These are passed down to the next level where they are appropriately adapted. This process continues until the lowest-level unit is reached. The plans prepared at each level other than the top are reviewed, coordinated, and integrated by the level immediately above.

Professional planners usually play a critical role in preactive planning. They generally formulate plans and submit them to the appropriate executives or managers for review. This differs from reactive planning in which managers do all or most of the planning, usually without professional help.

The deficiencies of preactive planning are subtle. They derive from a type of "uncertainty principle": The better we can predict, the less effectively we can prepare; and the more effectively we can prepare, the less need there is for prediction.

If the world were as Newton thought it was—a mechanism whose behavior is determined by its structure and the causal laws of nature—then we would be able to determine its state at any moment in time. In such a world nothing could happen by chance. Everything other than God, the first cause, would be determined by its cause. This view also precludes the possibility of choice, hence free will. This preclusion gave rise to one of the central problems of modern philosophy: How can our beliefs in free will and a mechanistic universe be reconciled? No generally accepted answer was found, but most scientists and many philosophers came to believe that free will was an illusion perpetrated by a merciful God who realized how dull life would be without it. As one philosophical wag put it: Man is like a fly who rides on the trunk of an elephant and thinks he's steering it. The elephant doesn't mind and it makes the ride more interesting.

Without choice there can be no preparation. With it, there can not be perfect prediction. Therefore, the mechanistic view of the universe precludes an ability to prepare. Then how can we explain the fact that we do predict the weather, however imperfectly, and prepare for it, also imperfectly, and are better off for doing so? The answer to this question is that our preparations for the weather have no effect on it; the weather is independent of what we do. But when a government predicts economic, political, social, and technological conditions, it attempts to foresee a future that will be affected by what it does. This leads to a vicious circle: To predict perfectly, we must know what we and others are going to do, but we and others do not know what we are going to do until we predict the future. It is precisely because our preparations and those of others affect what we forecast, and our forecasts affect what we do, that uncertainty and error arise. If we could predict perfectly the preparations of others, and they ours, then neither of us would have real choice; it would be an illusion.

The indeterminacy inherent in prediction and preparation can be seen in another way, one that requires a distinction between forecasting and prediction. A forecast is a description of the future obtained by extrapolating from a description of the past. It assumes that the kinds of changes that will occur in the future are the same as have occurred in the past. A prediction is not based on this assumption. It is a description of the future obtained by applying laws of change to a description of the present. The laws of change generate a prediction; extrapolation generates a forecast.

Forecasts are projections. Past data are fitted by some kind of a line (straight or otherwise) that is projected from now to a future then. Although there are many ways of fitting such lines, the logic employed in all of them is the same. It is based on the assumption that what will happen depends essentially on what has already happened, not on what will happen between now and then. This assumption clearly becomes less tenable the greater the interval between now and then.

If we assert that the future depends on what will be done between now and then, and that much of what will be done will be a matter of choice, we imply that the future is subject to at least some control. The more of it we can control, the less of it we need to forecast or predict.

Despite the arguments presented here, many people continue to predict and prepare because they believe there is no effective alternative. They are wrong. There is an alternative, even in the case of the weather. As previously conceded, we can predict and prepare for the weather and are better off for doing so. But we also build buildings and vehicles within which we control the weather, thus eliminating the need to predict or forecast it. Control is obviously more desirable than predicting and preparing for what we do not control. But how do we gain such control?

FROM "PREDICT AND PREPARE" TO "CONTROL"

We control or influence many causes or their effects. Curiously, the ways of controlling them are familiar but are seldom consciously considered as alternatives to prediction and preparation. There are five such techniques:

1. Vertical integration,
2. Horizontal integration,
3. Cooperation,
4. Incentives, and
5. Increasing responsiveness.

Vertical Integration

Buildings, as noted above, are built for the purpose of bringing the weather under control. The farmer who grows his crops in a greenhouse is not concerned about the weather. Therefore, an important way of gaining control over the future is by redesigning the system planned for so that an important uncontrolled variable is incorporated into that system.

Such a procedure is commonly employed in corporations; it is called *vertical integration*. For example, if the supply of a raw material is uncertain, a company can begin to produce its own. This is why some automobile companies produce their own steel and why many steel companies produce their own coke. For similar reasons, some nations have increased their self-sufficiency, their independence of imports.

Horizontal Integration

We control certain diseases by innoculation with vaccines that provide immunity. To immunize a system is to add something to it that precludes the effects of a cause that is not controlled. This can be done in a social system through *horizontal integration*. For example, a company's production efficiency may be significantly reduced because demand for its product is variable and unpredictable. It can reduce or eliminate this effect on production by adding a product that uses the same production technology and distribution system, and demand for which runs counter to that of the first product. This is illustrated by an old business joke: a rubber company that produces both nipples for baby bottles and contraceptive devices doesn't have to worry about which way things go. Hedging on the commodity exchange by simultaneously buying and selling futures of a grain does not control price of the grain but it does control the cost of acquiring it.

A nation can use such a strategy to make itself immune to damage from natural causes. By constructing dams and levees it can prevent floods, and by building irrigation systems it can avoid the effects of drought. The development of indigenous sources of coal is a way of protecting against arbitrary price increases by suppliers of oil. In general, development of indigenous sources of alternative materials is a form of immunization.

Cooperation

There are many variables that cannot be controlled by one nation or organization, but that can be controlled by several working together. Cooperation among nations can reduce, if not eliminate, uncertainty and the need for forecasting. The EEC and OPEC are good examples. Cooperation of organizations within a nation—for example, in voluntary price and wage control—can often bring something under more control than can legislation or regulation by government.

Incentives

Incentives and disincentives enable us to influence individual and collective human behavior. Influence is a weak form of control. To control something is to determine its properties or behavior. To influence something is to make a change of its properties or behavior more likely, but not certain.

Governments make considerable use of incentives and disincentives. Taxes, tariffs, duties, and exemptions from these are but a few among any common examples. Unfortunately, however, incentives and disincentives are often used counterproductively. For example, taxes on houses in the United States are generally proportional to their value, and permission to convert single-family houses into multiple-dwelling units is usually easier to obtain for less valuable properties. These two conditions provide an incentive for allowing houses to deteriorate and then converting them into tenements. Slums are the consequence. On the other hand, if investments in the maintenance and improvement of houses were tax deductible there would be fewer slums.

The large amount of solid waste generated in the United States, the largest per capita in the world, is a consequence of the fact that there is a very low, flat charge for its collection and disposal. If the charges were proportional to the amount of waste collected and disposed of, the solid-waste stream would be considerably smaller.

Responsiveness

There are cases in which none of the four preceding ways of gaining control can work. In such cases it is often possible to respond so effectively and rapidly to the unexpected as to remove the need for forecasting it.

Responsiveness can be significantly increased through contingency planning. By carrying a spare tire and tire-changing equipment in our cars, we make the effects of having a flat tire relatively insignificant. Note that we do not carry a spare tire because we forecast that we are going to have a flat. In fact, we usually drive with the expectation of not having one. But we assume one is possible. Therefore, contingency planning is based on assumptions of what can happen, not on forecasts of what will happen.

The ability to respond (hence adapt) quickly and effectively to uncontrolled events requires a readiness, willingness, and ability to change. Few nations satisfy this requirement, but they could. Such systems, including governments, can be designed and managed so as to be capable of rapid and effective response to change. This should be a major objective of national development planning.

The primary objective of such planning should be to gain control of the nation's future, not to re-create its past, preserve its present, or predict and prepare for a future it does not control. Interactive planning was designed to do just this.

THE INTERACTIVE APPROACH

Interactive planning, developed by Russell Ackoff (1981), is a systems methodology for designing the future. It is based on three beliefs: that an ounce of control is worth at least a pound of prediction and preparation; that a significant part of the future can be controlled; and much of what cannot be controlled can be responded to quickly and effectively. Therefore, such planning is conceived as the design of the most desirable future and the search for or invention of ways of approximating it as closely as possible.

To increase one's desire and ability to control the future is to develop. Development, not growth, is the primary objective of interactive social systems. Growth is desirable only if it contributes to development.

Interactive planners seek neither to satisfy, do well enough, nor optimize. Instead, they try to idealize, to act now so that in the future the system planned for will be able to do better than the best that is possible now. Put another way: they try to act so as to maximize the rate of future development.

According to interactivists and contrary to C. P. Snow (1964) who wrote that the arts and humanities and science and technology form two distinct cultures, these are two aspects of the same culture. For an interactivist, the opposing tendencies not only co-exist and interact but also form a complementary relationship. A complement is that which fills and/or completes a whole (Gharajedaghi 1983). The arts and humanities are seen as having the function of identifying differences among things that are apparently similar; science and technology, of identifying similarities among things that are apparently different. The arts and humanities identify problems yet to be solved and possibilities yet to be realized; science and technology deal with solving those problems and realizing those possibilities already identified. Therefore, effective management and planning require a continuous blending of these two aspects of culture.

Like preactivists, interactivists use quantification and experimentation wherever they can do so effectively, but, like reactivists, they also use experience and qualitative judgment where quantification and experimentation are either impossible or ineffective. They take morality into account, as do reactivists; manners, as do inactivists; and efficiency, as do preactivists; but they integrate these considerations by focussing on effectiveness. Effectiveness includes intrinsic as well as extrinsic values, quality of life as well as standard of living.

Interactivists seek neither to resolve nor solve problems, as the reactivists and preactivists do, but to dissolve them. This requires changing the system that has the problem in such a way as to eliminate the problem. For example, a nation that has an unreliable source of a critical material can eliminate the problem this uncertainty creates by developing an indigenous source or a substitute.

In Chapter 6 we examine in detail the content of interactive planning. Here, however, we consider the operating principles from which the interactive planning process derives.

The Operating Principles of Interactive Planning

There are three principles of interactive planning:

1. The participative principle,
2. The principle of continuity, and
3. The holistic principle.

The participative principle. To the interactivist the principal benefit to be derived from planning is the development of those who engage in it. In other words, the principal benefit of planning derives not from consuming its product, plans, but from engaging in the process. In planning, process is the most important product. Therefore, all those who are intended to benefit from planning should be given an opportunity to participate in it. Interactivists believe that more development takes place by engaging in planning than as a result of the implementation of plans. Therefore, it is better to plan for oneself, no matter how badly, than to be planned for by others, no matter how well. This set of beliefs does not imply that plans have no value, only that they have no more value than planning itself.

The participative principle requires that all those potentially affected by planning be given an opportunity to engage in it. How such broad participation can be organized in a nation or community is the subject of Chapter 5. In Chapter 4 we consider how development takes place in planning. It derives from the understanding that participants gain of how what they do affects the performance of the whole system of which they are part and how the performance of the whole affects them. They also become aware of possibilities of improving themselves and the system and learn how to realize such improvements. Acquisition of such knowledge and understanding is development.

The principle of continuity. Plans cannot work exactly as expected, and their results frequently deviate significantly from expectations. Such deviations occur because some of the many assumptions that underlie any plan turn out to be false. Therefore, effective implementation of plans requires that the critical assumptions on which they are based be explicitly formulated and checked frequently to determine if they continue to hold. For example, every national plan makes numerous assumptions about the behavior of other nations. When such an assumption becomes invalid, corrective adjustments should be made in the plan.

Since some of the effects of a plan are never foreseen, the actual effects should be monitored and controlled continually. Such control of a plan requires that (1) the expected effects and the times by which they are to be realized must be explicitly formulated, (2) actual performance must be checked continually, and (3) corrective or explorative action must be taken whenever a significant deviation occurs.

Finally, as we approach or arrive at a destination, an evaluation of it may change, and often does. We may find, for example, that we do not like a vacation resort as much as we had expected and that we want to go elsewhere. Moreover, as we move toward a destination along a planned route, we often learn of a better way to get there. Our knowledge and our values change with experience. These changes should be reflected in our plans. For these reasons, planning should be continuous. Moreover, since planning and implementation are a development process, why discontinue it?

The holistic principle. In most organizations, especially governments, there is a tendency to place responsibility for dealing with a problem in that part of the organization in which the problem is found. Therefore, if a problem is found in, say, a transportation ministry, it is said to be a transportation problem and responsibility for dealing with it is automatically assumed by that ministry. In contrast, although we call an ache in the head a headache, we do not try to cure it by manipulating the head; we swallow a pill.

Contrary to popular belief, adjectives used to characterize problems (e.g., transportation, health, finance, social, political, economic, etc.) tell us nothing about the nature of the problem. What they reveal is the point of view of the one looking at the problem. A variety of points of view can and should be brought to bear on every problem of any complexity, because only in this way can we determine which are the most effective.

Problems are still photographs clipped out of motion pictures. They are static abstractions extracted from dynamic experience by analysis. Problems are not objects of experience, but conceptual constructs. The objects of experience are large complex sets of interacting problems, dynamic systems of problems. They are called *messes* or *problematiques*.

Because a mess is a system of problems it cannot be treated effectively by breaking it into parts (problems) that are treated separately. Recall that the essential properties of a system (hence a mess) are properties of the whole that none of the parts have. Moreover, the parts of a system (e.g., the problems of which a mess is composed) lose their essential properties when they are separated from the system of which they are part. Therefore, when planners decompose a mess by analysis, they lose its essential properties. Furthermore, by treating its component problems separately, their essential properties are also lost. For these reasons, interactivists always imbed problem solving in planning and never reduce planning to solving a set of separated problems.

The performance of a system is never the sum of the independent performances of its parts: It is the product of their interactions. Therefore, in planning for national development, the objective should not be to develop the best plan for each part or level of society or government taken separately, but it should be to develop plans for each part and level that fit together to form the best whole.

CONCLUSION

We are practitioners and advocates of interactive planning. Thus, our description of the other approaches tended to emphasize their deficiencies. We recognize that each of the alternatives under specific conditions has merits and each can be effective in certain environments. However, current conditions in many less developed countries (see Part III) lead us to believe interactive planning is by far the most appropriate approach for such countries.

Reactivists value and preserve tradition and provide a sense of continuity with the past. They value scholarship, a knowledge of history, and experience, and through these they avoid reinventing wheels and repeating old errors. They do not adopt what is new just because it is new, however fashionable it may be. They are not susceptible to proffered panaceas and fads, technological or otherwise, as many preactive managers are. Because reactive organizations are paternalistic, they take care of their own provided they receive loyalty and obedience.

Inactive organizations preserve what is good in their current situations and tend to produce a stable environment that minimizes stress. Members of inactive organizations are not repeatedly confronted with disruptive changes, nor do they have to deal with many internal disagreements and conflicts. Such organizations tend to run smoothly and are relatively immune to disturbances from without. They generate a sense of security among their members because of the continuity of their practices. They have a high tolerance for errors of omission.

Preactive organizations are quick to take advantage of new technological developments. Their inclination to try out new things keeps them at the frontiers of technology where they are able to recognize and exploit opportunities that knock only once. Personal development is encouraged and facilitated and advancement comes early to those who perform well. There is a high tolerance for errors of commission; those who fail are usually given a chance to try again. Entrepreneurship is highly valued and encouraged.

In social-political-economic environments that are deteriorating, and many are, reactive management is progressive. The past was better than the present; to return to it is an improvement. In environments that are stable and satisfactory, inactive management is obviously effective, but such environments are increasingly rare. The preactive approach is well suited to environments that are subject to large but predictable changes and that provide opportunities for progress. Such environments were prevalent not too long ago, but today's environment is more turbulent and complex.

The interactive approach has no bias toward either the past, present, or future but is based on an appraisal of the nature of things as they are at the time at which planning is done. Intereactivists try to preserve those aspects of the past that are still valuable, and much of it is. They do not discard what is old merely because it is old, as preactivists are inclined to do. They are not disposed to change for sake of change but do not consider technology the devil, as reactivists do.

Interactivists search for diachronic compatibility between past, present, and future and they try to create environments with continuity but continuous challenges and opportunities to innovate.

At the present level of interdependence and complexity, developed nations do not have the luxury of dealing with their developmental problems in progressive stages as did the more developed nations. Less developed countries have to solve their production problems while facing increasingly pressing problems of distribution. They have to solve their marketing problems in view of shorter product life cycles, economies of scale and the challenge of obsolescence. They have to deal with sophisticated technology, and its increasing requirement for specialization, with an army of unskilled, impatient, demanding labor and inexperienced, mistrained, and incapable technocrats. They have to create social stability under the overwhelming pressure of opposing and antagonistic ideologies.

Ironically, the necessity for coping simultaneously with interacting sets of problems represents the most important opportunity for a less developed nation— the opportunity to avoid unforeseen consequences of suboptimization and to redesign the future with all its dimensions in mind. Interactive planning is a design methodology for creating this future.

Part **II**

Planning for Development

In the previous three chapters we have dealt with concepts of nation, development and planning separately, and have made our biases explicit. In Part II we would like to synthesize these concepts into a whole, and to show why and how social development can come about through interactive planning. We will address the role of the government in development planning specifically in the design of participative systems and then deal with the content of interactive planning in more detail.

4

Social Learning and Development

A DESIGN APPROACH

The development of a social system is a collective learning and creative process by which a social system increases its *ability* and *desire* to serve its members and its environment by the constant pursuit of an unattainable ideal, that of omnicompetence.

We have argued that dissatisfaction with the present, although a condition for change, is not sufficient to ensure development. What seems to us to be necessary is a faith in one's ability to partially control the march of events. Those who are awed by their environment and locate the shaping forces of their future only outside of themselves do not think that voluntary or conscious change is possible, no matter how miserable and frustrated they are.

But the ability to change cannot by itself assure development. In the absence of a shared image of a more desirable future the frustration of the powerful masses can easily be converted into a unifying agent of change—hatred—that, in turn, will result in the destruction of the present but will not necessarily be a step toward the creation of a better future. The recent Iranian case is a good example.

The two major components of development, therefore, are desire and ability.

Desire is produced by a vision enlarged through the interaction of creative and recreative processes.

The creative capacity of man, along with his desire to share, results in a shared image of a desired future and motivates the pursuit of more challenging and more desirable ends. Otherwise, life proceeds simply with setting and seeking attainable goals that rarely escape the limits of the familiar.

In most of the Midde Eastern countries a certain interpretation of the dominant religion—the fundamentalist—regards creation as a sole prerogative of God. Human beings are assumed not to be capable of, and therefore, not allowed to engage in, any act of creation. Art in almost any form—painting, sculpture, music, drama—is prohibited. Recreation is also considered sinful.

This antagonistic attitude toward aesthetics militates against development in that it does not provide much opportunity to articulate and expand one's horizon beyond the immediate needs of mere existence. This provides one explanation for cases of underdevelopment despite the availability of vast resources.

Ability, on the other hand, is the potential means of controlling, influencing, and appreciating the parameters that effect the system's existence.

Parameters that co-produce the future are found in the interaction of the five functional dimensions of a social system.

Economics. The generation and distribution of wealth; that is, the production of necessary goods and services and their equitable distribution.

Science. The generation and dissemination of information, knowledge, and understanding.

Aesthetics. The creation and dissemination of beauty—the meaningfulness and excitement of what is done in and of itself and the enjoyment derived therefrom.

Ethics. Creation and maintenance of peace, conflict, resolutions—the challenge of appreciating the plurality of value systems.

Politics. The generation and distribution of power—questions of legitimacy, authority, and responsibility—or, in general, the question of governance.

The interactive nature of these dimensions excludes the concept of a "single leading factor" which, for most development theories, seems always to be in the forefront. On the contrary, in the systems view, performance of the whole is not the sum of the performances of its parts. Rather, it is the product of their interaction. Therefore, the ultimate success and ability of a social system in pursuit of its desired future depends on its mode of organization. The mode of organization emerges out of interaction between integrative and differentiative processes for generation and dissemination of knowledge, wealth, power, beauty, and values.

This is so because for every level of differentiation there exists a minimum required level of integration below which a system would disintegrate into chaos. Conversely, higher levels of integration require higher degrees of differentiation in order to avoid sterility as manifested in a totalitarian state and other forms of oppressive systems.

Depending on the characteristics of a given culture, a social system can move from a state of chaotic simplicity toward organized simplicity, which in comparison with chaotic simplicity is a state containing less variety, more uniformity, stronger bonding among elements, all of which is produced by emphasis on integration at the cost of differentiation. It can also move toward chaotic complexity, a state with increased variety, reduced wholeness, increased diffusion produced by increased differentiation at the cost of integration. Or it can move toward organized complexity, signifying a higher level of organization achieved

Figure 4.1
Modes of Organization

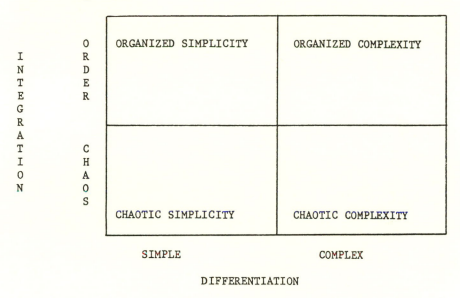

by a movement toward complexity and order concurrently. Note that movement toward complexity and order is the essence of the negentropic processes in living systems.

Movement toward organized complexity involves a participative process in selection of ends and creation of a collective commitment to their pursuit. This collective commitment is required if the aggregate of individuals are to function as a social system. Central to this notion of participation is one's ability to influence the system's behavior. There is no real participation if there is no sharing of power. In this context, alienation of members from the system is the most important obstruction for its development. Not surprisingly, underlying causes of alienation can also be found in one or the combination of the following factors, each corresponding to one of the same five dimensions discussed earlier.

Powerlessness. Powerlessness is equivalent to ineffectualness and impotency. When an individual feels that his contributions to the group's achievements are insignificant, or when he feels powerless to play an effective role in the system's performance, a feeling of indifference gradually sets in and he becomes alienated from the very system of which he is supposed to be a part. The feeling of powerlessness is due in part to the organizational setup, which is usually designed mechanistically, thus forcing a passive functioning of the parts. Furthermore, just as the strength of a chain is determined by its weakest link, so too, incompatibility between the strength of various elements in a developing system often causes the more dynamic units to retrogress to the level of the weakest, spreading a general feeling of ineffectualness and impotency.

Incompetence. Lack of sufficient knowledge and proper professional skills to carry out the responsibilities of a specific role (incompetence) result in excessive anxiety and frustration. To fulfill the role of a physician or carpenter requires certain expertise and mastery that must be learned. Otherwise, the individual to whom the role is entrusted will be alienated.

Meaninglessness. Lack of a meaningful, exciting, and challenging mission in life; suppression of an individual's need for creativity and achievement; and finally insensitivity toward the recreational aspect of the production process are among the main causes of a feeling of meaninglessness.

Exploitation. A feeling of injustice in the distribution of a system's achievements is another factor that can cause alienation. When an individual feels that he has somehow been deprived of his fair share of and recognition for contributing to a system's achievements, he becomes alienated and frustration will result.

Conflicting values. Finally, conflicting values within a social system contribute to alienation of its members. As mentioned before, the extent to which an individual's value image coincides with the "shared image" of his community determines the degree of his membership. The level of integration that a society will achieve depends on the means by which it deals with conflicts among its members. A certain degree of consensus with regard to desired ends is required for continued and productive membership in a given system.

A social system, in its ideal form, is a voluntary association of purposeful members. Emigration of a member from the system is considered to be the highest manifestation of his protest. However, because of a series of self-imposed or external constraints (there seem to be no more realistic chances for emigration), a dissatisfied member may not be able or willing to leave the system. He therefore becomes alienated from the very system of which he is supposed to be a voluntary member. This is a major obstruction to development witnessed in almost all developing nations.

As an open, purposeful system (system that manifests choices of both ends and means), a nation is part of a larger purposeful system—the international community. At the same time it has purposeful individuals as its own members. These create a hierarchy of purposeful systems of three distinct levels. These three levels are so interconnected that an optimal solution cannot be found at one level independent of the other two.

In contrast to machines and organisms in which integration of the parts into a cohesive whole is a one-time proposition, for social systems the problem of integration is a constant struggle and a continuous process.

The presence of an element of choice in the behavior of members places the social system in a class by itself. Lack of appreciation for the implications of the factor of choice in the behavior of members of social systems becomes the main source of the confusion and dilemmas encountered in organizations conceived as mechanistic or organismic systems.

In line with the assumptions of mechanistic and organismic models, the prime concern of every such organizational theory has been to define the criteria by which the whole is to be divided into functional parts. Major organizational theories have implicitly assumed that the whole is nothing but the sum of its parts and have conveniently ignored the fact that effective differentiation requires incorporation of a means that would integrate the differentiated parts into a cohesive whole. In this regard, the classical school of management depends solely on the unity of command and the imperative of no deviation. At the opposite end, the neoclassical school, advocating decentralized structure, relies on the assumption that perfectly rational micro-decisions would automatically produce perfectly rational macro-conditions. However, effective social integration requires that compatibility be continuously re-created, first between the different levels of purposeful systems (vertical) and, second, among purposeful members at the same level (horizontal). A third kind of compatibility should be included, a continuing concern for the interests of past, present, and future stakeholders in a social system (diachronic).

In a purposeful system with purposeful parts, interactions among the members take many forms that may co-exist simultaneously. Actors in a social system may cooperate with regard to one pair of tendencies, compete over others, and be in conflict with respect to different sets at the same time. In general, purposeful actors (individually or in groups), by agreeing or disagreeing with each other on compatibility of their ends, means, or both can create the following four types of relationships:

1) *Cooperation*:   Compatibility of both ends and means
2) *Competition*:   Compatibility of ends, incompatibility of means
3) *Coalition*:   Incompatibility of ends, compatibility of means
4) *Conflict*:   Incompatibility of both ends and means

In conflict, each party reduces the expected value of the outcomes for the others. The opposite is true of cooperation.

Competition represents a situation in which a lower-level conflict serves the attainment of a commonly held higher-level objective for both parties. It is a conflict of means, not ends.

Coalitions are formed when actors with conflicting ends agree to remove a perceived common obstruction. This is an unstable situation in which conflict is temporarily converted to cooperation only to be succeeded by possibly more severe conflict at higher level.

If organizations are to serve their members as well as their environments they must be able to deal with conflict among them. Creation of a conflict-free society may not be possible but one capable of dealing with conflict is. There are different ways of dealing with conflicts. One can either solve, resolve, absolve, or dissolve them.

To *solve* a conflict is to select a course of action that is believed to yield the best possible outcome for one side at the cost of the other, a win/lose struggle. To *resolve* a conflict is to select a course of action that yields an outcome that is good enough and minimally satisfies both of the opposing tendencies, a compromise. To *absolve* a conflict is to wait it out, to ignore it and hope that it will go away; to treat it with benign neglect. Finally, to *dissolve* a conflict is to change the nature and/or the environment of the entity in which it is imbedded so as to create a win/win environment.

Selection of any one of these courses of action depends on how the relationships between opposing tendencies are formulated. In contrast to solving or resolving, which is used whenever the conflict situation is conceived to be unidimensional, to dissolve a conflict requires a multidimensional conception.

In the unidimensional conception of conflict, the conflict situation is formulated as a zero-sum game, so that a gain for one player is invariably associated with a loss for the other. But the multidimensional conception of conflict characterizes a non–zero-sum situation, in which a loss for one side is not necessarily a gain for the other. On the contrary, this formulation permits both opposing tendencies not only to co-exist but also to increase or decrease simultaneously. Therefore, lose/lose as well as win/win in addition to win/lose struggles are strong possibilities.

To dissolve a conflict is to appreciate the systemic nature of the interactions between opposing tendencies. For example, security and freedom, usually considered dichotomous, are actually two aspects of the same problem. Freedom is not possible without security and security makes no sense without freedom. But if we choose to deal with each one of these aspects separately, then we should not be surprised to find them in conflict. The easiest solution to security, if treated in isolation, would be to limit freedom, and that of freedom would be to undermine security. To dissolve a conflict is to discover new frames of reference in which opposing tendencies are treated as complementary in a new ensemble with a new logic of its own. Despite seemingly contradictory requirements for pursuit of opposing ends, there are processes that would make the attainment of both ends feasible. For instance, both freedom and security are attainable by a process called *participation*, stability and change by *adaptation*, and order and complexity by *organization*.

Similarly, production and distribution of wealth form a complementary pair. Without an effective production system, there can never be an effective distribution system. To fail to note this important interdependency is to leave out the most important challenge of the problem. An obsession with distribution without a proper concern about production will result in nothing but an equitable distribution of poverty. Preoccupation with production without a similar concern for an equitable distribution will lead to an alienated society.

To sum up, it is important to note that Churchman's concern with "environmental fallacy" (1979), Boulding's rejection of suboptimization—"the name of the devil is suboptimization" (1975)—and Ackoff's concept of "separately infeasible parts making a feasible whole" (1978) are reflections of the same systemic principle. The principle is that expansion of the system to include other relevant and complementary variables will result in reformulation of the problem situation. This, in turn, will lead to shared higher level ends and will remove the contradictory requirements of suboptimization.

After all, ends and means are interchangeable concepts; an end is a means for a further end. Thus, the search for a shared higher-level end can continue up to and include the ideal, when ends and means converge and become the same. The probability of finding a shared objective increases by moving to higher and higher levels and is maximized at the ideal level.

Now, if even the ideal level cannot produce a common end for conflicting tendencies, then the conflict is considered nondissolvable within the context of existing world views. In this situation, dissolving the conflicts requires a change of world views, a most difficult change to make, but one that can occur. For example, it can happen without a design, as a reaction to frustrations produced by failure of the existing assumptions to deal with the emerging realities of a new era, a march of events nullifying conventional wisdom. Or it can be made to happen by an active learning and unlearning process of purposeful transformation.

This brings us to the role of the culture in the process of change.

As a prerequisite to survival it has always been necessary for man to observe and understand events that are constantly occurring in his environment. He does this so that he may utilize favorable opportunities and be prepared for antagonistic events. But understanding scattered phenomena in isolation, although necessary, is not sufficient for man to relate to his environment. Therefore, an additional struggle to find a logical relationship among these isolated findings impels him to synthesize this fragmented information into a unified, meaningful mental image and eventually into a world view.

Co-produced by the environment and man's unique process of creativity, the image establishes a link between man and his environment. It consists of a system of assumptions (possibly unconscious) regarding the nature of spatio-temporal-causal realities in addition to a concept of values, aesthetics, and finally his perceived role in the environment. A considerable part of this image or mental model of the universe is shared with others who live in the same social setting. The rest remains private and personal (Boulding, 1956). It is the *shared image* that constitutes the principal bond among the members of a human community and provides the necessary conditions for any meaningful interaction. The extent to which the image of an individual coincides with the shared image of a community determines the degree of his membership in that community. It is the shared image that we refer to as the *culture* of the people. It incorporates their experiences, beliefs, attitudes, and ideals and is the ultimate product and reflection of their history and the manifestation of their identity—man creates his culture and his culture creates him.

It is here that the key obstacles and opportunities for development are found, the collective ability and desire of the people to create the future they want. Therefore, human culture with all its complexity, ambiguity, and manifold potentialities stands at the center of a process of change. This process cannot be understood except against the background of the culture of which it is a part, which it builds upon and reacts against, so much so that the success of individual actions invariably depends on the degree to which they penetrate and modify the shared image.

The inertia of a culture is produced by the fact that public and private images act as filters, developing a selective mode of reception. This tunes the receptors for particular messages. Those consistent with the image are absorbed and further reinforced, while contradictory and antagonistic ones have no significant effect. This phenomenon, although an impediment to change, acts as a defense mechanism and structure-maintaining function.

Just like a high-level computer language that provides default parameters when programmers fail to provide one, the culture of a social system provides default values when actors fail to choose them explicitly. For example, if a man does not decide explicitly what kind of father he wants to be, the culture decides for him. The problem with this is that the implicitness of the underlying assumptions prevents actors from questioning their validity; therefore, they usually remain unchallenged and become obsolete. Furthermore, actors, by repeated use of default values, tend to forget that they have a choice and treat such values as "realities out there," undermining the fact that those "realities" will remain out there so long as no one is willing to challenge them.

On the other hand, the potentiality and vitality of the culture, and thus that of the social system, lie in its creative ability to meet the challeges of continuously emerging desires and ideals. This process demands conscious and active adaptation, not a passive acceptance of events. It is a struggle for the creation of new dimensions, appreciation of new realities, and, finally, enrichment of the common image. It is a learning process that entails collective and coordinated changes in motivation, knowledge, and understanding throughout the social system. This brings us to the notion of social learning.

The role of knowledge in social systems is analogous to that of energy in physical systems. As the energy level determines the mode of organization in physical systems, the knowledge level defines it for social systems. But unlike energy, knowledge is not subject to the "law of conservation." The ability to learn and create knowledge enables social systems to constantly re-create their structures. But the knowledge level of a social system is not the sum of the knowledge of its individual members. It is the shared implicit knowledge, or shared image, as manifested in the culture.

Although social systems learn through their members, who adjust their world views or mapping of reality by observing the actual or potential results of their actions, social learning is not the sum of the isolated learning of each member. It is a collective and participative process of generation and dissemination of knowledge, discovery of new dimensions and creation of successive modes of organization. This involves a joint and painful process of reconceptualization, reformulation, and integration of the relevant variables into a new ensemble with new relationships and characteristics of its own. This in turn demands a capability for second-order learning, which must be distinguished from first-order learning.

Consider a choice model in which actors are to choose among several courses of action. This choice model is formed by what actors collectively believe are the possible courses of action available to them. Inclusion or exclusion of alternatives in the choice model is not arbitrary. The choices in the set usually share one or more properties based on an explicit or implicit set of assumptions or constraints produced by the actors' previous experience with similar situations. In this context, first-order learning represents a quantitative change. It is a revision of probabilities of choice, modifying parameters, in a fixed structure. Underlying assumptions governing the selection of alternatives remain unchallenged.

Second-order learning, on the other hand, involves challenging assumptions. It represents a qualitative change that results in a reidentification of the available set of alternatives and objectives. This redefines the rules for first-order learning. Unfortunately, in societies polarized by antagonistic and rigid ideologies, social transformation takes place by a violent change of phase (a cusp). Retrieval from such a situation is often extremely problematic, since the relationship between members is irreparably damaged as happens in societies that are thrown into a perpetual state of civil disorder.

In this context, ideologies of any form or type represent a profound obstruction to second-order learning. Of course an ideology should not be mistaken for a cause or a vision. The significant and common characteristic of all ideologies is a claim to ultimate truth with a predefined set of ends and means. Underlying assumptions are not to be questioned by true believers. This makes ideologies incompatible with the requirements for second-order learning.

The formation of highly polarized political and social groups is the most destructive phenomenon confronting the majority of underdeveloped nations. Self-appointed guardians of the working class and cynical intellectuals, in their struggle for power and fame, manipulate the masses with slogans and demagoguery, pulling them from one extreme to the next like a pendulum.

In most Middle Eastern countries polarization takes the form of religious versus secular tendencies, with each of these further divided into groups of leftists and rightists, with national or international orientations.

The problem is that no one of the so-called opposing groups is strong enough to govern without the cooperation of the others, and yet each one is powerful enough to disrupt and undermine the effectiveness of the ruling group. This is partly due to increased complexity in the system, which makes it more vulnerable to sabotage, on the one hand, and more difficult to manage, on the other.

Once it seizes power, the ruling group sets out to monopolize power. This brings opposing groups together in a coalition to paralyze the government. The government in turn intensifies its efforts to eliminate the opposition through oppressive means. Hatred of the ruling group thus becomes the unifying agent, and the opposition movement erupts, causing destruction. New leaders who

Figure 4.2
Middle Eastern Polarization

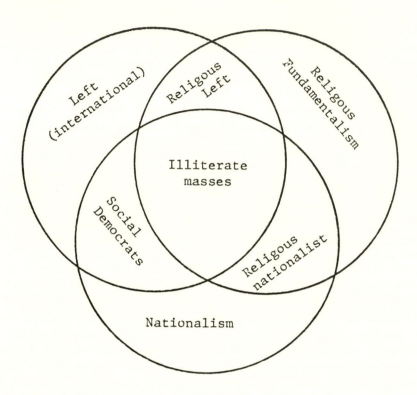

emerge soon renew the oppressive measures of the previous regime. Hatred grows anew, another cycle begins with opposing forces regrouping. Ironically, any conciliatory gesture by the oppressive regime toward the opposition is taken as a sign of weakness. This causes them to intensify rather than modify their attacks on the government. The regime is forced to tighten its control over the opposition until neither more pressure nor more freedom can save it from collapse.

Interestingly enough, this process does not depend on the ideology of the ruling group. There is no example of one that has been able to break out of this vicious circle. The secular left in Iraq and Afghanistan, the religious left in Libya, and both the religious and secular right in Iran and Pakistan provide new supportive evidence for this argument.

Polarization has resulted in increased terrorism, complete paralysis of government, and oscillation between extremes. The major effort of every new government has always been to undo every change instituted by the preceding regime, be it industrial projects or elementary school textbooks. The new regimes in Iran and Turkey have both set out to rewrite schoolbooks. Even the cultural heritage is not spared. Every new regime disbands existing historical accounts, calling them false and misguiding, and presents its own version as correct. The plan is always to destroy the old system completely before starting to construct a new order. Not surprisingly, the first part is usually more successful than the second, breaking the cumulative cultural and developmental continuity between one period and the next.

The oscillation will not end until opposing groups learn to modify their dogmatic positions, give up their monopolistic claim on power, and work toward creating a shared image and a consensus among people through processes of integration, not at the expense of differentiation, but alongside it.

The critical issues of qualitative change and development demand incorporation of second-order learning in social systems. This requires the creation of a new mode of organization in the form of an ideal-seeking system, in contrast to creating an ideal state.

Design of an ideal-seeking system is in fact at the core of any effective means for realizing the full potential of a purposeful social system. It requires creation of:

- A participative process that enables the members of a social system collectively to define and redefine their desired futures and relate their roles to the totality of the system of which they are a part,

- A learning and adaptive system that is able and willing to alter its course of action at any time in recognition of emerging values and new realities,

- A pluralistic social setting that encourages and facilitates questioning of sacred assumptions and challenges the implicit set of default values.

Interactive planning is a design methodology for creation of ideal-seeking systems through which the collective desire for and ability to pursue a more desirable future is increased.

It is our contention that the best way to learn and understand a system is to design it. In order to design a system designers must learn how to use what they already know, how to realize what they do not know, and how to learn what they need to know. Furthermore, producing a design requires an awareness of how activities of one part of the system affect and are affected by other parts. This requires understanding the nature of thee interactions among the parts. Thus, a design process involves all three questions of what, how, and why. This is holistic learning that results in increased levels of information, knowledge, and understanding.

Finally, this design approach explicitly recognizes the role of choice that we believe is the most critical element in the learning process. The generality and effectiveness of design as a mode of learning is also demonstrated by Churchman in his book *Design of Inquiring Systems*, in which he examines philosophy of science from a designer's point of view (Churchman, 1971).

In interactive planning an idealized design is used as a vehicle for collective learning and development. The reasons for this have to do with *participation, consensus, commitment, creativity,* and *implementability.* We consider each of these in turn.

> 1. Participation: idealized design facilitates participation in the planning process and such participation develops the participants.

Planning is an activity normally reserved for experts who are assumed to know best either how to react (if the planning is reactive) or how to predict and prepare (if it is preactive). But there are no experts on "what ought to be," which is what idealized design is all about. There are no authoritative "ought opinions." Therefore, all stakeholders can participate in idealized design with equal authority. In effect, involvement in the design process is its most important product. Therefore, those whom the design seeks to change should participate in the process.

Participation in idealized design is usually an exciting idea; engaging in it is fun (play); it facilitates and encourages learning. Thus, work, play, and learning are integrated in the design process. Each is enhanced by the presence of the others. It is in just such an environment that development best takes place.

> 2. Consensus: idealized design generates a consensus among those who participate in it.

The more ultimate the ends considered by two or more people, the more likely they are to agree on their desirability or undesirability. The shorter the range of ends considered and the greater the focus on means, the less likely they are to agree. Many fail to see this because they characterize the differences between opposing parties as ideological. Ideologies have less to do with ideals than with the means for pursuing them. (The similarity of those two words is misleading.) For example, the ideological questions involving who should own the means of production concern the selection of means for pursuing the ideal of plenty.

The idealized design of Paris (Ozbekhan, 1977) was forwarded to the cabinet of France with the support of every one of its large number of political parties. They agreed on what Paris ought to be. This may have been the first time they had ever agreed unanimously on anything.

Because the focus in idealized design is on what we would ultimately like, the process tends to generate consensus among its participants. Awareness of agreement on ultimate ends creates an atmosphere in which differences over more immediate ends or means can be negotiated in a conciliatory rather than a hostile mode. Moreover, those differences that cannot be settled by consensus can be subjected to resolution by an experiment that is incorporated into the design. Then consensus need only be reached on the nature of the experiment.

> 3. Commitment: participation in the preparation of an idealized design, the infusion of personal style and ideals into it, and the consensus that emerges from it generate commitment to the realization of that design.

Recall from the earlier discussion of the quality of life that one of its critical aspects involves the satisfaction that people derive from what they do and how they do it, independent of what they do it for. This involves intrinsic rather than extrinsic value. Preferences based on intrinsic value make up an individual's style.

In general, we develop stronger commitments to ideas and ideals that we have a hand in formulating than to those that we do not. Such commitments considerably reduce the number and difficulty of problems associated with implementation of plans. It is often more difficult to implement conventional plans than it is to produce them. The less developed a social system is, the harder it is to change; the harder it is to change, the more difficult it is to implement a plan. Therefore, one of the principal objectives of planning should be to overcome resistance to change. Involvement in idealized design often overcomes such resistance.

> 4. Creativity: the idealized design process stimulates creativity and focuses it on societal and individual development.

In most people, creativity is imprisoned behind walls built of self-imposed constraints. Such constraints convert simple problems into unsolvable puzzles. A puzzle is a problem that cannot be solved because of an incorrectly made assumption. Once this assumption is removed, finding a solution is generally easy. Creativity, like solving a puzzle, begins with the removal of self-imposed constraints that take the form of unquestioned assumptions. Idealized design relaxes, if it does not remove, such constraining assumptions, particularly those associated with implementability. Implementability is not a requirement imposed on an idealized design. Therefore, it tends to liberate the imagination and stimulate the desire to innovate and invent.

> 5. Implementability: the idealized design process enlarges the designers' conception of what can be implemented.

In conventional planning it is assumed that unless each part of the plan taken separately is implementable, the plan as a whole is not. This is not the case. A plan is a system of decisions and hence can have properties that none of its parts do, including implementability. The implementability of the whole can derive from the interactions of parts that, when viewed separately, appear to be unimplementable.

For example, the plan for Paris previously referred to included many changes that appeared to be infeasible when examined separately. One was that the capital of France eventually be moved out of Paris. Another was that Paris be converted into a self-governing open city not subject to the government of France. Because the idealized redesign of Paris focused on making it the informal capital of the world, these changes were viewed not only as feasible, but necessary. For this reason, the government of France has taken significant steps toward their realization.

Those exposed to an idealized design of a system with which they are familiar frequently note with surprise that there is very little in the design that could not be brought about now if the stakeholders would put their minds to it. The design reveals that the principal obstruction between man and the future he most desires is man himself. Idealized design helps remove this self-imposed constraint.

Role of the Government in Development Planning

Government is the management of society. The development efforts of the governed require coordination, encouragement, and facilitation by their government. We have argued that development most effectively takes place in situations in which individuals can participate in making decisions that affect them. Central to this notion of participation is one's ability to influence the system's behavior. There is no real participation if there is no sharing of power, and the key to sharing power is the decentralization of control over the resources. The way by which a government is selected, organized, and works is a matter of power, of who has control over whom. The practice of government with respect to distribution of power defines its mode of organization. It is our contention that the principal role of the government in development planning is the design and implementation of a participative system. This is the subject of our next chapter.

5

A Design for Participation in Planning

We have called for the participation in development planning of all those who have a stake in it. This is easier said than done. How can one organize national development planning so that all stakeholders who so desire can participate in it in a meaningful way? An answer to this question lies in the concept of a "circular organization." First we explain this concept in a very simple context. Then we show how it can be adapted and applied to a nation. Next, we consider the role of the professional planner in the participative planning process and illustrate this role by use of a community development project. Finally we consider how the large number of competent planners required by our design can be produced and made available.

THE ELEMENTS OF A PARTICIPATIVE DESIGN

Consider a simple three-tiered organization such as is shown in Figure 5.1. The tiers could be federal, state, and local governments, or a ministry, subministries, and directorates. Each box in Figure 5.1 represents a unit—the collection of people who constitute that unit. The small circle at the top of each box represents the head of that unit.

In the design that follows, each unit prepares a plan for itself and all members of that unit, regardless of their rank or status, are given an equal opportunity to participate in that planning.

The most critical element of the design is the planning board, represented in Figure 5.2 by the larger circles. Every unit has such a board. Each board, except the one at the top and those at the bottom, which we treat separately below, consists of the following members:

1. The head of the unit reporting to it (thus the head of unit 2.1 is a member of planning board 2.1),

Figure 5.1
An Organizational Design for Participative Planning

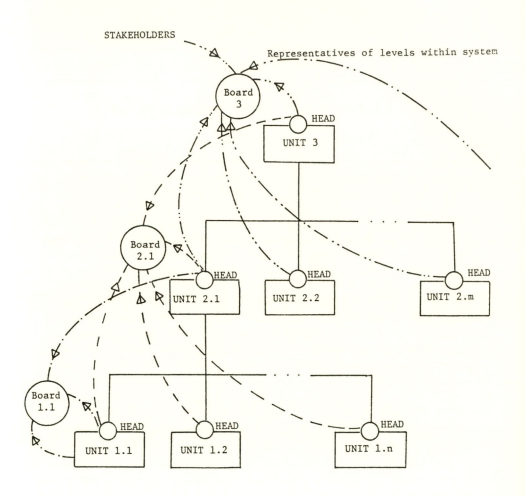

Figure 5.2
A Design for Participative National Development Planning

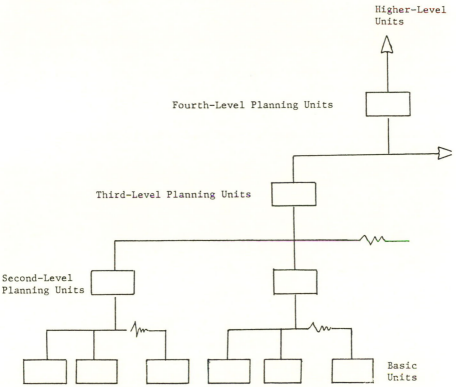

2. The immediate superior of the head of the unit (thus the head of unit 3 is a member of board 2.1), and

3. The heads of the units immediately subordinate to the head of the unit whose board it is (thus heads 1.1, 1.2, . . . , 1.n are members of board 2.1).

Three levels are represented on each board except the one at the top. Every unit head, except those at the top and bottom, are members of the board to which his superior reports, his own board, and the boards to which each of his immediate subordinates report. This means that in an organization of five levels, the heads of units in the middle (third) level would interact with unit heads at all five levels. In their superior's board they would interact with their superior, his superior, and all other unit heads at the same level. In their subordinates' boards they would interact with their subordinates and their subordinates' subordinates. The extensiveness of such vertical interaction makes effective integration of planning performed at different levels possible.

At the lowest level, all members of a unit are members of that unit's board.

Thus, there are three levels in these boards. The lowest does not consist of only unit heads, but includes those who are under the lowest-level head.

The board at the top includes the highest authority (head 3), his immediate subordinates (heads 2.1, 2.2, . . . , 2.m) and elected representatives of each other level of the system. The number of representatives from each level clearly depends on the number of levels and the number of units at each level. The composition of this "top board" is what makes the organization circular.

Each board has the following responsibilities:

1. Coordination of the plans made by those units at the level below that report to it. (Since the majority of the members of all boards except the one at the top consist of those from the level below, coordination is essentially self-coordination.)
2. Integration of the plans made at the level of the board with higher- and lower-level plans, where such levels exist.
3. Control of the implementation and effects of the plan made at its level. (Later we consider what is involved in such control.)

These are the essential elements of the design. Now let us see how they can be extended and adapted to national planning.

A DESIGN FOR PARTICIPATIVE NATIONAL PLANNING

The design that follows is idealized; hence it requires adaptation to fit particular conditions. Furthermore, it is not intended to be a universal design—good for all times and all cases. On the contrary, we believe a comprehensive design of a social order that would be appropriate for a given culture requires active participation of its members in the design process itself. However, the proposed design presents a concept around which many different variations can be constructed.

We begin by considering the spatial or geographical organization of a nation's population into the planning process. Then we extend the design to include various social dimensions other than location. The objectives of this design are, first, to expose every important planning decision to participative public scrutiny and, second, to provide every member of a society with an opportunity (but not an obligation) to participate in those aspects of planning in which he or she has a stake.

The Geographic Organization of Planning

Each box in Figure 5.2 represents a planning unit. The lowest-level units (basic units) are such that everyone who so desires can participate in one or more of these units depending on where he or she resides and the number of residences that he or she has. For example, in an urban area the lowest level may consist of all the residents of a city block; in a rural area, all the residents of a village. The units should be small enough to allow for meaningful participation of each member. We have arbitrarily set this number at 100. It can be changed where appropriate. Not all lowest-level units need have the same number of participants, but all the members of such units should have a common geographical area of concern.

Each of the first-level units should plan for its own future. It should be free to make and implement any decision that has no effect on any other unit. It would be the responsibility of the second-level units to determine which of the decisions made at the first level have no such external effects. Second-level approval would be required for decisions that have such external effects.

Each first-level unit should have funds made available to it by government for use at its own discretion. The amount of funds made available to units should be large enough to make a difference in their development of quality of life. Decisions that involve use of these resources should satisfy two conditions: They should be agreed to by a majority of the unit's members, and the funds should be used either for development or improving the quality of life in the unit. It should be the responsibility of the appropriate second-level unit to see to it that these conditions are satisfied. A unit could legitimately use its funds to purchase technical assistance from either public or private sources.

Each first-level unit would elect a chairman. The chairmen of approximately ten contiguous first-level units would form a second-level unit. This unit would coordinate and monitor the planning of the first-level units of which it is composed. It would deal with all matters that affect two or more of these first-level units. However, plans that affect more than two second-level units would have to go up to the third level, and so on up to the top.

Second-level units should also have funds made available to them. In addition, first-level units might turn over part of their funds to the second level for use on matters that affect them jointly. The conditions imposed on use of resources at the first level would also apply at the second and higher levels. These conditions would be monitored in each case by the next higher level unit.

The third-level unit would consist of the elected chairmen of the second-level units of which it is composed. The chairman of any unit above the first level should be relieved of his or her lower-level chairmanship, and replaced by another, also elected. However, the chairman at each level should participate in the planning of all units that are part of the unit they chair.

The number of levels required would be dictated by the number of adults in the nation. In general, no more than ten units should be combined in a higher-level unit. The units above the first level should be small enough to permit full participation by each of their members. Figure 5.3 shows the approximate numbers at each level. These numbers are only suggestive. The structure might well require adjustment to existing political and geographical conditions. The highest level would, of course, be national.

This design applies to a nation looked at geographically. However, people may want to participate in planning from the point of view of one or more special

Figure 5.3
Number of Levels and Sizes of Units in a Participative National Development Process

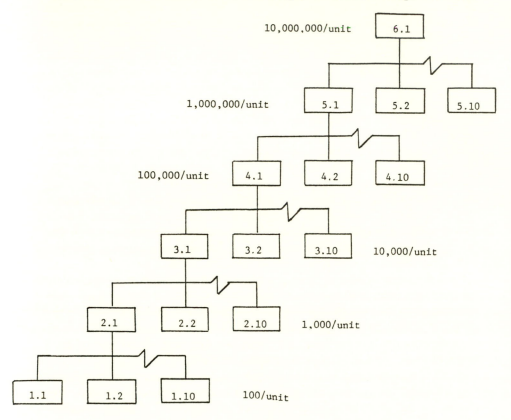

interests they have; for example, industrial, agricultural, educational, health, and so on. Therefore, some provisions should be made for sectoral planning that can be superimposed on the design already presented.

Sectoral Planning

The design just presented is organized spatially; hence, the focus is on geographically defined areas and those who occupy them. However, our social lives are organized in many other ways: by profession, occupation, avocation, and so on. Comprehensive development planning should therefore enable institutions, associations, organizations, and other collectivities to plan their futures and integrate their output with that of geographically based planning units.

Consider, for example, how educational planning might be organized by, say, a ministry of education. (What follows could apply to any ministry.) The educational system of most countries is organized as a multilevel hierarchy—for example, individual schools as the basic unit collected into school districts, then regions, and finally into a national unit. Each unit at any level would plan participatively for itself and be subject to the same constraints as apply to geographically based units: It could act unilaterally on anything that had no effect on any other unit in or out of its sector.

Each unit would also have a board constituted as for geographically based units, and they would function in the same way with one difference: They would have to coordinate their planning with the appropriate geographically based planning boards. For example, each educational planning board would submit its plans to the lowest level geographically based board that has jurisdiction over all the areas affected by the relevant educational plan. This means that educational planning at, say, the city level would have to be coordinated with geographically based city planning and be approved by the city's planning board. This would be equally true for planning units in every sector; for example, health, transportation, industry, housing, and so on, as well as education. This would preclude any agency of government at any level from imposing its plans on an area without its approval or that of the lowest level geographically based planning board covering all of the areas affected.

Organizations or associations that have no geographical effects—for example, ones that affect only their members—would require no such approval or coordination. Professional societies, recreational clubs, or religious groups might be in such a position.

Comprehensive sectoral planning could also be organized along the five functional dimensions of science, economics, ethics, aesthetics, and politics. Obstructions and opportunities for development associated with each of these dimensions are discussed in Part III of the present work.

Coordination and Integration of Multisectoral Planning

The coordination and integration of planning carried out simultaneously in a number of sectors with that which is geographically based requires a national planning support and monitoring system. This system should have a national headquarters with a director who reports directly to the head of the government and is a member of his or her cabinet. The system should have units at lower levels; for example, regional and state. The number of levels and units would depend on the geography and population of the country. In a country that is large in both respects, four or five levels might be required. Lower-level service units would be tied together by a communication network with on-line, real-time access to each other's files.

Each service unit would maintain records of all planning carried out within its area of responsibility. These records would be accessible to all. Users could be charged a fee sufficient to cover the marginal costs of retrieval. Each unit would also maintain a bank of data relevant to planning, and it would provide,

Figure 5.4
Coordination and Integration of Planning Boards

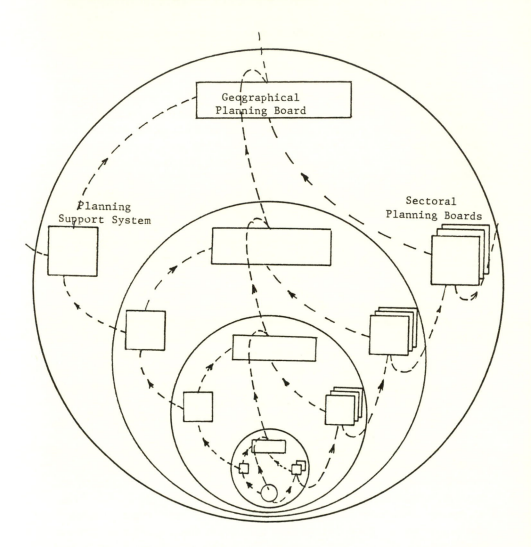

on request and at a fee, data-processing and analytical services. The data bank would include a register in which relevant information on each planning unit in the area would be maintained.

The service units would publish a planning newsletter or journal periodically to inform those involved in planning about what was going on, where, and when. It would also call to their attention any relevant methodological or substantive developments that they should consider.

The service units would also inform planning units about other units that they should consult or whose approval they require. These units would analyze all plans prepared in their domains to be sure all units affected by any plan were aware of such effects and had been appropriately consulted. They should be empowered to prevent implementation of any plan that does not meet the participative requirements.

Each service unit would have a board consisting of its own director, the director of the higher level unit to which it reports, the heads of any lower level units reporting to it, and a number equal to the sum of those three of the lowest level geographically based planning board covering the area of its responsibility.

Service unit boards would review and settle complaints of stakeholders arising from their being denied an opportunity to participate in any planning affecting them. They would also arbitrate any unresolved conflicts arising across sectors within their areas of jurisdiction. They would review requests by planning units for exemption from public scrutiny. Plans, or portions of them, could be exempted from such examination but only if doing so were in the public's interest. Records of decisions to exempt would be open to public examination.

THE ROLE OF THE PROFESSIONAL PLANNER

The role of the professional planner in the type of participative development planning advocated here is very different from the traditional one. It does not involve planning for others, but enabling them to plan more effectively for themselves. Rather than decrease the task of the planner, this approach increases it, as the following case involving an underdeveloped black urban neighborhood in an American city illustrates. The planners in this case were members of the university-based research center of which the authors are a part.

The community involved, called Mantua, lies just to the north of the University of Pennsylvania, close to the center of Philadelphia. At the time this story began, in 1968, the neighborhood was referred to by blacks in the city as "The Bottom." It contains about eighty city blocks and had an official population of about 15,000, but an unofficial one of at least a third larger. About 98 percent of its population was black. By almost any standard it was a critically depressed and disadvantaged area. About 25 percent of its housing units were overcrowded, and more than 50 percent were in substandard condition. Its male unemployment rate was between 15 and 20 percent during the 1960s, more than three times the rate in the city as a whole. Thirty-seven percent of its families earned less than $3,000 per year during this period. More than a third of the Mantuans who were over twenty-five years old had less than eight years of education. About 50 percent of its minors received some type of public assistance, more than six times the city's rate. Sixteen percent of its population from seven to seventeen years old were arrested in 1964, nine times the rate in the city as a whole. Its adult crime rate was more than twice that of the city. Uses of narcotics was widespread.

The approach taken to the development of this neighborhood was based on an assumption that history seems to support strongly: A developed community cannot solve an underdeveloped community's problems. Only the underdeveloped can do so. Development of a community requires development of its members' ability to solve their own problems. Therefore, the less developed must plan and manage their own development. They can benefit more from their own mistakes than they can from consuming the development plans made for them by the developed.

What the less developed have been most deprived of is not the fruits of development, but the opportunity to develop themselves. Only self-development can bring with it the self-confidence, dignity, and self-respect that makes continuous development possible.

This set of beliefs does not imply that those who are developed should sit by idly while the less developed go it alone; they cannot go it alone in a developed society. They need access to human and material resources that are controlled by the developed. They need the developed working for them, not on them. This requires the developed placing themselves and some of their resources at the disposal of the less developed, to be used as the less developed see fit.

Resources should be made available to the less developed not only as an investment in their development, but also as an investment in the further development of the developed. Like all investments, some will fail to pay off, but the ability of the less developed to provide satisfactory returns on such investments increases with each failure because of what they learn from these failures.

Control and management of investments, financial and intellectual, should be placed in the less developed community because so doing maximizes its learning and that of the giver as well. The solution lies in investment, not charity. Charity breeds dependency in the receiver and even hostility to the donor. It also breeds resentment in the donor. Development can be neither given nor received; it must be generated from within.

The Mantua Story

Early in 1968 Forrest Adams, a Mantuan, came to the Busch Center at the University of Pennsylvania for help in preparing a request for neighborhood assistance from a city agency. This help was given to him but he was asked if he would be willing to bring his neighborhood's principal leader to the University to discuss a proposal that the Center would like to make to him. This proposal had been carefully worked out in the hope that just such an opportunity would arise. The funds needed for it had already been obtained from the Anheuser-Busch Charitable Trust of St. Louis.

The next day Forrest Adams brought Herman Wrice, president of the recently formed Young Great Society (YGS), to the University for a meeting. YGS was an indigenous group dedicated to the development of Mantua. The Center offered to employ any three people selected from the community by Mr. Wrice. They were to work on the development of their community in any way they saw fit. There were no constraints on how, when, or where they worked. They were not required to be present at the University at any time, but the personnel and facilities of the Center were made available for them to use as they desired, and they were encouraged to use them. The Center would do nothing except by request, but it would attempt to fill any request even if it involved competencies and resources not available to it by trying to obtain these from other sources in or out of the University.

There was considerable discussion of the question: What is in it for the Center? The answer was: the chance to learn how to be helpful to a neighborhood such as Mantua. This was not very convincing coming from members of a university that had previously demonstrated lack of concern for its surrounding neighborhoods and whose physical expansion was a major thorn in the side of these neighborhoods. But, since the proposal involved little risk to Mantua, Mr. Wrice accepted it. He and Forrest Adams selected three Mantuans before the day was over. They signed in on the following day.

The two men and one woman selected from Mantua were hired on a Friday. The following Monday they asked for a meeting with the Center to review a work plan they had prepared over the intervening weekend. The Mantuans found the discussion helpful but, more important, they found a willingness on the part of the University's personnel to pitch in where asked to do so. As a result, the Mantuans asked for regular weekly meetings to review plans and accomplishments. In the weeks that followed, requests for meetings and participation of Center personnel became increasingly frequent. Before long, more than thirty people from the University, faculty members and graduate students, were involved in providing the assistance asked for. It became necessary for the Center to assign one of its senior staff members and a graduate student to the effort on a full-time basis so that the diverse activities could be coordinated.

In order to stretch the small initial grant to cover the salaries of the three Mantuans for nine months, the faculty members involved did not bill the grant for their services. This turned out to have an unexpected advantage. Subsequently, many other faculty members who were too busy to "sell" their time to the Center gave some of it to this effort.

After about six months of collaboration the Mantua team and the Center jointly prepared a proposal for continued support of their efforts. It was the Mantua team's decision that any additional funds that might be obtained should continue to be administered by the Center. They preferred this for two reasons: It relieved them of responsibility for keeping the books and it assured them continued involvement of the Center. The proposal was submitted to two foundations. Grants were obtained from both.

When one of these grants was announced one of the members of the Mantua team was asked by a local television interviewer what he thought were the University's motives in the collaboration. He replied: "When the project started I couldn't figure out the University's angle and it worried me because we had been screwed by the University in the past. I'm still not sure what it's up to but I don't think about it any more." Before long the community knew very well what the Center was up to, perhaps better than did the Center itself.

Over the next ten years a great deal was accomplished in Mantua by YGS and members of the community, much of it with help from the Center. We review it only briefly here. A more detailed treatment can be found in Ackoff (1974).

Economic activities. The Mantua Industrial Development Corporation was formed as a subsidary of YGS. It created and operated a black industrial park that housed eight minority-owned and two white-owned industrial enterprises. The employees of these companies were drawn primarily from Mantua. This part was described in a feature article in *Business Week* (Jan. 16, 1971).

With the help of the Center, a number of small businessmen obtained loans from local banks. The Center provided them with managerial and technical assistance.

YGS established an employment service that placed about 250 Mantuans each year. It also initiated and operated a number of job training programs for young people.

Housing. YGS and its subsidiaries redeveloped two apartment houses, one with fifty-eight units and the other with twenty-nine. Thirty-nine townhouses were built on a parcel of land returned to the community by the University. It also brought to Mantua a large federally funded housing project.

Health. YGS established and operated three medical facilities: a medical center that provided general medical and dental services, a healthmobile that brought services to those who could not come for them, and a half-way house, a heroin addiction treatment center that provided methadone maintenance.

Education. YGS established and operated seven schools, which began with infant care and went through undergraduate college. By means of these schools, dropout rates were drastically reduced and the number of young Mantuans who went on to universities was dramatically increased. YGS personnel worked for the School District of Philadelphia in three high schools and one middle school, providing motivation and incentives to minority students and working to reduce tension among gangs in the schools. They also assisted the Board of Education in selecting and orienting new teachers for these and other schools serving the black community.

In January of 1969 the Community–Wharton Educational Program was initiated at the University of Pennsylvania. Using volunteers—faculty members and students—from the Wharton School, this program offers courses in business to students who do not have the financial resources required to attend a regular college and have a desire to learn business and seek a career in it. A large number of its graduates have moved on to degree-granting programs at the University of Pennsylvania and other local universities. A number of others are now usefully employed in business and industry.

In 1970 YGS and the University's Center conducted a twenty-two–week Urban Leadership Training Program (ULT). The following is a description of the program written by one of its participants, Ronald E. Thompson, for the *Mantua Community Newsletter* of April 1970:

On February 9 started the greatest event that ever happened in urban history. The event I'm talking about is the starting of the Urban Leadership Training Program. The program started with 21 gang leaders from the Mantua community. The Young Great Society and Mantua Community Planners are affiliated with the program. The 21 leaders were picked from different corners which consist of 36th Street, 39th Street, Lancaster Avenue, 41st Street, and 42nd Street.

A few months ago, before the program started, these corners were at war with each other. Many times before the start of U.L.T., social workers tried to gather the corners together, but the problem that would result would be more conflict between the young men. As always, somebody would end up getting hurt.

So far the program is doing very good. The great thing about the program is that the young men have unity among each other. You know yourself that it is good because without unity you do not have anything.

The University of Pennsylvania provides space for the young men. Members of the University faculty and community workers of various fields volunteer to teach the young men different courses. Some of the courses the young men are taking consist of criminology, sociology, black studies, community health services, community planning, housing rehabilitation, radio and TV, and communications. The purpose of these courses is to prepare for future black leadership in all fields. . . .

The program is the first I have known to even understand gang problems.

I used to be affiliated with one of the gangs before I went into service. I have been home from the service since January. I was in Vietnam. I compare the fighting in Vietnam with the fighting in the streets and find it almost the same. The only thing is that in the streets you are fighting your own brother.

The brothers are not fighting now. This is why the program might be the greatest event in urban history.

Of those who went through the ULT program, about half went to work for community development groups or government agencies. Most of the rest took positions in business or industry.

YGS personnel were invited to give courses and lectures at a number of universities, and they provided university students with opportunities to do field work in Mantua.

In 1971 YGS and the Center conducted two programs for corporate executives to familiarize them with the black ghetto, its problems, and what they could do about them. This program was also written up in *Business Week* (June 19, 1971).

Recreation and culture. YGS established an athletic program that covered every major sport and several minor ones. These served both boys and girls. Its teams competed in leagues throughout the city and won a disproportional number of city championships. Mantuan teams competed out of state, giving many young people their first chance to travel.

Each summer YGS conducted extensive recreational and work programs for young people, including summer camps located on nearby university campuses. Four hundred thirty-five youngsters were kept constructively busy on community projects involving repair, maintenance, and cleaning up of community facilities.

In cooperation with students from the Philadelphia College of Arts, YGS established a program in which classes in drawing, painting, sculpture, and pottery were given in the neighborhood. In addition, the Mantua Academy of Theatrical Black Arts was founded in which some fifty young men and women were trained in dance. They performed widely throughout the city.

YGS and the Center were increasingly asked by other neighborhoods in Philadelphia and as far away as California to assist them to set up similar programs. Many of these were successfully established.

The Significance of the Story

There were four essential characteristics of the collaboration between "planners and plannees" described here, characteristics that have been subsequently incorporated into projects in other communities, many in other countries. First, the university-based planners did not plan for the community; the community planned for itself using the professional planners as resources in whatever ways they saw fit. In so doing they solved the planners' problem of determining how to be useful to the community. Center personnel would have been rejected by the community if they had tried to plan for it, but even if they had not, they would not have penetrated it as deeply as they eventually did. They developed an expertise on black ghetto problems by working on them under the supervision of those who had them.

Second, only a little of what Center personnel did for the community in the first year or so required use of their special technical skills. But they never rejected a request for aid because it fell outside their field or interests. When they did not have the skills required, which was often, they either obtained the help of others or developed the skills themselves. Center personnel were not above chauffeuring or acquiring empty used oil drums or dirty pond water for a school's fish tank. Gradually they earned the right and ability to participate in the planning of the community. They even got the chance to use their special skills, but it took several years before the trust and knowledge required for such involvement were developed.

Distinctions between disciplines and jurisdictional issues that are important to academics, professionals, and government bureaucrats have no importance to the underdeveloped. They cannot be bothered trying to sort out the types of help that are available, and they have no patience with those who "pass the buck" on jurisdictional grounds. They want HELP, not help. They are "turned off" by those who want to help only in prescribed ways. Because of their willingness to do whatever was asked of them, the planners discovered that they were competent to do many things of which they had previously been unaware.

The third essential characteristic of the relationship between the Center and Mantua was that no ideas generated in the Center were ever imposed on the community. Once the willingness of Center personnel to work for the community was well established, their suggestions and criticisms were sought. In time the difference in color became irrelevant to the interactions that took place. Deep friendships between blacks and whites were formed. Their families began to interact and their joint activities extended well beyond the bounds of Mantua.

Fourth, it became apparent to the Center that what the black community wanted from the whites were not gifts or charity, but investments and involvement. Blacks had learned that white donors cannot be counted on for sustained interest because they are subject to many competing demands for their resources and attention. But an investor does not lose interest once he has made his resources available, and the community found that it often benefitted more from the continuing investment of an investor's time than from the resources he provided. Hence, whenever possible, the community sought partnerships because these provided the strongest kind of bond between the benefactor and the community, and it gave the community an opportunity to help its benefactor. Obligation is not a nice feeling.

It became increasingly apparent over time that the community and YGS could be as helpful to those who helped it as they could be to the community. Nearly all organizational donors had some kind of black problem of their own. The staff of YGS was often able to help them solve their problems in ways that benefitted blacks as well as the donors. This led the Center and YGS to look jointly for opportunities to help others without knowing in advance how the community might benefit. A number of corporate problems were thus identified and solved with YGS and Center intervention. This effort culminated in an invitation by the governor of Pennsylvania to establish YGS as a special task force to intervene in every racial crisis that arose in the state. Over the three years in which this task force was required, not a single one of the many crises that arose ripened into violence.

Is the Mantua Experience Reproducible?

It is natural to ask whether the relationship between Mantua and the University's Center is generalizable to other communities and cultures. Fortunately, the answer need not be speculative because such extensions have already taken place. As already indicated, similar programs were successfully initiated in a number of other cities in the United States. But what about communities in less developed countries?

Miguel Szekeley, who was a member of the Center when it was active with Mantua, initiated similar efforts in the state of Nayarit in his native Mexico. He and others made themselves available to about twenty communities in rural areas for their use in their development efforts. The improvements were often dramatic. These communities learned how to deal with those persons and institutions in both the public and private sectors who obstructed their development. They increased their agricultural production through cooperative efforts and learned how to perform a number of the functions required to get their products to consumers, thereby obtaining a larger share of what the consumer paid for their products. They provided themselves with services that should have been but were not provided by the government. Most of all, they provided themselves with hope, aspirations, and the conviction that they could improve their quality of life by taking their lives into their own hands.

The Postgraduate College of the National School of Agriculture in Mexico provides similar services to rural communities in the state of Puebla. And a group at the Institute of Engineering at the National Autonomous University of Mexico, under Jorge Elizondo, have carried out a completely participative planning project on the island of Cozumel.

Scaling up to National Development

There are two ways of enlarging the scope of such efforts to a scale that would have a significant impact on national development. First, the number of rural and urban communities receiving support in their self-development efforts can be significantly increased. There are about 100,000 rural communities in Mexico; hence, considerable manpower is required to initiate and sustain self-development efforts in each. However, it could be provided as follows.

There are about 500,000 students in federally supported universities in Mexico and this number is increasing rapidly. The students are required by law to put time into what is called "social service." This is supposed to be an activity that contributes to national development. With few exceptions, however, the program is not effective. For the most part it is poorly organized and administered; only a small percentage of the students engage in any socially useful activity. In addition, there is considerable resistance from the students to such service because it comes at the end of their university education when they are anxious to start their careers.

We believe this program can be salvaged, students' attitudes converted, and a massive self-development program initiated. Here is how.

Many Mexican universities operate on a semester system as most universities in the United States do, but there is little climatic justification for doing so in most of Mexico. With a climate that is mild most of the year in most of the

Table 5.1
Proposed University Schedule

Quarter

Year	1	2	3	4
1	C	C	C	S
2	C	C	S	C
3	C	S	C	C
4	S	C	C	C

C = Classes

S = Social Service

country, there is little justification for summers off. Furthermore, it leaves expensive buildings and facilities virtually unused for a third of the year.

Our proposal is based on using four academic quarters per year. The quarters would be used as is shown in Table 5.1.

The proposed schedule would make 25 percent of the university students available for organized social service at any one time, enough to provide coverage of every rural community. The communities served would have a constant number of assistants, but they would change quarterly. Each outgoing group or individual would be responsible for orienting his or her replacement(s). The activity could be operated much as the Peace Corps or Project Vista is in the United States.

In addition to the benefits the communities would receive from such assistance, the education that the students would receive in the problems of development would be invaluable and would be likely to have a considerable effect on their attitudes toward the disadvantaged throughout their lives. It is very likely to make a more equitable distribution of wealth possible.

A very thoughtful Mexican friend whose opinion we respect a great deal reacted to this proposal as follows:

. . . many professors experienced in social service programs shudder when presented with a proposal like yours. They are conscious of the naive romanticism of the young, of the radical politicizing they have put into practice, of their advice to home owners in the aftermath of the Puebla-Orizaba earthquake to tear their houses down "so as to get better compensation from government bodies," of the similar experience of Portugal in the Azores Islands, and so on. This does not mean that the program should not be implemented. It means that the young are easily manipulated by the shrewd. It means that the young can be guided and should be guided in a constructive direction. This is not easy. Think of all the professors we have in our . . . system. Most of them are as immature as when they helped lead the 1968 revolts but they are now more resentful of society. . . . And think of the vulnerability of some of our institutions. By all means, let us implement a social service program, and your calendar scheme is attractive for the purpose, but let us beware of the very dangerous pitfalls and warn the unwary.

We accept this warning but do not believe the Mexican peasants are as susceptible to ideological arguments as the warning implies. We believe that influence is much more likely to flow the other way. Furthermore, with the rotation of students that our plan calls for, there is hardly time to impose an ideology on the peasants. Nor do we believe that university professors are the best qualified to supervise such a program. We agree that the students are being manipulated by shrewd adults, but most of them are doing so to maintain, not disrupt, the status quo. There is no way of trying to produce fundamental changes in a nation without some risks being run, but in poorly developed countries we can think of nothing more worth running risks for.

CONCLUSION

The design for widespread participation in national development planning that is described in this chapter is meant only to be suggestive, to serve as a guide to preparation of a design that fits the unique characteristics of a particular country. Moreover, the design is idealized, hence, can at best only be approximated. However, even a poor initial approximation can be guided toward the ideal over time.

It should be borne in mind that people will not persist in participative planning unless they can obtain concrete results in a reasonable amount of time. Therefore, two characteristics of the design are essential. First, any unit should be able to implement any part of its plan that has no effect on any other unit, and do so unilaterally. Second, every public planning unit should be provided with enough resources to implement a significant part of its plan. In effect, each unit that engages in participative planning should have a meaningful measure of self-control and the resources required to realize some of its aspirations.

The type of planning set forth in the chapters that follow does not come naturally. It must be learned. Therefore, planning units will require aid from some who have the requisite knowledge. The training of these professionals or semiprofessionals is itself a monumental task. We suggested a way of providing it: through courses and periods of social service required of all who attend a university. The development orientation that such exposure and experience would provide should have significant benefits beyond providing the assistants required. It should orient all professionals toward national development and keep it in the forefront of their consciousness in both their public and private activities.

6

The Content of Interactive Planning

Planning is at least as much an art as it is a science. It requires a great deal of improvisation because it should be responsive to the unique characteristics of both the system planned for and those engaged in the process. Therefore, it cannot be reduced to a rigidly specified procedure. Our concern here, however, is not so much with how to do it as with what should be done and why.

In the discussion that follows we use "the system" to refer to the system planned for, whether it be a nation, region, state, city, neighborhood, village, government, government agency, enterprise, or any other type of organization.

Interactive planning is directed at gaining control of the future. It is based on the belief that an organization's future depends at least as much on what it does between now and then as on what is done to it. Therefore, this type of planning consists of the design of a desirable future and the selection or invention of ways of approximating it as closely as possible.

Interactive planning has two parts, idealization and realization, and these can be further broken down into the following five phases:

1. Formulation of the mess,
2. Ends planning,
3. Means planning,
4. Resource planning, and
5. Design of implementation and its control.

These phases overlap, interact, and require frequent adjustment to each other. In continuous planning no phase is ever finally completed; all completions are tentative, subject to subsequent revision.

The first two of these phases—formulation of the mess and ends planning—which culminate in an idealized redesign of the system, constitute the idealization process. The last three phases—means planning, resources planning, and design of implementation and its control—deal with the realization of the idealized design.

FORMULATION OF THE MESS

To overcome underdevelopment a country must deal with a complex set of strongly interacting threats and opportunities, a system of problems that we can appropriately refer to as a mess. Because a mess is a system, its essential properties are ones that none of its parts has. These properties are consequences of the way its parts interact. Therefore, comprehension and appreciation of the mess as a whole cannot be obtained by the common practice of listing the threats and opportunities it contains. It is out of their interactions that a mess arises.

Neither a mess nor a problem is directly experienced. What we experience lies somewhere between them. Similarly, we do not have direct experience of either a house as a whole or its individual furnishings separately. Problems, like pieces of furniture, are extracted by analysis from what we experience. Messes, like houses, are constructed out of our experience by synthesis. Put another way: Messes have to be composed out of our experiences; problems come from their decomposition.

Formulation of the "underdevelopment mess" is essential for effective planning because the independent solutions to each part of a mess do not add up to an effective solution to the whole. The effectiveness of treatment of the whole depends on the way the solutions to its parts interact, not on how they act independently of each other.

Because underdevelopment messes are very large and complex, they are usually difficult to formulate in a way that is useful in planning. Ordinarily, they are treated much like the elephant of the familiar allegory in which blind men, each feeling a different part of the animal, describe the whole differently. It is easy but dangerous to attribute to a whole those properties that we perceive in only a part.

A mess is not merely a system of problems. We hardly characterize as a mess a situation that we believe will improve if left alone. Therefore, "mess" connotes a situation that we expect will deteriorate unless there is an intervention. For this reason a mess can be understood and appreciated by perceiving the future that is implicit in it, by comprehending the consequences of no intervention. Thus, we get at the essential nature of a mess by extrapolating from it and its recent past the future that it contains. This is the future that would come about if there were no interventions, no deliberate or accidental changes that would alter the "normal course of events." It is the future that the system currently is in.

Formulating a mess requires three types of study that are normally conducted simultaneously. They are:

1. A system analysis—a detailed description of the state of the system, how it operates, those it affects and how it affects them, and how it is affected by its environment.

2. An obstruction/opportunity analysis—identification and definition of obstructions to the system's development, and analyses of these to identify and define the opportunities inherent in each.

3. Preparation of reference projections—extrapolations of the system's performance from its recent past into the future assuming no significant changes in the behavior of either the system or its environment.

These studies are normally conducted by, or carried out under the supervision of, professional planners. To be effective they require a detachment from the system that those who are part of it seldom have but can often obtain with the help of a professional.

The outputs of the three types of study are synthesized into one or more pictures, reference scenarios, of the future(s) that the system would have if both it and its environment were to continue in their current directions. Such scenarios are not forecasts of the system's future because the assumptions on which they are based—no significant change in either the system's or its environment's behavior—are known to be false. They are contrary-to-fact extrapolations, what-if projections.

Every operating system contains the seeds of its own destruction. Therefore, the purpose of reference scenarios is to identify the nature of its self-destructive tendencies and to suggest changes that can increase its ability to survive and develop. A good formulation of a system's mess provides planning for that system with a focus.

SYSTEMS ANALYSIS

Effective system planning requires for its foundation a detailed, comprehensive, and cohesive description of the current state of the system, how it operates, whom and what it affects and is affected by, and how. It also requires a complete description of the system's environment.

It is crucially important to have a clear image of the system planned for because only that system is subject to control by the planners. The environment is both a source of constraints and opportunities, and the system has to be planned in such a way as to adapt it to its environment. Too often the boundaries between the system and its environment are blurred. This results in impractical recommendations, ones that require major modifications of the environment and, as a result, lead to a design of the system that is not capable of operating in the world of which it is part. For example, the planning for national foreign-trade policies is often limited to suggesting revisions of international procedures with little or no attention given to what ought to be done if these procedures are not reformed. The result frequently is chronic inactivism.

Much of the information required for analysis of the system may be available but is usually scattered about; hence, requires collection and organization. Available descriptions are usually partial and lacking in depth. What is required is an extensive description that should cover the following properties of the system and its environment.

1. Define the system—the set of variables that are subject to the control of those doing the planning, those for whom it is done (if these are different), and those who authorized it.

2. Define its transactional environment—those things that can affect the system's performance and that can be influenced but not controlled by the system.

3. Define the contextual environment—those things that can affect the system's performance but that cannot be affected (influenced or controlled) by the system.

4. Identify the functions of the system and those who are affected by each, the stakeholders, and their relevant needs and desires.

5. Identify the resources required by the system for carrying out its functions, and describe how it acquires or generates each.

6. Describe the products, facilities, and/or services provided by the system and how and by whom they are used.

7. Describe how the system carries out its functions, its operations.

8. Describe how the system is organized and managed.

9. Describe the rules, regulations, and laws that affect the system's behavior and determine the internal or external source of each.

10. Describe the culture of the system—its style, folkways, and mores.

The collection of the information required for such a description is often facilitated by the use of outsiders who do not share insiders' prejudices and preconceptions. The description, once completed, should be widely disseminated for discussion and criticism. Differences of opinion are particularly important because they often indicate possible obstructions to the system's development.

Obstruction/Opportunity Analysis

Study of the obstructions to and opportunities for development is best initiated by a phenomenological immersion in the system and its environment. A good way of doing so consists of getting the stakeholders to describe their perception of the system, its environment, and the mess. This can be done in either individual or group sessions. The objective is to gather impressions that later can be subjected to a formal analysis. The stakeholders' perceptions of the mess are useful both in generating working hypotheses about it and in indicating how the stakeholders obstruct the system. Obstructions are often revealed in statements made about the system by its stakeholders. For example, it is not uncommon to hear from one in a position of authority that his subordinates are not responsive enough to his initiatives and to hear from the subordinates the same about him. When put together these statements indicate a classical obstruction to development, organizational paralysis.

It is often difficult to get those who are part of a system, and particularly those who manage it, to face the truth about the system. Their unwillingness to do so can be a major deterrent to the system's development. It must be overcome if effective development planning is to take place. The revelation of discrepancies between what people believe about a system and what is actually the case, and between what they practice and what they preach, can be perceived as very threatening. It can even be dangerous to those making the revelations. The threat and danger can be diminished by the use of group processes that enable participants to share responsibility for their disclosures.

The crude empiricism of the phenomenological approach should be refined throughout by analyses carried out by professional planners (or surrogates, as when analyses are already available in the literature). In these analyses the impressions gathered from stakeholders are organized and examined. Redundancies are consolidated, and contradictions are highlighted. Conflicts of value and style are separated from those of fact. Factual discrepancies can be resolved by research.

The analysts should not limit themselves to inputs provided by stakeholders during the phenomenological immersion. They can and should use prior analyses carried out by others: research reports, statistics, newspaper and magazine articles, books, speeches, and so on.

The immersion phase of obstruction analysis should be terminated when either time has run out (for example, when there is pressure to produce results) or the analysts feel that little additional knowledge or understanding will be generated from its continuation. Then it is necessary to produce a composite picture of the obstructions and opportunities. This can be done in much the same way as will be done in the general analysis of Part III of this book. The content required is shown in Figure 6.1. A table such as is shown can be used to initiate the process. Obstructions should be identified first and entered in the table. Then the opportunities corresponding to each obstruction can be identified and entered in the table. Finally, detailed descriptions of each entry can be prepared.

It should be borne in mind that obstructions to a system's growth are primarily found in its environment, but obstructions to its development are more likely to be found within the system, to be self-imposed. Recognition of this fact is reflected in the common practice of listing the system's weaknesses (as well as its strengths). Such lists, however, are usually quite superficial because they include only those obstructions disclosure of which is permitted or considered to be "in good taste." Such lists seldom reveal more than the tip of the iceberg.

Reference Projections

A reference projection is an extrapolation of a performance characteristic of a system from its recent past into the future, assuming no significant change in

Figure 6.1
A Table for Initiating Obstruction/Opportunity Analysis

	Obstructions			Opportunities		
	Scarcity	Maldistribution	Insecurity	Scarcity	Maldistribution	Insecurity
Science & Technology						
Economics						
Ethics & Morality						
Aesthetics						
Politics						

either its behavior or that of its environment. Such a projection is, in effect, a glimpse of the future that is implied by continuation of the system's recent history.

Reference projections are normally made using the principal measures employed in characterizing the state of the system; for example, for a nation, its GNP, its population and population density, foreign trade deficit, distribution of wealth, consumer price index, per capita income, unemployment, and so on. Similar projections should be made for those aspects of the environment that have a significant effect on the system's performance; for example, the cost of imported oil, foreign exchange rates, foreign demand for the nation's products, and so on. An examination of the relationships between projections usually reveals one or more future states that are impossible. For example, projections made in the 1950s of the population of the United States and the number of scientists in it revealed that there would be more scientists than people before the end of the century. Thus, the inevitable reduction in the then current rate of producing scientists in the United States could be foreseen. Unfortunately, it was ignored by many universities whose subsequent financial difficulties could have been avoided.

The projections of the population growth of the major city in one less-than-well-developed country, and of the country as a whole, showed that the entire population of that country would be in that city well within 100 years.

A reference projection is not meant to be a realistic prediction of future problems. If prediction at all, it is one of what is not likely to happen. It serves, like a resonance box or microscope, to amplify the latent contradictions in the system here and now. It is an aid to an evaluation of the present. It is intended to reveal the potential crises that are inherent in the current behavior of the system planned for. By identifying such crises, reference projections focus the attention of those engaged in planning on those characteristics of the system that are most in need of change. Therefore if appropriate changes are made, the projected future will not occur. Put another way: The objective of reference projecting is to identify those crises that are likely to occur without planning, but that can be avoided with it.

Reference Scenarios

Those reference projections that turn out to be revealing can be combined with the outputs of the system and obstruction analyses into a scenario of that future the system would have if there were no significant changes in its behavior and that of its environment. It is in such a scenario that the mess confronted by the system is best revealed.

Not every reference projection reveals a crisis; for example, population projections do not reveal problems in every country. Therefore, in order to find the major threats to national development, it is usually necessary to project a number of properties of the current situation, and to explore their interactions creatively.

Individual projections seldom reveal such threats; they ordinarily become apparent only when the joint implications of a number of projections are explored. A composite picture of the future or a part of it is based on a study of such interactions. We call such a picture a *reference scenario*.

A useful reference scenario has to be based on the choice of those variables describing reality that are most pertinent to the planning at hand. In other words, planners have to have an idea of the mess before even attempting to make it explicit through the use of a reference scenario (hence the value of the working hypotheses generated by the phenomenological immersion). Otherwise, they run the risk of carrying out an analysis of little relevance to their main purpose.

It should also be noted that a decision has to be made as to how much time and effort to invest in developing a reference scenario. Recall that its only purpose is to provide a point of departure for planning and to motivate stakeholders to engage in planning. How much time and effort this requires depends largely on how "obvious" the mess is and on how much is needed to motivate the planners.

For example, *The Limits to Growth* (Meadows et al., 1972), a study sponsored by the Club of Rome, was a reference scenario of the future of the world. The conclusion that it reached—that unconstrained growth in a finite universe is limited—was largely self-evident. It is hard to justify the cost of the study in terms of this result. However, there are few studies that have had a larger impact on public and governmental opinion or a larger mobilizing effect on governments and researchers, setting them off in search of alternative growth—and alternatives-to-growth—strategies. In the eyes of many this justifies the Club of Rome effort.

The term *reference scenario* is usually reserved for exercises that involve formal though not necessarily complicated techniques. It is important, however, to observe that in many cases a less formal or even impressionistic evaluation of reality may be more useful than a formalized reference scenario. The works of Illich (1972, 1973), Freire (1970), Ward (1968), Ward and Dubos (1972), and Thurow (1981) uncovered in imaginative and provocative ways some basic contradictions and deficiencies of contemporary societies and can be considered to be formulations of messes in education, health, and economics.

The reference scenario should make it apparent that the mess the system is in is at least as much a consequence of what that system has done and is doing as of what has been done and is being done to it. It can also be used to reveal the changes that can be made to evade the mess. For example, a reference scenario prepared in 1959 and again in 1971 by Sagasti and Ackoff showed that the entire surface of American cities would be covered by streets, highways, and parking places by the end of this century if the automobile industry continued on its then current trend. This, of course, was impossible. Subsequent studies of the effects of automobile sizes on the people-carrying capacity of streets and highways revealed that a two-person vehicle in which the passenger sat behind the driver would increase that capacity by about 500 percent. This would remove the need for any new urban streets and highways in the United States until after the end of the century. In addition, it was shown that by relocating facilities within cities, about 80 percent of the mechanically aided trips taken would be eliminated. Such location of facilities was incorporated into the design of Cuautitlan Izcalli, a new town in Mexico.

Finally, the composite formulation of a reference scenario should point out the interrelationships among the problems identified. For example, it is not population growth alone that creates a problem; it is such growth coupled with lesser growth of production that creates a mess. The importance of viewing the mess systemically is illustrated by the fact that several less developed countries have considered population growth as positive until recently. With a narrow view of international competition it is easy to reach such a conclusion. It is only when other factors are introduced that one sees the potential crisis, if not catastrophe, inherent in unchecked population growth.

It is very important that a reference scenario not be presented as a forecast of what will happen. The confusion that arises from its being taken as a forecast is apparent in the way *The Limits to Growth* was received. The purpose of a reference scenario is to reveal the future implications of a system's current behavior. It is intended to focus attention on the right problems and to produce a shared perception of the nature of these problems and their interactions. It is against a background provided by a shared perception of an undesirable future and shared understanding of its sources that the process of redesigning a system's future can be initiated.

ENDS PLANNING

Ends planning consists of designing a desired future and extracting from it those ends to be pursued that the remainder of the planning process addresses. Ends, which are desired outcomes, are of three types:

1. Goals—ends that are expected to be obtained within the period covered by the plan.
2. Objectives—ends that are not expected to be obtained until after the period planned for, but toward which progress is expected within that period.
3. Ideals—ends that are believed to be unattainable but toward which progress is expected within that period.

Goals, therefore, can be considered to be means relative to objectives, and objectives can be similarly considered relative to ideals.

The procedure for setting ends that is developed here begins with specifications of ideals and works backward through objectives to goals. This procedure is based on the idealized redesign of the system planned for.

Idealized Redesign

An idealized redesign of a system is one with which the designers would now replace the current system if they were free to replace it with any system they wanted. Therefore, the process begins by assuming that the current system was destroyed last night, but everything else remains as it was; the environment, the needs and desires served by the system, and those who have them remain unchanged.

The only constraints placed on an idealized design are that it be technologically feasible, operationally viable, and capable of rapid learning and adaptation. Consider each of these in turn.

Technological feasibility. This requirement means that the design must not incorporate any technology that is not currently known to be usable. Nevertheless, available technologies can be used in new ways. This constraint is intended to prevent the design from being an exercise in writing science fiction.

Operational viability. This requirement means that the system designed should be capable of surviving in the current environment if it were brought into existence. However, this does not mean that it should be capable of being brought into existence. The implementability of the design should not be considered in the design process for reasons discussed below.

Learning and adaptation. The requirement that an idealized system be capable of rapid learning and adaptation translates into three subrequirements.

(a) The system's stakeholders should be able to modify the design whenever they care to. This is desirable because their relevant information, knowledge, understanding, and values change over time, particularly as a result of their efforts to realize the design.

(b) Design issues that arise that cannot be settled by consensus among the designers should be dealt with by incorporating into the design of the system experimental processes for settling the issues. This endows the system with the ability to learn systematically from its own experience and to improve itself over time.

(c) All decisions made within the system and the critical assumptions on which they are based should be subjected to control. This means that the expected effects of each decision that affects the system and the assumptions on which these decisions are based should be explicitly formulated and subsequently monitored. When actual effects are found to deviate significantly from the expected effects or conditions the deviations should be diagnosed and corrective action taken where appropriate.

Therefore, the product of an idealized design is an adaptive-learning system that is capable of improving its own design over time. Because it is subject to improvement, it makes no pretense at perfection, hence is neither utopian nor ideal. What it is, however, is the best ideal-seeking system that its designers can currently conceive. Therefore, it should be subject to subsequent revision by its stakeholders.

There are three steps involved in the idealized-design process:

1. Selecting a mission,
2. Specifying desired properties of the design, and
3. Designing the system.

Although these steps must be described sequentially here, in practice they interact and overlap a great deal.

Selecting a Mission

A mission is an overriding purpose for the system being designed, one that can unify and mobilize all of its parts and members in its pursuit. The mission should capture an aspiration that can activate a society and give meaning and significance to all it and its members do. It should integrate the many roles that the system plays, thereby making it possible to plan for the system comprehensively and cohesively. Without a mission the various roles of a system are likely to be planned for independently of each other, and priorities are likely to be set in response to political pressures and social crises. Missionless planning tends to be reactive: to focus on getting rid of what is not wanted rather than on pursuit of what is.

A mission is a vision of something strongly desired accompanied by a strong commitment to its pursuit. It should inspire planning and provide a basis for evaluating design and operating decisions that take place in and out of the planning process.

For example, the large number of Frenchmen who engaged in planning for Paris in the early 1970s (Ozbekhan, 1977) selected as the city's mission: to serve as the informal capital of the world, the location of most public organizations and institutions that operate transnationally. Achievement of this mission was seen as equivalent to reinstating Paris as "the queen of cities," as the place from which the ideas that will dominate interactions of nations in the future are generated today.

In contrast, a group planning for Mexico City selected as its mission: to serve as development capital for, first, Mexico, then for Latin America, and ultimately for the Third World. Mexico City has long been obsessed with taking resources from the rest of Mexico, not with giving them to others. Paradoxically, this has produced a rapidly deteriorating quality of life while providing an increasing standard of living. The city has been preoccupied with its own growth, not its own development or that of others. Therefore, the intent of the mission statement was to convert the city from a destination and a receptacle to an origin and a source.

A mission statement, then, should be much more than propaganda or an advertising slogan; it should provide a concept on which the redesign of the system can focus and that can have a significant impact on that design.

Specifications

The idealized-design process is usually greatly facilitated by specifying in advance those properties that the designers would like to incorporate into their design. Such specifications can be very qualitative in nature, leaving their operationalization for the design process. For example, one might specify for a city that "it be so designed as to minimize the number of trips within it that require mechanical modes of transportation." It would then remain for the design to show how this could be accomplished.

Preparation of specifications is usually facilitated by a set of questions that cover the major aspects of the system to be designed. For example, for a city or nation one might first formulate the following questions.

1. What functions should the nation/city perform; that is, what products and services should it provide?
2. How should it provide them; that is, in what activities should it engage?
3. How should these activities be managed and how should the managers be selected?
4. What resources should be used in carrying out its functions and how should these be acquired or generated?
5. How will the outputs of the system be distributed and to whom?
6. How should the system interact with other systems in its environment?

An example of specifications may be helpful.

An idealized city. The following is a set of specifications prepared by a group of graduate students in connection with an idealized design of a prototype city.

1. Segregation of people based on any of their characteristics over which they have no control should not be possible. This includes race, sex, national origin, religion, and age.
2. The city should provide complete equality of opportunity to everyone within it, regardless of the characteristics of their parents. This is not equivalent to economic equality—what a person becomes depends not only on what opportunities he has but also on what he does with them and on his personal abilities—but it does imply the elimination of poverty.
3. Most trips within the city would be able to be made by walking, but efficient mechanical aids would be available to those who need them, when they need them.
4. Everyone within the city should be within walking distance of natural open space in which one could find outdoor privacy in a setting of natural beauty.
5. The city should have a participative democratic government, but it should have as little government as is necessary, not as much as is possible.
6. The city should deliberately experiment with itself to find ways of improving itself. It should continuously evaluate its own performance, detect deficiencies, and correct them.

The design itself. The conversion of specifications into an idealized design requires determining how the desired properties of a system can be realized. For example, the specification that a city require minimal mechanically aided transportation must be transformed into a physical design that makes this possible.

This was done in the example cited by designing the city from the bottom up. The basic unit of the city was defined to be a neighborhood that consisted of eight blocks covering about one-ninth of a square mile and housing about 1,750 people. All the publicly and privately provided facilities and services that the neighborhood's population can justify are located in the center of the neighborhood. (See Figure 6.2.) Then eight neighborhoods are clustered into a section (Figure 6.3) consisting of about 14,000 people in one square mile. All the publicly and privately provided facilities and services that the section's population can justify are located in the center of the section. The longest distance to be walked within a section to reach any facility or service is well under a mile. Eight sections are similarly clustered to form a district (Figure 6.4) that contains about 112,000 people in an area of nine square miles. Each district has its center. Even in a district most facilities and services are within a mile of most people. Districts are then clustered to form cities of various sizes (Figure 6.5).

Design is a cumulative process. It is usually initiated by using a very broad brush; hence, the first version is a rough sketch. Then details are added and revisions are made as, for example, by adding the transportation system to the city described above. This process continues until a significantly detailed design is obtained to make it possible to "construct" the system.

Once the design has been tentatively completed, it should be checked for its technological feasibility, operational viability, and adaptive-learning capabilities. Should it be found to be wanting in any of these respects, appropriate revisions should be made. Once such revisions are completed, the design should be exposed to critical review by as many stakeholders as possible. Their suggestions, when compatible with the design, should be incorporated in it; when not, an experiment should be designed to resolve the issue and be incorporated into the design.

An unconstrained idealized design. The environment of a system contains any larger system of which the smaller system is a part. It will be recalled that the environment of the system subjected to idealized design is left unchanged. Whether the system being redesigned is autonomous or subordinate to another larger system it is subject to constraints imposed on it by other autonomous and/ or superior systems. For example, a nation's redesign is constrained by what other nations do or do not do, and are willing or not willing to do. A city is constrained by the nation that contains it and possible by what cities in other nations are doing.

Because of such constraints it is desirable and useful to prepare a second version of a system's idealized redesign, one in which there are no externally imposed constraints and in which the containing system is as supportive as reasonably can be. This, in effect, involves a redesign of the relevant aspects of the system's containing system and other parts of its environment.

There are three important benefits to be derived from preparing such a design. First, a comparison of the constrained and unconstrained idealized redesigns reveals just how constraining the environment is and what the critical constraints are. It has been our experience that in most cases such a comparison reveals

Figure 6.2
A Neighborhood
(Schematically)

1,760 people
1/3 mix 1/3 mi.

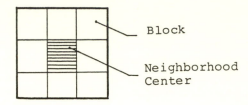

Block

Neighborhood
Center

Figure 6.3
A Section
(Schematically)

14,000 people
1 mi. × 1 mi.

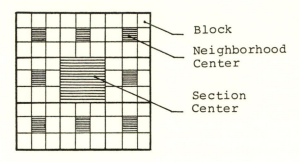

Block

Neighborhood
Center

Section
Center

Figure 6.4
A District
(Schematically)

112,000 people
3 mi. × 3 mi.

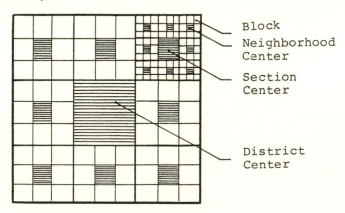

Block

Neighborhood
Center

Section
Center

District
Center

Figure 6.5
The City
(Schematically)

2,000,000 people
15 mi. × 15 mi.
16 Districts

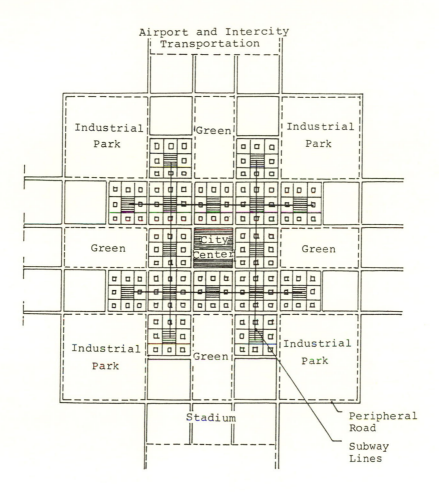

that most of what a system's stakeholders would ideally like to do to a system can be done despite externally imposed constraints. Put another way: The comparison usually reveals that most of the obstructions to changing a system toward what its stakeholders most desire lie within that system and its parts, not in its environment.

Second, many of the constraints that appear to lie in the environment do not really exist except in the minds of the designers. For example, we have often been told by participants in a system being redesigned that their containing system prohibits their doing something they would like to do. Subsequent investigation has often revealed that there is no such prohibition. People who do not want to change but who do not want to appear in this light, frequently claim, and often sincerely believe, that they are precluded from doing so. This avoids any sense of guilt for inactivity.

Third, where externally imposed constraints are found to be real, there are three options available to the system's designers:

1. Accept and work within them,
2. Try to "beat the (containing) system," and
3. Try to change the containing system in such a way as to remove the constraints.

The first alternative requires no elaboration; the second and third do. Rules, regulations, laws, policies, practices, and so on are written by human beings who try to cover all of the relevant domain, but they seldom if ever succeed. This helps keep the legal profession busy telling people how to break the intent of the law without breaking the law itself. This is particularly true in the domain of taxes.

In general, a great deal can be gained by learning the art and science of beating the system—of evading, getting around, obstructions.

Third, a system normally has some, and sometimes considerable, influence on the system that contains it. Therefore, once the constraints imposed by the containing system and their effects have been identified by comparing the constrained and unconstrained designs, a program for inducing the larger system to change can be developed and will succeed not infrequently. A redesign of the containing system can also induce those in control of that system to initiate their own redesign effort.

MEANS PLANNING

Once goals, objectives, and ideals have been extracted from a comparison of a system's idealized design and its reference scenario, planning toward their realization can begin. The more innovative and creative the design is, the more innovation and creativity are required to realize it. But these are not enough; detailed knowledge of the current system is also necessary. Some of this knowledge is supplied by the system analysis carried out earlier in the planning process.

To obtain the rest a variety of experts are usually required as consultants, if not participants in means planning; for example, experts in law, public finance, agriculture, transportation, education, housing, and so on.

In general, experts should not be allowed to control the formulation and selection of means because they tend to be more conservative than creative. The manner in which they should be used is well illustrated by an incident in which a corporate executive asked a law professor why, whenever he asked a lawyer whether he could do something new, the answer was almost always "no." The professor replied: "Because you ask the wrong question." He went on to explain: "You consult a lawyer to keep you out of trouble. When you ask him if you can do something new, he knows you are not in trouble at the time. Therefore, he can most easily keep you from getting into it by keeping you at what you are already doing. If you want to innovate, tell him what you intend to do and ask him how to do it so as to avoid legal problems. Then you will get what you want." This advice is useful in dealing with any type of expert in the context of planning.

Realization planning has a great deal in common with what occurs once an architect has produced a design of a building that is acceptable to his clients. He must then show how to translate that design into a building. He does so by taking the following three steps.

First, he prepares detailed working drawings and specifications of the materials and construction methods to be used. These provide graphic and verbal instructions that cover what is to be done, how it is to be done, and what materials and equipment are to be used in doing it. Preparation of working drawings and specifications often requires or suggests modifications of the design.

Second, the working drawings and specifications are used by those who will construct the building to estimate the kinds and quantities of materials, equipment, and labor that will be required, and to derive an estimate of the total cost of construction. If the estimated cost is too high, then changes are made in either the design (ends to be sought) or the working drawings and specifications (means to be used); or a part of the building is selected for construction and the rest is delayed or dropped. If the estimated cost is lower than expected, then the design, working drawings, or specifications are reexamined to determine if they can be improved with use of more or better resources.

Third, once the design, working drawings, specifications, and resource requirements have been brought into harmony, planning for implementation begins. This consists of:

1. Organizing the work to be done—dividing it into tasks that can be performed either at different times or at the same time by different agents,

2. Scheduling these tasks,

3. Determining who is to perform them, and

4. Designing a way of managing and controlling their performance.

Plans for implementation may also require or suggest changes in the outputs of any of the previous stages of the planning process. Furthermore, as construction proceeds, unexpected problems arise and also require or suggest changes in the outputs of one or more of the previous steps.

The phases of realization planning for development are the same as those involved in planning a building, but development of a community or a society is more like constructing a city than a building. Many different but interdependent facilities and services must be designed, planned for, and constructed or otherwise provided. Many different relatively independent agents are involved. This and the complexity of the system to be developed require a higher order of coordination and integration than is required in the building process.

Each unit of society or government that prepares an idealized design should also prepare a plan for approximating that design as closely as possible.

The two basic steps in means planning are formulation or identification of alternative means, and evaluation and selection from among them.

Formulation of Alternative Means

The formulation of alternative means normally begins by listing those means known to be relevant and available. It is also desirable to uncover any relevant means of which the planners are initially unaware; for example, ones involving new technologies or recently developed in other places. In many cases, however, none of the alternatives, known or uncovered, are good enough; and even where one is, there is often an opportunity for considerable improvement. In either case better means than were initially formulated should be invented. This requires creativity.

Creativity is largely a matter of identifying self-imposed constraining assumptions, removing them, and exploring the consequences of doing so. (See Ackoff, 1978, for a more complete discussion of this subject.) Unfortunately, creativity is not easily "turned on," but it can be encouraged and facilitated by such measures as the following.

1. Involve people with as many different types of background and experience as possible. Different points of view tend to reveal different types of alternatives.

> For example, a very poor old woman who lived in one room of the fourth floor of a tenement in an urban ghetto died of a heart attack climbing the stairs to her room when returning from a periodic health examination at the only free medical clinic in her neighborhood. There had been several such incidents in her neighborhood. A group of professionals were asked to help find a way of preventing them.

> A professor of community medicine suggested increasing the staff at the neighborhood clinic so that house calls could be made. An economist suggested that welfare payments be increased to cover the cost of house calls

by private medical practitioners. An architect suggested that elevators be required in such buildings. A social worker pointed out that the old woman had a son who was a successful lawyer and lived in a bungalow in a nice suburb with his family. Therefore, if the woman had not been alienated from her son, she would have lived where climbing steps would not have been required and she would have been able to afford house calls by private practitioners.

2. Use creativity-enhancing techniques in groups assembled to formulate means. Among the more prominent of these techniques are the following:
   (a) *Synectics* (Gordon, 1962, 1972; Reitman, 1964)
   (b) Brainstorming (Noller and Parnes, 1972 and 1973; Noller, Parnes, and Biondi, 1976; Osborn, 1963; and Parnes and Noller, 1972),
   (c) TKJ (Kobayashi, 1971),
   (d) The search conference (Emery and Emery, 1978; and Williams, 1979), and
   (e) The dialectical approach (Churchman, 1966; Mason, 1969; and Emshoff and Mitroff, 1977).

3. Enlarge rather than contract the context in which choice is considered. In the common practice of "cutting problems down to size," effective means are frequently precluded from consideration.

   For example, in one European city in which double-decker buses are the principal means of public transportation, conflict between the drivers and conductors broke out because of delays produced during rush hours by the conductors collecting fares. These delays prevented the driver from keeping to schedule. His income was decreased when he failed to maintain his schedule.

   Efforts to have representative drivers and conductors work out an acceptable *modus vivendi* ended in complete failure. The problem was subsequently solved by enlarging the system considered: taking the stops into account. During peak hours when there were more buses in operation than there were stops, conductors were taken off the buses and located at the stops. Then they could collect fares from passengers while they were waiting for a bus. Conductors could signal drivers when to start by using a button located at the rear entrance to the bus, and passengers could signal the driver when they wanted to get off by pulling a cord around the sides of the bus. Not only did this reduce delays, it also made fare collection easier. When the number of buses in operation is less than the number of stops, at off hours, the conductors return to the buses.

   Apparently uncontrollable variables can frequently be brought under control, particularly when they are imbedded in the behavior of others. One or more of the following procedures can often help in doing so.

4. Obstructive and apparently uncontrolled behavior of others is often the result of one or more incentives, usually concealed, that produce their behavior. These incentives can frequently be changed so as to modify the undesirable behavior.

Automobile congestion is often very heavy at toll booths located at bridges and tunnels leading into and out of cities. Studies have shown that the average number of people in automobiles affected is less than two. Some cities have reduced or eliminated tolls for those cars carrying a specified number of passengers, and provided them with an express lane. This encourages car pooling and reduces the number of cars using the facility. The suggestion has also been made that tolls be made proportional to the number of empty seats in a car, thus encouraging both car pooling and the use of smaller cars.

5. The apparent inability to control or influence the behavior of others is often based on what appear to be "obvious facts." No matter how "obvious" such "facts" appear to be, their validity should be checked. Denial of the obvious and exploration of its consequences are one of the most powerful ways of creating new means.

For example, birth control was a major objective of foreign reformers in India during the 1950s and 1960s. The birth rate prevented average income from increasing significantly despite significant increases in GNP.

A study conducted by Balakrishnan and Camp (1965) revealed that the average size of an Indian family was based on the requirements that there be enough sons in the family to support parents when they were too old to be employed. Since no other form of old-age security or unemployment benefits was available to most Indians, their behavior was rational to continue to have children until there were enough sons. For this reason, Balakrishnan and Camp designed a publicly supported social security system in which payments to the elderly were inversely proportional to the number of sons they had. (Daughters were virtually unemployable at the time.)

The selection of variables to be controlled and those that are uncontrolled (but are to be taken into account) is based on criteria of relevance. Such criteria, in turn, are derived from what is believed to be causally related to desired outcomes and how these causal variables interact. Too frequently we assume causal relationships where they do not exist. Such errors are often made because we assume that variables that are associated are causally related. Association is usually determined by use of correlation and regression analysis from which causality cannot be correctly inferred.

For example, a number of years ago environmentalists in one American city found a high correlation between the amount of sootfall in neighborhoods and the incidence of tuberculosis in them. From this they argued a causal connection and managed to get a smoke-abatement ordinance enacted. No reduction in tuberculosis followed. Subsequent researchers found that rents were low in high sootfall neighborhoods, hence low-income families lived in them. Such families had a higher incidence of dietary deficiencies and these were causally related to tuberculosis.

The strongest inference that can be drawn from a significant correlation or regression is: If two variables are found not to be significantly associated, then it can be inferred that they are not causally connected under the conditions of the analysis and if the form of the association assumed in the analysis (e.g., linear or quadratic) was correct.

Causal inferences require establishment of more than associations; they require demonstration that in some specified environment a change in the "effect" invariably follows a change in the "cause." In other words, one thing is the cause of another if it is both necessary and sufficient for the other. Ordinary experience may suggest such a relationship but only experiment can provide confirmation.

Experimentation in the social domain is often assumed to be either too costly or infeasible. Such an assumption is frequently wrong. Moreover, the cost of not conducting experiments often far exceeds the cost of conducting them, and the appearance of infeasibility is often the product of ignorance with respect to experimental design.

> Some societies impose capital punishment on capital crimes because they believe it deters their commission. Other societies do not use such punishment because, among other reasons, they believe it does not act as a deterrent. Since in some nations different states have different punishment practices, and change them from time to time, it is possible to determine experimentally whether capital punishment deters capital crimes. The cost of not conducting such an experiment may be the loss of many lives needlessly, either of victims or criminals.

The cost of an incorrectly assumed causal connection can be very large. For example, in many of the more developed economies of the West it is assumed that an increase in the cost of money (interest rates) will decrease the rate of inflation. Policies based on this assumption have been failing at a very high social cost. Also costly are such assumptions as the illegalization of harmful drugs will decrease their availability and use.

Evaluation of Alternative Means

Selection of one from a set of alternative means obviously requires a comparative evaluation of them. There are three types of approach to such an evaluation.

Satisficing: to look for a means that is good enough. It is obvious that we use this approach in much of our everyday decision making. *Satisficing* judgments usually rely on common sense, past experience, and current trial and error. They are qualitatively rather than quantitatively oriented.

The satisficing approach to choice is essentially clinical. Clinicians, of course, occasionally use research, even quantitative research, but they seldom use it in a decisive role. Research output is seldom more than a minor input to their choices. Such output tends to be based on surveys of opinion, attitudes, and other characteristics of people. Therefore, tests, questionnaires, and interviews are their principal instruments of inquiry.

Most reactive officials, executives, managers, administrators, and planners are satisficers. They defend this approach by citing the lack of the time or resources required to do anything more. They assert that real choices are so complex and are normally made under such constraints as to render alternative approaches either impossible or impracticable. Furthermore, they claim that because satisficing is based on conventional wisdom and common experience, it minimizes risk, hence maximizes the chances for survival. Finally, because the choices this approach yields tend to be conventional, they require little ''selling''; hence their implementation is usually easy.

Optimizing: to look for the best possible means. We call this the research approach because it is largely based on the use of scientific methods, techniques, and tools. It makes extensive use of quantitative analyses and real or simulated experiments. It attempts to base itself on objective observation and measurement rather than subjective judgment as satisficing does.

This approach is used most heavily by preactive officials and planners whose principal organization goal is growth rather than mere survival. They seek to be the best, the largest, or ''number one.'' Good enough is not good enough for them.

The principal scientific instrument used in the search for optimal choices is the mathematical model, a symbolic representation of the choice situation. In it an attempt is made to relate choice variables and environmental variables explicitly to the value of the outcome of any choice that is made. Such models can often be manipulated mathematically to determine which choice will yield the ''best outcome.''

However, the structure and content of choice situations continuously change, particularly in turbulent environments. Because optimal solutions are very seldom made adaptive to such changes, their optimality is generally of short duration. They frequently become less effective than were the often more robust satisficing solutions that they replace. Let us call this cross-over point the moment of death of the solution. Schon (1971) has convincingly argued that the life of solutions to many critical social problems is shorter than the time required to find them. Therefore, more and more so-called optimal solutions are still-born, and with an increasing rate of social change this situation will become even worse.

For this reason there is a greater need for systems that can learn and adapt quickly and effectively in rapidly changing situations than there is for optimal solutions that deteriorate with change. Most optimizers have failed to respond to this need. As a consequence, the use of optimization is increasingly restricted to those choices that are relatively insensitive to their environments. These usually involve the behavior of mechanical rather than purposeful systems, and societies are purposeful systems.

Idealizing: to design a means and a way of monitoring and adjusting it so that it will perform better in the future than any available means can today; that is, to design an adaptive-learning system. Such systems are seldom available; they usually have to be created. Therefore, we call this the design approach to choice. It is used primarily by interactive officials and planners whose principal social objective is development rather than growth or survival.

The designer makes use of the methods, techniques, and tools of both the clinician and the researcher, but he uses them in a different way. He uses them either to develop a capacity for improving whatever means are selected, or to so redesign the system planned for that the need for the kind of choice being considered is eliminated. Put another way: He tries to dissolve problems rather than resolve them as the clinician does or solve them as the researcher does.

An example may help clarify the differences between satisficing, optimizing, and idealizing. Coming into the 1960s the urban public schools of the United States were racially segregated. This followed from the facts that residential areas were racially segregated and children were assigned to the nearest school. Those schools that served minorities were generally of poorer quality than the others. Thus, opportunity for education was inequitably distributed. This maldistribution became a national issue.

Using common sense, some sought to resolve the problem by increasing the amount of funds available to "minority schools." This, of course, had no effect on racial segregation in education, but was intended to improve the quality of education in these schools enough to eliminate minority pressure for better education. It failed to do so. The minority insisted that segregated education was incompatible with equal educational opportunity. The resolution did not work.

A law was then passed that required desegregation of schools by changing the way children were assigned to schools. Educational planners went to work on solving the following problems: how to assign children to schools so as to meet desegregation standards, busing them to schools that were more than a specified distance from their homes, and doing so in such a way as to minimize the costs involved. That is, they sought an optimal (least cost) solution to the problem through research. The solution thus obtained failed to attract widespread support, particularly from the white majority, for a number of reasons including the fact that the average quality of public education continued to deteriorate.

A design approach was taken by Christopher Jenks of Harvard University, who invented a new way of distributing and financing educational opportunity. He called it the "voucher system." The following is one variation on such a system.

The parents of each school-age child are given an educational voucher worth a specified number of dollars payable by the government to a school that receives it. This voucher covers tuition and transportation (if necessary) to any public school, and part or all of tuition in private schools. Parents can apply to any school for admission of their child; they do not have to use one to which their child is assigned because of proximity or political jurisdiction. In other words, children can apply to any primary or secondary school much as young adults do to college today. Cost would not be a factor unless a private school were selected.

Schools that have more applicants than they can accommodate are required to select from among them at random. This assures equal educational opportunity and as much heterogeneity of student bodies as the applications permit.

Public schools have no source of income other than what they receive by cashing in the vouchers they receive. Therefore, if they do not attract and retain students, they go out of business. Private schools can charge whatever they want but parents have to pay any amount over the value of the voucher. Private schools that accept vouchers must select from among applicants at random. This creates competition between and among public and private schools. Such competition induces schools to learn more effectively from their successes and failures and to become more responsive to the needs and desires of their stakeholders.

As this example shows, improvements obtained by satisficing tend to have shorter lives than those obtained by optimizing. Optimal choices, however, tend to have shorter lives than ones obtained by idealizing. Nevertheless, few if any problems are ever permanently resolved, solved, or dissolved. Every choice generates new choice situations. The consequences of the choices made in means planning interact. Therefore, evaluation of means should consist of more than a set of independent evaluations of different choices; it should also include a detailed analysis of their interactions and the effects of these. For example, conversion to a voucher system in education significantly affects the transportation needs of school-age children. This in turn affects fuel consumption, and so on. It is not unusual for separately desirable programs to come into conflict. In the United States, for example, the federal government simultaneously conducts a campaign to discourage smoking and subsidizes the growing of tobacco. A detailed analysis and evaluation of the interactions of the means selected is absolutely necessary for effective means planning. This is best done by identifying at least the major consequences of each means selected and identifying their interactions and evaluating them.

Means should be evaluated after, as well as before, their full-scale implementation.

RESOURCE PLANNING

Resource planning is directed at determining what resources are required by the means selected, when and where these requirements will occur, and how and where those resources that are not already available are to be acquired or generated. These determinations should involve five types of resources:

1. Inputs (materials, supplies, energy, and services),
2. Facilities and equipment (capital investments),
3. Personnel,
4. Information, and
5. Money.

Money can be considered to be a "meta-resource" because its only value lies in its use to obtain other resources.

Each type of resource other than money and information should be divided into relevant categories; for example, facilities into schools, hospitals, office buildings, roads, and so on. Personnel can be similarly categorized using occupational classes and grades.

Using knowledge of the means selected and the environment in which they are expected to be used, the following questions should be answered about inputs, facilities and equipment, and personnel:

1. How much of each type of resource will be required? When and where will they be required?

2. How much of each of these types of resources will be available at each relevant location at each relevant point in time, assuming no changes in current resource plans and policies?

3. What are the gaps between requirements (as determined in 1) and availabilities (as determined in 2)?

4. How should the gap (identified in 3) be filled: by developing or generating them internally or by acquisition from external sources? How much will it cost to fill the gaps?

Once these questions have been answered the following questions should be answered about money:

1. What is the total amount required at each relevant point in time?

2. How much will be available at each relevant point in time?

3. How large are the gaps between what is required and what will be available?

4. If the required amount of money is not expected to be available, then how can it be obtained or how should previously made planning decisions be modified so as to be able to finance them with the funds that will be available? If more than the required amount of money will be available, how should previously made planning decisions be modified to use all of the funds available?

Since facility and equipment decisions depend on assumptions about future demand, and since these are almost always subject to error, it is desirable to hedge against such error. One of the most effective ways of doing so is by acquiring plant or equipment that can be converted to uses other than the ones for which they are originally intended. Flexibility, expandability, and contractibility are obvious hedges against uncertainty of demand. However, these properties can only be obtained at a cost. This cost should be weighed against the expected cost of error associated with assumptions about demand.

Effective financial planning requires a financial model of the system planned for. Such a model consists of a set of interconnected equations that can be used for estimating the financial consequences of employing different means under the same or different conditions. There is no one financial model that applies to all systems or even to different parts of the same system. Nevertheless, most financial models consist of four submodels:

1. A model that shows how income is generated,
2. A model that estimates the cost of operations,
3. A model that estimates how much capital is required to support the operations, and
4. A model that uses the outputs of models 1 and 2 to calculate net internal funds available.

By combining the outputs of models 3 and 4 and using information on the amount of funds available from previous years, the additional funds required from external sources can be calculated.

The usefulness of financial models is greatly enhanced when they are computerized. This facilitates rapid exploration of the financial consequences of a large number of alternative means and environmental conditions. Such explorations obviously have great value in the planning process. (For further details of resource planning see Ackoff, 1984, Vergara Finnel, Gharajedaghi, 1984.)

IMPLEMENTATION AND CONTROL

When the previous phases of planning have been completed, decisions should be made as to who should be responsible for doing what and by when. Such decisions require the translation of previously made planning decisions into a set of assignments with a schedule for each. The assignments and schedules should be prepared jointly by those who are responsible for carrying them out, those to whom they report, and those who report directly to them.

Implementation planning can be initiated by preparing a PERT (Program Evaluation and Review Technique) chart of the activities required for pursuit of each goal and objective. Such a flow chart identifies the activities required, their sequence, and the time allocated to each. If different activities in the chart are to be assigned to different individuals or groups, those to receive such assignments should be designated. These charts should also be prepared by those who will be responsible for the implementation, those to whom they report, and those subordinates who will be involved in the process.

They should specify the following:

(a) The nature of the task to be carried out,
(b) The relevant goal or objective,
(c) Who is responsible for carrying it out,
(d) The steps to be taken,
(e) Who is responsible for each step,
(f) The timing of each step,

(g) The money allocated to each step (if any),

(h) The critical assumptions on which the schedule is based,

(i) The expected effects on performance and the time by which they are expected, and

(j) The assumptions on which the expectations are based.

When assumed and actual conditions or expected and actual performance agree, nothing need be done. When they do not agree an effort should be made to determine what has gone wrong or unusually right (diagnosis). Although the producers of unfavorable deviations may be difficult to identify, they are only of four types:

(a) The information used in selecting the means was in error.

(b) The means-selection process was faulty.

(c) The implementation was not carried out as intended.

(d) The environment changed in an unexpected way.

The effective conduct of such diagnoses and prescriptions can assure both effective learning and adaptation. Without effective learning and adaptation there is no need for continuous planning. Without continuous planning continuous progress toward organizational objectives, let alone ideals, is not possible. Without a sense of progress toward ideals, the quality of work life deteriorates. With such deterioration work loses its meaning and becomes nothing but work.

Part III

Obstructions to and Opportunities for Development

7

Introduction to Part III

An obstruction is normally thought of as something outside ourselves that makes it difficult or impossible for us to do or attain something we want. For example, a bridge that is closed may prevent our reaching a destination. Conventional wisdom has it that there are only two ways of dealing with an obstruction: either remove it or go over, under, around, or through it. But there is another way: Convert it into an opportunity. To do this we must think of an obstruction not as an external deterrent but as an internal deficiency, as a handicap; for example, we must focus not on the ability of the closed bridge to block an automobile, but on the inability of the automobile to cross the river without a bridge.

To take another example: A job application form may be an obstruction to an illiterate person who wants a job. We can focus on changing either the employer's requirement for literacy or the applicant's illiteracy. Although it may be easier to remove the obstruction, it is often preferable to remove the handicap because doing so increases the ability of the one obstructed to satisfy his needs and desires. Therefore, removal of an obstruction viewed as an internal deficiency is an opportunity for development. The possibility of converting obstructions to development into opportunities for it has long been neglected. It is generally easier to excuse one's disadvantages by blaming them on external deterrents than to remedy internal deficiencies.

The effective conversion of obstructions to a nation's development into opportunities for it also requires understanding the useful functions that the nation's internal deficiencies may have. For example, illiteracy is widely taken to be a functional deficiency that retards development. It keeps people economically disadvantaged, scientifically and technologically naive, and culturally deprived. Some argue that illiteracy is deliberately maintained by exploiters to preserve the advantages they enjoy at the expense of exploited illiterates. But this is only part of the story: Illiteracy also has some useful social functions. It helps preserve a culture, that is, traditional values and ways of doing things. It necessitates oral and demonstrative teaching and learning; this makes for family, clan, and tribal cohesion. It serves religion by perpetuating ritual and pagentry. It also preserves common sense, conventional wisdom, and such skills as are used in hunting, fishing, navigation, animal husbandry, agriculture, and, of course, a variety of arts and crafts. It protects a culture from dilution by foreign influences. In sum, illiteracy conserves culture.

The unreflective reduction or elimination of illiteracy can weaken unifying social values and lead people to abandon effective, traditional ways of doing things. It may even produce deficiencies more obstructive than illiteracy, for example, greed. All this does not imply that illiteracy should be preserved, but that its removal or reduction should be viewed as an opportunity to produce desirable cultural changes.

Recall that in the earlier discussion of reactive planning we observed that the removal of a deficiency does not assure an improvement; it can make things worse. Therefore, it should be viewed as a means, not an end. This requires specifying ends for which a deficiency is to be removed and determining how to remove it so as to assure attainment of these ends.

Just as obstructions can be converted into opportunities, opportunities can be converted into obstructions. For example, an opportunity to import advanced technologies is often taken to be an opportunity for national development, especially by less than well developed countries. But even well-developed countries are beginning to have second thoughts about such technologies and regard some as mixed blessings. For example, use of some of these technologies pollutes the environment and decreases employment.

There may also be negative consequences associated with taking advantage of an opportunity to import an "advanced" political-economic ideology such as autocratic communism or democratic capitalism. Each of these ideologies in combination with advanced technology has produced economic growth, but they are also responsible for worldwide fear of atomic annihilation and shortages of critical resources. Capitalism's preoccupation with economic growth is increasingly viewed as dangerous even to its well-developed proponents. (See, for example, Meadows et al., 1972.) Moreover, economic growth of one country often, if not always, takes place at the expense of other countries, usually ones that are less developed. On the other hand, communism has yet to deliver the standard of living and quality of life it has promised. It has often dictated to the proletariat and suppressed their rights. Neither capitalism nor communism has had any notable success in raising less developed countries to higher levels of development. It is not necessary to belabor this point. We know from experience that what comes labelled as an opportunity is often an obstruction.

In the context of development, a deficiency is the absence of something that is either required for, or very helpful in producing, development. When such a shortage pervades a society we call it *scarcity*, a condition in which the amount of a resource, service, or opportunity available within that society is insufficient to provide each of its members with the amount needed for development. For example, a scarcity of food means there is not enough available to prevent widespread malnutrition or starvation. The other side of this deficiency is the inability to produce enough food. Because scarcity is a very general and pervasive type of national deficiency from which many other deficiencies derive, we treat it as a primary obstruction to development.

Even in nations in which there is more than enough of something required for development, some or many of the nationals may not have enough of that resource because it is maldistributed. Some may have more than they need and others less. For example, in some very affluent nations maldistribution of income, discrimination, and segregation deprive many of opportunities for development. Because maldistribution, like scarcity, is pervasive and the source of many other deficiencies, it too is treated as a primary obstruction to development.

Even where a resource, service, or opportunity required for development is available in sufficient quantity and is well distributed, it may not be used for development. Misuse, abuse, or nonuse of an essential resource, service, or opportunity may be due to ignorance or conflict, which, as we will try to show, are types of scarcity. But nondevelopmental use of an essential resource may also derive from insecurity, a fear of losing what one has for reasons unrelated to what one does. Insecurity in this sense means the fear of being fired regardless of how well one performs or because of a declining demand for one's services or products. It does not apply to losing what one has because of what one does, for example, fear of losing one's job because of poor performance.

Insecurity leads to protective measures. For example, nations use the military to protect their resources from unjustified appropriation by external forces, and they use the police, courts, and prisons to protect themselves and their members against hostile internal forces. However, nations that are the targets of such defensive and deterrent measures often perceive them as aggressive, thus increasing their insecurity. These nations respond in kind and the spiral of defense spending takes off, continuing until each country spends at least as much as it can afford. All these consequences of insecurity obstruct development by consuming resources that could otherwise be used to facilitate it.

Nature is also a major source of insecurity; for example, fear of floods, hurricanes, tornadoes, and earthquakes. Societies and individuals subject to the possibility of such events usually spend some of their resources to either prevent their occurrence, reduce their potential effects, or ensure against them. The greater the insecurity, the more is spent. The more spent, the less is available for investment in development.

Some of what is spent to increase security is well spent, some is not. There clearly is such a thing as overspending on security, and it is pervasive. This is why we consider insecurity to be the third and final primary obstruction to development.

In the next five chapters we consider the intersection of each of the three primary obstructions to development (scarcity, maldistribution, and insecurity) with each of the five ideal pursuits necessary for development: truth, plenty,

Table 7.1
Secondary Obstructions to Development

IDEALS PURSUED	TRUTH	PLENTY	GOOD	BEAUTY	POWER
RELEVANT SOCIAL INSTITUTIONS	Scientific, Technological, and Educational	Economic	Ethical and Moral	Aesthetic – Creative and Recreative	Political
OUTPUT OF PURSUITS	Information, Knowledge, and Understanding	Goods and Services	Peace and Cooperation	Fun and Inspiration, Excitement	Influence and Participation
SCARCITY	Ignorance	Poverty	Anxiety Conflict	Boredom and Ugliness	Impotence
MALDISTRIBUTION	Elitism	Disparity, Exploitation	Discrimination, Social Castes	Segregation	Autocracy
INSECURITY	Fear of Obsolescence	Fear of Appropriation	Fear of Aggression	Fear of Isolation, Hopelessness	Fear of Illegitimacy

good, beauty, and power. These intersections produce secondary obstructions, some of which are shown in Table 7.1. Each of these ideal pursuits is treated in a separate chapter, but their interactions figure prominently in our discussions of them.

Finally, a few words of caution: While reading the discussions of opportunities for development, it should be kept in mind that none of the measures presented are intended as panaceas. Although each can contribute to development, it is only when they are used in combination and their interactions are carefully orchestrated that maximum benefits can be obtained. Such orchestration requires comprehensive planning.

8

Science, Technology, and Education

Development requires a continuous supply of information, knowledge, and understanding. Information is descriptive; it consists of answers to questions that begin with such words as *who, what, which, when, where,* and *how many.* Knowledge is instructive; it consists of answers to "how-to" questions. Understanding is explanatory; it consists of answers to "why" questions. In general, science provides the best way to obtain answers to any of these types of questions. Technology provides applications of the outputs of science to practical affairs. Education, among other things, disseminates the products and methods of science and technology.

SCIENTIFIC, TECHNOLOGICAL, AND EDUCATIONAL SCARCITIES AS OBSTRUCTIONS TO DEVELOPMENT

Scarcity of Science

The absence of information, knowledge, and understanding is ignorance, which, of course, is a major obstruction to the development of individuals and the societies of which they are part. There is no well-developed society that ignorance pervades. Nor is there any less developed society in which information, knowledge, and understanding are plentiful.

The information, knowledge, and understanding produced by science are contained in and are transmitted by messages that, in general, are publicly available. Although the production of new information, knowledge, and understanding by science may be costly, the acquisition of most of what already has been produced is not. Access to the output of technology is another matter, one that is discussed below. However, scientists are usually the only ones who can understand, evaluate, and translate much of the output of science. Moreover, because there is a large international flow between scientists of information about work not yet published, access to this can also only be obtained through a scientific establishment. Without such an establishment the output of science is not accessible.

Any country that fails to acquire most of the output of science does so as a matter of choice. This choice is often made by those in control of less developed countries because the ignorant are the easiest to exploit, their labor is the easiest to obtain, and they are the least likely to challenge established authority and the existing social order.

The presence of science and widespread familiarity with it usually has a profound effect on a society's culture. It replaces myth and superstition with more effective ways of dealing with reality. It produces such concepts as evidence and proof, and these spill over into other-than-scientific areas. Science tends to become the ultimate arbiter of truth and weakens the foundation under those who claim some other special access to it and who use this claim to seize and hold on to power. A free science weakens claims to authority based on anything but competence.

Put another way: Science is a way not only of thinking and dealing with what we experience, but of extending that experience. It increases the ability of man to penetrate what were previously deep mysteries, dispelling fatalism and counteracting resignation to "forces beyond our control." It provides an ability to control at least part of one's destiny. It is an antidote to hopelessness, helplessness, stagnation, and decay.

Even in countries in which science is plentiful, its various disciplines may not be equally represented, and "pure" science may dominate applied. Some types of science may be scarce even when others are not. The social sciences are generally the least developed in autocratic countries because these sciences can challenge the status quo more than any other type of science. They tend to reveal abuses of power and exploitation, organizational inefficiency and ineffectiveness, and hypocrisy. The physical and biological sciences pose a less direct threat to established authority and the way society is organized and managed. For this reason, the more repressive a society is, the less support it gives to the social sciences. Moreover, in such societies, the more abstract the work of its scientists and the less obvious its practical applications, the safer the scientists are.

Suppression of the social sciences is often based on the apparently convincing but false claim that they are less precise than the older natural sciences. This claim ignores the relative nature of precision. Safety factors of at least 100 percent are incorporated into bridges, ships, airplanes, and buildings. However, such large margins for error are almost never available in organizations and, in general, are not needed. It can be argued, contrary to popular belief, that the "social engineer" receives and requires less margin for error than the "physical engineer."

Whether or not this is true is not nearly as important as the fact that to initiate and sustain national development a great deal of information about, and knowledge and understanding of society and its institutions are required. If any part of science can be spared in the early stages of development, it is the natural sciences, not the social.

Another argument frequently used to maintain a scarcity of science in less developed countries is that these countries are in a state of crisis, confronted with emergencies, and science is of little value in such circumstances. It is viewed as a luxury, an indulgence that less developed countries can ill afford. This argument ignores two important facts. First, science has been very useful to well-developed countries precisely at times of crisis. The role of science in World War II (as recorded in Crowther and Whiddington, 1947) is illustrative. Many scientists left their laboratories to go into the field and apply the scientific method to urgent operational problems. Their success is a matter of undisputed record.

Second, the countries that have the greatest ability to cope with emergencies are ones that are equipped with the products of science and technology. To be sure, when emergencies arise there is seldom time for research, but the products of research carried out for such contingencies often make the difference between survival and death.

Scarcity of Technology

Access to the know-how produced by technology is more limited than access to the output of science. Technology is not freely exchanged because, unlike much of the output of science, it is widely regarded as private property. Therefore, it usually has to be purchased and frequently at a high price. The alternative, development of an internal ability to produce technology, is also very expensive, hence it is not feasible for small, poor, and less developed countries. Moreover, in many less developed countries those who govern and/or exploit the governed feel threatened by technological change because it is often accompanied by significant social change.

Technology is know-how: knowing how to provide useful goods or services inexpensively, how to maintain them, and how to use them effectively. The acquisition of technology is not merely a matter of acquiring its products. Without knowledge of the technology that produced these products, a country's dependence on those who have it increases, and this opens that country to abuse by those on whom it depends. In sum, possession of the products of technology without the knowledge that produced them can be an obstruction to development. It is much better to have the knowledge without the products than the products without the knowledge. Norway has taken considerable advantage of this fact by sending specialists of various kinds and industrialists abroad for their education (Bergh et al., 1980).

Awareness of this fact has also led some less developed countries to insist that foreign suppliers of products produce all or some of them in the country in which they are sold and teach natives how to produce them. Going further, "the Japanese government's policies demand . . . that foreigners give help to Japanese companies in return for access to Japan's markets'' (Gross, 1983, p. 46). To be sure, such requirements are often economically motivated, but the requirement for technical education of natives by ''invading'' foreigners is primarily an effort to reduce the scarcity of technology.

Scarcity of Education

Education is the principal means for disseminating both science and technology. It can spread awareness of the fact that a better and more satisfying life is possible and the knowledge of how it can be obtained. By so doing it can stimulate an ignorant society or a segment of it to seek development. But compulsory publicly provided education is normally very costly. This is particularly true of the way education is provided by the more developed countries. The major portion of the cost lies in school buildings and salaries of teachers and administrators. The need for developing ways of providing education more efficiently and effectively is apparent. The prevailing model of education is not good enough.

Jules Henry (1963) and Ronald Laing (1967) have argued convincingly that education can also be used to preserve an established social order, thus discouraging development. When it does this, it ceases to be education. Perhaps it should be called ''schooling.'' Little wonder that Illich (1972) advocated ''deschooling society.'' A great deal of what is called education is misinformation as well as information and misunderstanding as well as understanding. It can demotivate learning by suppressing curiosity and creativity.

A great deal of what educators present to students as science is not science or is poor science; and a great deal of the technology taught is ineffective, inefficient, and inappropriate. Science, technology, and education are means, not ends. They can be used either to promote or obstruct development; they are necessary but not sufficient for it. The blessings they bring may be mixed. Therefore, their effective use for development requires careful planning and control. Effective control, as we will see, does not imply an external expert authority. In fact, such an authority is usually a major obstruction to development-oriented education.

SCIENTIFIC, TECHNOLOGICAL, AND EDUCATIONAL MALDISTRIBUTIONS AS OBSTRUCTIONS TO DEVELOPMENT

Maldistribution of Science

The maldistribution of resources means that some have less than they need and others have more. Those who do not have enough often suffer additionally from the use to which it is put by those who have an excess. The excess is frequently used to exploit those who are already deprived.

Science not only contributes to development, but development contributes to the growth of science. The percentage of a nation's population that is engaged in scientific activity is generally proportional to its level of development. In addition, the percentage of a nation's population that knows what science is and how it can be used is also proportional to development. This means that in less developed countries science-policy issues and other issues that have scientific content cannot be debated intelligently by most of the population, including many politicians. Therefore, such issues are usually handled with unqualified politeness or by a few politically influential scientists whose judgments tend to be biased in their own favor; that is, they tend to strengthen the scientific status quo.

No practical problems are purely scientific, not even those of national science-policy. Therefore, if left to scientists alone, the nonscientific aspects of such problems are likely to be overlooked. Consider, for example, the allocation of public resources to the development of science. Where there are not enough scientists to cover all the disciplines and interdisciplines of science, which is the case in most less developed countries, some sciences are either not covered or are covered inadequately. The slighted sciences are almost always those having more relevance to practical affairs. Such "pure" sciences as mathematics, astronomy, physics, chemistry, and biology are the best cared for. The sciences dealing with purposeful human and social behavior are neglected.

As a result, many public issues, to which some branches of science can contribute, go without assistance from science or receive it from scientists who are not qualified to provide it. But of even greater importance are the consequences of a shortage of scientists. The few there are usually attain advantaged positions in society that they are loathe to relinquish or share. Therefore, they try (by means we discuss below) to detach themselves as much as possible from even those controversial public issues to which they can contribute, and they resist efforts to increase the number of scientists who could make such contributions.

The worse the maldistribution of science in a society, the more its scientists tend to hoard their knowledge and refrain from using it on public issues that affect development. This obstructs the development of relevant sciences and of development-oriented scientists.

Maldistribution of Technology

The relevance of technology to development is much more apparent than that of science. As a result, the need for technology and technologists such as engineers, agronomists, and medical doctors is well recognized in less developed countries. Moreover, technologists are generally much less reluctant than scientists to become involved in public affairs. In fact, they often migrate into politics and public administration. In Mexico, for example, the proportion of engineers who hold public office is much greater than in most developed countries.

Maldistribution of technology means the uneven and inequitable allocation of technology over different sectors of an economy and segments of a population. In particular, technology is usually concentrated in the urban industrial sector in an effort to industrialize the country. This is done despite the fact that the industrial revolution succeeded in most developed countries because it was preceded by an agricultural revolution. Technology was first used to mechanize agriculture, increasing the productivity of the land and the amount of land that could be used productively. This resulted either in enough food to eliminate the need to import some of it or in a surplus that could be exported and converted into capital to finance industrialization.

Currently, most less developed countries have not gone through an agricultural revolution and, as a result, are short of food and must import it. This, together with the cost of importing the products of technology necessary for industrialization, leads to unfavorable balances of trade, heavy borrowing, inflation, and devaluation of currencies, all of which obstruct development. Moreover, the lack of appropriate mechanization in agriculture promotes a rural population explosion because children are needed to provide the low-cost labor required by manual farming.

In many of the less developed countries in which technology has been brought to bear on agriculture the effects have not been conducive to development. Ward Morehouse (1982) has reflected on such failures:

For the past three decades, much economic growth in the Third World has been based on the proposition that the way to reduce poverty is to improve productivity, and the best means of doing that is to provide new and advanced technology to increase the efficiency with which productive resources are used. Thus has been created one of the particularly egregious myths of the modern world; that complex, deep-rooted social problems can be solved through "technological fixes."

This leads to what C. T. Kurien of the Madras Institute of Development Studies in India has called the "refraction effect" of technology in rural development. Technology itself may be "scale neutral," but its consequences are seldom socially neutral for the rural communities in which it is introduced. When it is passed through a filter of an established social order, it is bent, as a ray of light is refracted when it passes through a body of water. More and more evidence suggests that the "natural" direction of this refraction effect is to *increase*, rather than reduce, disparities within social communities into which substantial technological inputs have been provided. . . .

It is a melancholy fact that all too often the "refraction effect" of technological inputs into rural development magnifies economic disparities within rural communities, making the lot of the poor still worse than it was. [pp. 71–72]

While industrialists and government officials of less developed countries fly abroad on domestically owned airlines equipped with the latest technology and large operating losses, peasants haul their supplies and crops in ox carts over rut-filled dirt roads. City dwellers cannot get to where they want to go because there are too many mechanized vehicles, most of which are underutilized. Peasants cannot get to where they want to go because there are too few vehicles of any kind to take them there, and those vehicles that are available usually do not have the needed capacity.

Cities provide water, electricity, gas, sewage disposal, paved streets, and so on, while in rural areas people do without any of these "luxuries." They often live without any publicly provided utilities or services. The leading city in most less developed countries is a museum of modern technology, while their rural areas are museums of antiquity.

Architects and civil, mechanical, and electrical engineers combine their skills to produce modern office buildings, factories, hotels, expensive homes, and so on in cities, while peasants live in no-cost housing that has not improved in centuries.

The infrastructure required to support industry is built in cities because in the short term it is more economical. For the same reason this is done in as few cities as possible. The result is a high concentration of industry in a small number of urban areas to which many of the rural population migrate in the hope of finding jobs. This migration is usually excessive and results in a large underclass that constitutes a potential threat to political stability. For this reason, and because taxes on urbanized industry become a major source of government income, an additional and disproportional amount of public resources is poured into a few urban industrial centers, leaving little to invest in the development of rural areas.

Urban concentration is often accompanied by land reform that increases the number of farms and decreases their size so that their mechanization becomes impractical. Efforts to solve this problem by creating large cooperative farms, as were carried out successfully in Israel, usually fail because the organizational skills required are not available.

Medical doctors (i.e., biological technologists) who usually have been trained at public expense tend to congregate in large urban industrial centers where affluent people congregate and facilities exist in which medicine can be "practiced." The rural areas are left largely unattended. As a result, rural infant and child mortality is often very high. This stimulates high birth rates. And so the vicious circle turns, becoming more and more vicious.

All of this occurs despite a significant increase in technology planning. According to Frank Long (1979):

Heavy costs are said to be borne by Third World countries in terms of prices paid for technology, conditions under which technology is transferred, and in terms of absorbing foreign technology. One upshot of all this is the pronouncement of technology plans in a number of Third World countries. . . .

Some countries which have already produced such plans include Mexico, Brazil, Venezuela, India and Pakistan. The plans so far confirm the established, but not wholly desirable, social scientific tradition of looking at technology in the development process— namely the overriding importance of economic considerations. . . .

Several researchers in the area of development have drawn attention to the increasing inequalities between "haves" and "have nots" in spite of spectacularly high growth rates induced by modern technology. For example, Brazil and Venezuela. The introduction of local technology into the equation, for instance, is no guarantee that the "have nots" can increase their development prospects. It is therefore a source of surprise that the technology plans concerned have failed to provide any meaningful scope through which science and technology can bring about real improvements in the quality of life of the masses. [pp. 10–11]

Maldistribution of Education

There are few societies in which everyone is ignorant. Even in the least developed countries there is usually an elite who have either been educated abroad or in well-run native schools accessible only to the children of the elite. Those educated in this way enjoy and hoard advantages unavailable to the rest of the population. National wealth and power are usually concentrated in those who are well educated.

Such inequity in the distribution of education is sometimes rationalized by claims of special personal endowments; for example, superior blood or brains, favors granted by nature, destiny, or God, not by man. In such ways, the educated absolve themselves of responsibility for the ignorance of others.

Knowledge is power; its inequitable distribution breeds dependency of the uneducated on the educated. This paves the way for the exploitation of the former by the latter. Each dollar spent on schooling means more privileges for the few at the cost of many. At best it increases the number of those who, before dropping out, have been taught that those who stay longer earn the right to more power, wealth, and prestige. What such schooling does is to teach the schooled the superiority of the better schooled (Illich, 1973, p. 360).

Power and status are transmitted to the children of the elite through education. Little wonder that education available to the children of the elite is significantly better than that available to others. The public universities in Mexico City, for example, spend several times as much per student per year as do public universities in other Mexican cities. In addition, Mexico City has more private schools of quality than there are in the rest of Mexico, and opportunities for education abroad are disproportionally allocated to those who have been educated in that city.

Such maldistribution of education converts power and poverty into inherited characteristics, thereby spuriously supporting claims by the educated to genetic superiority. It also makes for low social productivity and considerable waste of human and physical resources that could be used for development. It enables the advantaged to continually improve their quality of life while precluding similar improvements for the underdeveloped masses. Maldistribution of education tends to become worse, not better, over time.

What has been said here of the maldistribution of science, technology, and education within nations also applies between nations. A nation's ability to conduct scientific inquiry, develop technology, and educate its population is a source of power and status in the community of nations. It also equips those nations that have this ability to exploit nations that do not.

SCIENTIFIC, TECHNOLOGICAL, AND EDUCATIONAL INSECURITIES AS OBSTRUCTIONS TO DEVELOPMENT

Because information, knowledge, and understanding are sources of privilege and power, many of the societies, organizations, and individuals that possess them fear their "loss." "Loss" in this case does not mean what it does where objects are involved. It refers to the advantages brought by having more information, knowledge, and understanding than others. Such losses occur either when others acquire the same information, knowledge, and understanding, or when these become obsolete. Protection against such losses is obtained by denying others access to what information, knowledge, and understanding one has, and preventing or obstructing efforts that could make these obsolete or reveal their obsolescence when they have become so.

Scientific Insecurity

Scientists who feel their advantaged position in society is insecure hoard their information, knowledge, and understanding, and see to it that only a select few gain access to their store. They hoard these resources by refusing to popularize them, to make them understandable to, hence useable by, laymen. Scientists in less developed countries almost always present their work in journals published in more developed countries, usually in a foreign language. This virtually assures its inaccessibility to their lay countrymen, but it enhances their image among their "enlightened" compatriots.

Scientists in less developed countries generally restrict the number of students to whom they transmit what they know; they demand intense loyalty and even subservience from their students. Skeptical students are not tolerated. Moreover, by sending students abroad for advanced work and research experience, their number is kept small and their selection can be rigidly controlled. Finally, the ability of young scientists to find jobs is controlled by scientific patrons who thus maintain their own security. The consequences of such patronage are a scarcity of scientists and a lack of development orientation among them.

As already noted, scientists in less developed countries tend to avoid involvement in public issues. Such involvement exposes them to evaluation and criticism by others, particularly by those in political power. This retreat from practicality is defended by proclaiming the need to keep science "pure" and "objective." The ability to remain detached and uninvolved, they claim, has been responsible for the success of science in more developed countries.

Most scientists in less developed countries tend to emulate their counterparts in more developed countries. This, they believe, helps secure their position in their own countries. The problems they choose to work on are generally drawn from the prestigious "pure" sciences in more developed countries. They ignore the fact that many of even these problems derive from practical considerations. Technology often advances without the benefit of science. Science then tries to understand and extend these advances. It is this exchange back and forth between science and technology in more developed countries that is responsible for their greater contribution to the development of their countries than occurs in the less developed. Therefore, "pure" science in less developed countries tends to be even more "pure," and applied science tends to have even less repute.

"Pure" science in developed countries usually has only a short wait before application of its output is found. This is not true in less developed countries. As a result, and ironically, pure science from less developed countries contributes more to the development of relevant technologies in developed countries than it does in the countries of its origin.

Objectivity is widely regarded as a virtue among scientists, particularly those in less developed countries where it is believed to reduce chances of intrusion into their work by politicians and laymen. Objectivity is taken to mean the exclusion from research of the researcher's ethical-moral values. Objectivity so conceived is not possible.

All scientific research involves the balancing of two types of error, one of which increases as the other decreases. For example, as the probability of accepting a false hypothesis is reduced, the probability of rejecting one that is true is increased. As the probability of overestimating the value of a variable or constant is decreased, the probability of underestimating it is increased. Therefore, the decision as to how to conduct scientific research always involves a value judgment about the relative seriousness of these "conflicting" errors. The fact that scientists usually make this value decision unconsciously does not attest to their objectivity but to their ignorance.

Those who conduct research in which the consequences of error are very difficult to identify often excuse themselves from giving these errors conscious consideration by calling their research "pure." This label does not change the fact that in drawing any conclusion from any type of research, "pure" or otherwise, a judgment about the relative seriousness of different types of error is necessarily involved.

The prevailing concept of objectivity is based on a distinction between ethical-moral man (who is believed to be emotional, involved, and biased) and scientific man (who is believed to be unemotional, uninvolved, and unbiased). The scientist is expected to deposit his "heart" at the door to his workplace, but take his "head" with him. This expectation obviously assumes the separability of head and heart, of science and values. This is completely contrary to what philosophy and science have revealed about the nature of man. To assume the "head" and "heart" can be separated is like assuming that because we can look at and discuss the head and tail of a coin separately, we can separate them.

Objectivity is not the absence of value judgments in research, but the product of an open interaction of a wide variety of subjective value judgments. Objectivity is a property of science taken as a whole, not a property of individual researchers or research. It is obtained when all possible values have been taken into account; hence it is an ideal that science can continually approach but never attain. That which is true, works; it works whatever the values of those who put it to work. Truth is value-full, not value-free.

Therefore, scientists who seek security by claiming the need for detachment and uninvolvement in practical affairs preclude their chances of attaining the objectivity they seek and reduce their ability to contribute to the development of the society of which they are a part.

Finally, scientists in search of security tend to enclose themselves within the protective walls of a traditional scientific discipline. They prohibit or discredit any effort by their colleagues to probe the exterior of their disciplinary cells and try to prevent any intrusion by outsiders. They discourage or prevent the development of interdisciplinary scientific activity. It is precisely through such activity—for example, cybernetics, decision sciences, information and communication sciences, policy sciences, operations research, management sciences, and systems sciences—that science can contribute most to national development.

Technological Insecurity

Technologists who feel insecure try to induce their countries to undertake large public projects involving advanced technologies. The more they succeed, the more need there is for their services. The projects selected for "promotion" are often not in the best interests of the country, however well they serve the interest of the technologists. These projects frequently involve technologies that are inappropriate to the country, however appropriate they may be in the countries in which they were developed. Moreover, they often exacerbate the problems they were intended to solve. For example, the large expansion of the transportation system in Mexico City has increased, not decreased, congestion and the time required for travel.

As already noted, engineers in less developed countries often move into politics and public administration. The ease with which they can do so depends on a number of large public projects that require their skills. The power they gain need not involve increased accountability for success of these projects. Such responsibility can be easily avoided by importing foreign experts at considerable cost to approve the projects. Their approval provides security to the indigenous imitators, even though the experts seldom know enough about the country involved to make good judgments about the appropriateness of the projects. Moreover, since these experts cannot be held accountable for project failure, responsibility is buried in a bureaucratic cemetery.

Technologists also protect themselves by closing ranks. Stiff qualifications are imposed on those seeking entry. Access is restricted to those who are not likely to disturb the status quo. Qualifying examinations, professional certification, and licensing procedures are used to filter out potential troublemakers.

Professional associations are used to police the practice of members of technological disciplines and to assure conformity to restrictive standards. Heresies in technology, as in religion, result in excommunication and disgrace. Under the guise of maintaining professional standards, innovations are discouraged and the threat of obsolescence is reduced. These associations not only preserve the competence of their members, but protect their incompetence as well. They do not disclose evidence they have of the imcompetence. They propagate the myth of their members' infallibility. On the other hand, anyone attempting to practice the profession without approval of the association is subject to attack, whatever his competence.

There is considerable resistance from professionals to the training and use of "barefoot" or paraprofessionals, as China has used so successfully. Despite claims to the contrary, a great deal of what technologists do requires little skill or professional education. It can be performed more than adequately by technicians, for example, drafting, surveying, computing, considerable laboratory work, and much of the practice of medicine. Nevertheless, training of para-technologists is generally opposed by professionals because they believe it lowers regard for their skills and diminishes their status. This opposition keeps the cost of technology high and deprives many of access to it, hence it obstructs development.

Educational Insecurity

In every country the well educated enjoy opportunities not available to the poorly educated. This education and opportunity gap is greatest in less developed countries. The less developed a country is, the greater is the advantage of a good education. The educated in these countries often devote considerable effort, consciously or unconsciously, to preserving their advantages. The most effective protection consists of denying a good education to "others." Publicly provided education is kept low in quantity and quality for almost all but the children of the well educated. Better education is provided in cities than in rural areas, where often none is available. Furthermore, the quality of the public education provided in cities tends to be proportional to the number of educated in it. For example, as previously noted, public universities in Mexico City are provided with several times as much money per student as are public universities in other Mexican cities.

Private schools, to which only the educated can afford to send their children, usually provide a better education than public despite the fact that they often pay their teachers less. Opportunities for education abroad are available to only a select few and provide access to the highest status in society.

Little if any effort is made to encourage and facilitate informal education;

what there is of it is usually discredited by the well educated. There are exceptions, of course, for example, the open-school system in Mexico.

SCIENTIFIC, TECHNOLOGICAL, AND EDUCATIONAL OPPORTUNITIES FOR DEVELOPMENT

Recall that the function of science and technology is to enable us to pursue our ends more efficiently. They capacitate, hence develop. Some consider them to be sufficient for development and treat them as ends rather than means. This was the case in Iran where the late Shah focused on absorbing all the science and technology of the developed world as rapidly as possible almost to the exclusion of anything else. A large number of young Iranians were sent to foreign colleges and universities to acquire and return with science and technology. Ironically, it was among these retrievers of science and technology that the seeds of the revolution against the Shah were sown, nurtured, and brought to fruition. "Westernization" (the uncritical adoption of the science and technology of the more developed nations) is neither an unmitigated good nor evil. It does not assure development.

Nevertheless, to the extent that science and technology (but not necessarily of the Western variety) are not present in a culture, its development is obstructed. This does not imply a need to absorb all the science and technology possessed by others. Less developed countries have an opportunity to design scientific, technological, and educational institutions that can serve their development better than the corresponding institutions in more developed countries.

Scientific Opportunities

As previously noted, during World War II science was very effectively mobilized in a number of more developed countries to serve national purposes, but this mobilization terminated with that war. The development of science was not retarded during the war; on the contrary, it was greatly stimulated. There is no reason why science cannot be mobilized as effectively for constructive national purposes as it was for destructive purposes and why it cannot develop rapidly under these conditions. Herein lies an opportunity for less developed countries, an opportunity not yet grasped by the more developed.

The institution of science in less developed countries is usually relatively small, confined to the traditional disciplines, concentrated in a few locations, and underfinanced. It also tends to be conservative and resistant to change. However, because government is usually its sole source of support and survival, it can be directed by government into development-related activities. Such redirection requires an explicit national science policy. This policy should make national support of science proportional to its dedication to national development. Government and scientists should work together in selecting areas in which research should be done and in allocating resources to them.

A principal objective of a government's science policy should be the infusion of the scientific attitude into the population at large. This means that the public should come to know and understand science as a powerful method of inquiry as well as an organized body of knowledge. This method can easily be learned and used by laymen, particularly if helped by professional scientists.

Science education should not be preoccupied with memorization of terminology, facts, and laws, but should focus on development of the scientific attitude and understanding of its method of inquiry. Such education should not be restricted to schools or young people. Radio, the press, motion pictures, and particularly television, if available, also should be used. To facilitate this process, scientists should be encouraged to translate the method and findings of science into ordinary language. A high value should be placed on such efforts. Foreign literature and films that effectively popularize science should be translated with government support and made available at low or no cost.

Science museums and exhibits should be made available. Where possible, they should be made mobile to increase access to them. Fairs and competitions can be used to encourage young people to become involved in science.

Scientists themselves should be encouraged to become familiar with the development-oriented interdisciplinary research conducted in more developed countries. They should be induced to initiate teaching and research in these areas, and a major portion of those students who are sent abroad for advanced education should be directed into these areas.

In sum, science can be made a vital and pervasive aspect of national development efforts. Governments can bring this about if they understand and appreciate what science can do, and stop treating it as a luxury or type of conspicuous consumption of scarce national resources. There is no reason that science cannot be put to work, that the funds involved in doing it cannot be increased by making it useful, and that the number of people engaged in or making use of it cannot be greatly increased.

Technological Opportunities

There are two aspects of the way technology has developed in more developed countries that are widely overlooked by planners in less developed countries. First, the problems to which technology has been addressed have been culturally and environmentally determined. This was clearly shown by Crowther and Whiddington (1947). For example, the diseases on which the medical sciences focus are usually indigenous. Therefore, to the extent that problems differ between cultures and environments, the technological solutions obtained in one culture may not be suitable in another. More significantly, the criteria employed in evaluating technological solutions in one culture may be inappropriate in another. For example, an industrial technology developed in a country that has expensive labor and inexpensive capital is not likely to be well suited to a country that has expensive capital and inexpensive labor. Nor will a technology that requires a highly skilled work force work well in a country whose work force is low skilled.

Technological products. Technological products once useful in the country in which they were developed often become dysfunctional in that country at a later time. Because less developed countries so frequently imitate the more developed, they often adopt technologies that are not even appropriate in the countries of their origin. The automobile is a conspicuous example. It was designed for use in developed countries at a time when their average family size was much larger than it is now, when cities were much smaller than they are now, when energy was plentiful and inexpensive, and air pollution was not a problem. Today, the traffic, congestion, pollution, energy, and safety problems created by automobiles plague developed countries. But this has not deterred less developed countries from importing the same difficulties. These difficulties are often magnified in less developed countries. Witness the congestion and pollution in Mexico City, Rio de Janeiro, São Paulo, Calcutta, and Teheran, to mention only a few.

In a state of underdevelopment there is a tendency to try to fit problems to predetermined solutions rather than solutions to problems. The automobile is such a predetermined solution. Yet less developed countries could design and produce automobiles that function well under their conditions. It would probably be a two-passenger vehicle (because more than 80 percent of the vehicles used in cities carry only one or two people), have a maximum speed of about forty miles (sixty-five kilometers) per hour (because at approximately this speed the maximum density of transported people is obtained on city streets), seat the passenger behind the driver (because this yields between a 200 and 500 percent increase in the number of cars that can be accommodated), and be capable of being coupled to each other to form trains (to accommodate more than two people and to facilitate the removal of cars stalled on city streets). If such a vehicle were made available, it would increase the number of people who could afford automobiles (because it would be much less expensive than current automobiles and would use much less fuel), and it would reduce congestion and pollution. It would also be likely to find large export markets, even in more developed countries.

Glass-walled skyscrapers no longer function efficiently in the countries of origin because of increased costs of heating and air conditioning. Yet they continue to be reproduced in less developed countries.

Excessive packaging of consumable products and one-way nonreusable containers contribute to serious solid-waste and litter problems in more developed countries. They need not be imported by less developed countries.

Less developed countries need products that are not currently available; for example, low-cost do-it-yourself housing of decent quality, and inexpensive easy-to-maintain pumps, generators, tractors, trucks, and industrial production equipment. The government can conduct studies to identify such products and assign priorities to them and create incentives to encourage their development.

Processes. Less developed countries should evaluate imported production processes as well as products. The productivity of a technology varies with culture, the characteristics of workers, and availability of materials and energy.

Furthermore, the types of plants being imported are increasingly nonproductive in their countries of origin and are producing widespread alienation from work. As a result, there is a growing effort in more developed countries to design work and workplaces to fit the capabilities and aspirations of workers. There is an increasing amount of experimentation with completely new designs; for example, the Volvo plant at Kolmar, Sweden, the Buick plant at Flint, Michigan, and the Alcoa plants outside Knoxville, Tennessee. But even these newer types of factories may be completely inappropriate in less developed countries.

The opportunities available to less developed countries to avoid the mistakes of the industrial revolution are great, but perhaps nowhere more than in rural industrialization. While factories in the developed world are increasingly emigrating from urban areas, less developed countries continue to locate them in cities. Rural rather than urban industrialization is especially needed in less developed countries if for no other reason than to retard migration to already overcrowded cities. Mexico City, for example, has already become an unmanageable monster of more than fourteen million people. The more jobs created within the city, the more migration from the countryside.

Where rural industrialization is taking place in less developed countries, factories and production processes originally developed for urban settings are used. To do this is to lose a great opportunity. With forethought, rural industrialization could enhance agricultural development, an almost universal need among less developed countries. Products made in the countryside can be selected so they use agricultural raw materials and have production cycles that run counter to that of agriculture; that is, require heavier production in the nongrowing season.

If rural factories were designed as an integral part of rural development their contribution to such development could be significantly increased. For example, they could be used to generate electricity, pump and supply water, and provide do-it-yourself workshops, recreational and educational facilities. They could also house daycare centers for children of employees, health clinics, and space for community activities.

In general, the opportunity that a low level of development in science and technology presents rests precisely on the underdevelopment that is ordinarily regarded as an obstruction. Highly developed countries can do relatively little to redirect their advanced science and technology so that it better addresses their changing needs. A high level of development is usually accompanied by an inability to make significant changes in science and technology because they are relatively autonomous. It is only in time of war, catastrophe, or crisis that science and technology in a developed country can be made to adapt quickly to changing needs. Less developed countries need not be so handicapped.

Finally, national or multinational collaborative efforts can be directed at developing appropriate new technologies. Such efforts should not focus exclusively on products to be exported to more developed countries, as has so often been the case, but on products for export to other less developed countries. Countries in this condition that do not help each other can hardly expect to be helped by more developed countries without exploitative strings attached.

Educational Opportunities

Education is the key to development. When conducted properly, it is development. Nevertheless, a number of experts in the field believe that institutionalized education, particularly in many of the more developed countries, is deteriorating at an alarming rate. (See, for example, Friedenberg, 1971; Illich, 1972; and Silberman, 1970.) Despite repeated studies that proclaim the crisis in education, the systems that provide it in most countries continue with only cosmetic changes or, at most, modest reforms.

What is needed is a frontal assault on the existing school structure that will replace outmoded teaching methods, impersonal and authoritarian teacher-student relations and obsolete behavior codes with new forms and ideas more in tune with the times. [*Newsweek*, Feb. 16, 1970, pp. 65, 69]

This need has yet to be met. Educational institutions are paralyzed by vested interests of teachers, archaic ideas about the nature of education, and proliferating bureaucracy. In the United States, for example:

The number of pupils per administrator has dropped from 523 in 1949–50 to 295 in 1979–80. Teachers' salaries comprised 52.4% of current expenditures per pupil in 1959–60; by 1979–80 they were 38.8%. [Brimelow, 1983, p. 62]

The basic structure of educational systems has remained essentially the same for centuries. Radical inquiry into this function arouses deepseated opposition and, where initiated, does not last long and has little if any lasting effect. For example, the educational experiments of the late 1960s and early 1970s in the developed world have long since been washed away by a wave of reaction.

Educational administrators and planners find it almost impossible to depart from old models even though many radically new ones are readily available. Some of the new models have been used successfully, but usually on a small scale. This plus the inevitable differences between their circumstances and those under which the experiments were conducted provide educators and educational administrators and planners with all the excuses they need to ignore these innovations. Nevertheless, the possibility of significantly increasing the efficiency and effectiveness of publicly provided education is great, particularly in less developed countries in which educational bureaucracies and the self-interests of professional educators are not so deeply entrenched.

Most educators blame the plight of education on the family, the public, politicians, and everything else in sight other than themselves. But mostly they blame the lack of funds. The institutional structure, the type of facilities and equipment required, and educational content are assumed to be fixed. Therefore, the amount of money available determines the amount of instruction and facilities available. Thus, the quality of education is equated to the amount spent per student per year and the number of years of education provided. This is a terrible distortion of the meaning of "quality of education." For example, in the city of Philadelphia where this is being written, the amount spent per student per year has been increasing sharply, but the quality of education, measured by what has been learned, has been decreasing precipitously. It costs more to educate students poorly in this city's public schools than it does to educate them well in private schools.

Leaving quality questions aside, [U.S.] public school productivity, measured by the number of employees required to process a given number of students, seems to have declined by 46% between 1957 and 1979. Even the poor old steel industry managed to increase its output per worker-hour 36¢ during this period. Overall business sector productivity rose 65%. [Brimelow, 1983, p. 62]

Opportunities for increasing the contribution of formal education to national development can be revealed by identifying the fundamental assumptions on which it is currently based, denying these assumptions individually and in a variety of combinations, and exploring the consequences of these denials. This has been done with very different results, for example, by Ackoff (1974, Chapter 5), Illich (1972), and Freire (1973).

However, the task of national development planners is not to redesign the educational process; this should not even be the task of educational planners. It is to redesign the educational system so as to make it ready, willing, and able to experiment with new pedagogy, new educational content and organizations of that content, and new designs of the facilities and equipment used. Such a redesign requires at least two fundamental changes: the educational system must be debureaucratized, and students and their parents or guardians must be given an opportunity to participate in determining the content of education, its method of delivery, and how the system is managed and planned for.

Debureaucratizing Education

The problems of education are . . . the problems typical of any socialized monopoly. . . . Symptoms include: the persistent tendency . . . to treat capital as a free good and all possible uses of it as equal; constant mismatching of supply and demand . . . ; prices administered without regard to incentives . . . ; an absence of internal checks and balances to prevent wholesale imposition of officially favored enthusiasms . . . ; a pervasive politicization, a search for panaceas, and inexorable growth. [Brimelow, 1983, p. 64]

Institutional and organizational development derive to a large extent from the struggle for survival. Public schools have not had to engage in such a struggle;

they are subsidized and provided with captive consumers. They need not compete for or satisfy their consumers. School-age children and their parents and guardians have no choice of public school. They must use the one to which they are assigned, usually on the basis of location.

Any supplier of a service who has assured income and assured consumers has little or no incentive to provide a satisfactory service. Public schools are no exception. To survive, all they need to do is comply with regulations. Bureaucracy is the inevitable consequence. Innovation and experimentation are discouraged. As a result, most educational systems are less capable of learning than their worst students.

The debureaucratization of public education can be accomplished by making survival of individual schools depend on the satisfying of students and their parents and guardians, by providing students and their parents and guardians with a choice of schools, and by making the income of each school depend on the number of students enrolled in it. This can be accomplished by use of the "voucher system," first formulated by Jenks (1970). What follows is our design of a voucher system.

The parents of each school-age child would be given an educational voucher worth a specified amount of money payable by the government to the school that receives it. This voucher would cover tuition and transportation (if required) to any public school and part or all of tuition to a private school. Students, or their parents or guardians acting for them, could apply to any school for admission. They would not be constrained by location or political jurisdiction.

The main reason for advocating an education voucher system . . . is that vouchers would greatly enlarge freedom of choice for parents, children, and teachers. . . .

We should ask what overriding benefits we get from forcing people of limited means to accept only one alternative. . . . [Pear, 1983]

Schools that have more applicants than they can accommodate would be required to select from among them in the following way. They would have to accept applicants who live within their designated areas of responsibility. The remainder would be selected at random. This would provide students with assured access to the nearest school or equal access to any other school.

Public schools would have no source of income other than that obtained by redeeming the vouchers they receive. If they did not attract and retain enough students, they would go "out of business."

Private schools could charge whatever they wanted, but parents or guardians would have to pay the difference between the charge and the value of the voucher if that charge exceeded the value of the voucher. These schools would be able to redeem vouchers only if they selected among applicants at random. This would create competition between public and private schools as well as between schools in either sector.

The voucher system would encourage differences among schools. Needed specialization would take place. For example, if there were a large number of retarded children requiring education, schools would specialize in serving them, particularly if their vouchers had a higher redemption value.

By introducing the market mechanism into the educational system, parents or guardians as well as children would be encouraged to become familiar with alternative schools available to them. Each community should provide a clearing house of information about schools, including evaluations by children and parents.

In this system, schools would learn more than they do now from their successes and failures and do so more rapidly. They would also become more adaptive. Individual schools would tend to be more responsive to the needs and desires of students, parents, guardians, and the communities of which they are part. Their administrators would be more likely to involve parents, guardians, and students in planning and policy making.

This would encourage and facilitate the development of the participants as well as make the schools more responsive to those they serve.

Participative education. Suppliers of a service (e.g., education) who are not subject to control by those served (e.g., students and their parents or guardians) assume an infallibility that deprives them of the ability to think creatively about their services or to learn from those who do. Most educators believe that laymen, and certainly children, cannot contribute to improvement of institutionalized education. This is nonsense.

There is widespread realization that the process of development can be very much accelerated by prompting the participation of the concerned people on both designing and implementing such activities. An educational activity designed to promote such participation cannot itself be conducted in a non-participative way. The traditional way of imparting education to children, in which the teacher talks and others listen, will not be conducive to education of the adults. This itself has to become participative in which the learners become active partners in the process of educating themselves. Newer educational methods are obviously needed here. The process and methods of education cannot be separated from the intended content and objectives of education, particularly in the context of development activities. It is becoming increasingly clear that the concerned rural poor themselves have to play an active role both in their education and in their development. The adult educators and others involved in such activities can play at best the role of facilitators of this process and as resource persons for various content inputs. Participation in the process of education is vital even when functional literacy is involved because even simple literacy cannot be separated from the life problems of the learners—in this case the rural poor. The more they become aware of the deeper socio-economic problems and develop readiness for confronting such problems, the more motivated they become to take part in educational activities, including functional literacy. [Mehta, 1979, p. 5]

Even educators who accept adult involvement in educational design are likely to argue that children are not competent to do so. There are many experiments that refute this, for example, the *Gruppo Futuro* and similar experiments in Naples, Italy, and Oxford, England.

Our intention was to try to create a procedure (process) in which children could actively experiment with as many media as possible in order to express, propose, question and build alternative futures with minimal interference/domination from adults (especially those likely to specialize and profess). . . .

Our role became that of providing an initial spark of an idea that change and different futures are possible. We found that most of the childlren already knew this but that schooling prohibited thoughts about many kinds of change, especially any change not of a scientific or technological nature. We became not only facilitators but intervened in the school setting.

This ''intervention'' consisted of handing over communication tools to the children. . . . The intervention also consisted of creating an environment where change is acceptable; most often the changes expressed by the children had to do with community, feelings and institutions. [Nicholson and Lorenzo, 1981, pp. 66–67]

Such participation as we have suggested would assure the relevance of education. It would tend to be directed to more realistic prospects of the students. For example, students in rural areas would learn how to engage more productively in agricultural activities. Their education would not force them to migrate to cities to find employment in which their education is relevant.

Participative schooling expands rather than contracts the horizons of children and adults. It unifies work, play, and learning, rectifying the harm done by societies that encapsulate each in different institutions and put them into different time slots. It is only by making life whole for children as well as adults that each aspect of living can be engaged in satisfactorily and developmentally.

CONCLUSION

Development involves an increased ability to satisfy one's own needs and desires and those of others, that is, increased competence. Such an increase in turn requires an increase in knowledge and the ability to produce it (science), in the ability to use it effectively (technology), and in the ability to disseminate both knowledge and know-how efficiently. Scarcity, maldistribution, and insecurity with respect to any of these constitute obstructions to development. Like most obstructions, however, they benefit a few at a high cost to many. Even if those who benefit would benefit more in the long run from removal of obstructions, they are likely to resist removal efforts. It is difficult to induce those who are essentially satisfied with their currently advantaged position to make short-term sacrifices, no matter how small, for long-term benefits, no matter how large. In practice, therefore, the possibility of accelerated development reduces to the possibility of those obstructed gaining control of national policies, rather than those obstructing. This means that participative planning is the key to accelerated development.

We have tried to show that each obstruction in this area can be converted into an opportunity, an opportunity either to avoid an error committed in the developed world or to take desirable action omitted in that world. Less developed countries can create scientific, technological, and educational institutions that serve them better than do counterpart institutions in more developed countries. To accomplish this, the less developed must critically evaluate the science, technology, and education they intend to import and, minimally, adapt these to local conditions and needs. Such institutions in the developed world may pretend to internationalism, but they are as culturally biased as national politics.

Scientific, technological, and educational institutions should be reinvented to suit each society. This need not be done from "scratch," but it does require taking nothing for granted.

9

Economics

Continuous development requires pursuit of plenty, abundance. Pursuit of this ideal in turn requires production, distribution, maintenance, and protection of those material resources required to satisfy human needs and legitimate desires. Responsibility for these activities lies in society's economic institutions. Therefore, the field of economics is expected to provide the information, knowledge, and understanding required to manage a nation's economy and economic institutions effectively. Recently, however, belief in the ability of economics to meet this expectation has seriously eroded because national economies increasingly appear to be out of control.

To many economists and those under their spell, national development is either exclusively or primarily a matter of economic growth. The distinction between development and growth, and the relevance of ethics and aesthetics to development completely escapes them. They take science and technology to be relevant but only because these fields are seen to affect economic activity.

Economists measure economic growth in a way that even they increasingly criticize. One of their more articulate opponents, Henderson (1978, p. 119), noted that the social and environmental costs incurred because of economic growth "are added to their Gross National Product, rather than subtracted." Because of this, these costs "grow unnoticed until they begin saturating real productivity."

It does seem peculiar that money spent to clear an oil spill or a polluted river adds to growth of a national economy, and that a hired maid or babysitter contributes to gross national product while the unpaid housewife who performs these functions does not. Perhaps the economist's addition to gross national product is a consequence of adherence to an old adage: "If you can't measure what you want, want what you can measure."

Economists have led us to believe that natural resources are required to support development. Such resources include arable land, supporting climate, potable water, minerals, rivers, harbors, and so on. It is quite apparent, however, that the presence of these resources in and of themselves does not guarantee growth, let alone development; nor does their absence prevent either growth or development. Development can take place even where most such resources are lacking. One would hardly include Japan, Switzerland, Holland, and Israel among those nations favorably endowed by nature. Most of the resources used by these nations are not given to them by nature, but have to be generated internally or acquired from others.

Economists seldom take account of the quality of human resources. They do not know how to quantify its value. Therefore, they tend to ignore it.

Particular professional groups deprecate approaches that are essentially nonquantitative. The response is typified by a comment such as: "If you cannot measure it, it does not matter," or "If there are no data on it, leave it out."

A more powerful form of this pressure appears in the idea that qualitative approaches are non-scientific and non-professional, so whoever attempts to break away from the use of quantified variables puts himself beyond the pale and will be ignored by the scientific community. [Meadows et al., 1972, p. 199]

Human resources are the ultimate source of development. Natural resources do not develop people; people develop resources.

We now turn to consideration of scarcity, maldistribution, and insecurity of economic resources as both obstructions to and opportunities for development.

SCARCITY OF ECONOMIC RESOURCES AS AN OBSTRUCTION TO DEVELOPMENT

Poverty is a condition of people in which there is a scarcity of those resources essential for their surviving as long as is biologically possible. These resources include food and water, health services and drugs, and, in most environments, clothing and shelter. Survival is obviously essential for development. Therefore, scarcity of the resources required for survival obstructs development. However, because development involves "thrival" as well as survival, it requires more than biologically essential resources.

Resources are either natural or man-made, but even natural resources require man to make them available and usable; for example, to move water from its source to where it is needed or to convert clay into ceramics. The acquisition and conversion of natural materials into resources usually requires other resources; for example, fuel is required to convert sand into glass and chemicals to purify water.

Scarcity of a needed resource is an obstruction to development only if there is no suitable substitute for it. Moreover, the amount of a resource that is needed depends on how efficiently it is used. Therefore, substitution of one resource for another and waste reduction are important ways of reducing or removing scarcity, but they too require resources that may be scarce. For example, the current search for economic, safe, and environment-conserving sources of energy as a substitute for oil requires a large number of highly trained technologists and large amounts of money, equipment, and materials. In general, these are only available to more affluent countries. Should these countries succeed in finding suitable substitutes for oil, the maldistribution of wealth among nations may be increased.

Affluent nations are also engaged in efforts to reduce their requirements for energy and scarce materials (e.g., development of close-to-closed system houses like the Arks at Cape Cod, Massachusetts, and Prince Edward Island, Canada; see McRobie, 1981, pp. 173–174, and Starrs, 1979, pp. 27–42). These efforts also require the use of technology and resources not generally available to less developed countries. Their success in the case of oil has produced at least a temporary oversupply of it at a cost to less developed oil-supplying nations.

The high cost of oil and lack of suitable alternative sources of energy have made more developed countries (MDCs) aware of how energy and resource wasteful many of their technologies are. This should make less developed countries (LDCs) more cautious in their importation of these technologies, but it has not always done so.

Waste of Material Resources

The more affluent a country is, the more it tends to waste material resources. Convenience takes on a disproportionate value, a "throw away" society emerges. Incentives for conservation and recycling of materials and maintenance of products tend to diminish. Superficial model changes of hard goods and changes of fashion in soft goods lead to disposal of products long before their usefulness has ended. This led Octavio Paz (1972) to observe:

In the West the young rebel against the mechanisms of the technological society, against its tantalizing world of objects that wear out and vanish almost as soon as we possess them. . . . [p. 9]

Less affluent countries tend to be more conserving, but out of necessity rather than choice. Where possible, they imitate the consumption patterns of more affluent nations. Even though they waste less, they can less afford to waste what they do.

Waste of limited nonrenewable resources drives their prices up. In addition, collection and disposal of waste is costly. The amount of solid waste generated per capita normally increases with income; therefore, costs of collection and disposal do as well. Since these are usually borne by government, the cost of government increases and this is inflationary.

Waste of Human Resources

As already noted, the reduction of scarcity requires resources that are often not available in LDCs. The only resource with which most such countries are oversupplied is unskilled labor. Therefore, for them the key to the elimination of economic scarcity must lie in the use of labor to create needed material resources.

It is precisely where human labor is most abundant that it is most wasted. In some LDCs people are employed to "operate" automatic elevators. Others are paid to push "up" and "down" buttons for those waiting for elevators. There are those whose only task is to prepare and serve coffee and tea to persons of rank or to carry their packages. There are lavatory attendants who dispense toilet paper and paper towels. Worse yet, governmental organizations are choked with excess people who make work by creating red tape that obstructs those who have real work to do. All this creates employment and distributes income, but it also reflects the bankruptcy of the minds of the employers. With all that needs to be done they cannot put people to work usefully. Their excuse often is that those so (mis)used are not capable of doing anything useful and that to increase their capability would require more resources than are available. What a vicious and obstructive circle this argument takes. It can and must be broken.

Scarcity of Income

Employment is the principal means by which societies distribute income as well as produce goods and services. In a free-enterprise system the private sector is expected to provide employment to many, if not most, who seek it. This expectation has seldom been fulfilled, even in MDCs.

Because high unemployment is politically destabilizing, governments feel obliged to preserve and create employment or otherwise provide income to the unemployed. There are a number of ways governments have done this, but these have generally either obstructed development or had little effect. We review some of them briefly here.

Welfare. Government support of those who are unable to work because of age, disabilities, or other good reasons, and are not otherwise supported, can be justified on purely humanitarian grounds. Support of those who are able to work but are involuntarily unemployed can also be justified in this way. Nevertheless, welfare consumes wealth; it does not produce it. It improves the distribution of wealth but reduces the amount available for distribution. It is also argued by some that suppport of those who can work reduces their will to work and contributes nothing to their development.

Few LDCs can afford much if any support of their unemployed. Those without jobs have to rely on family, friends, begging, or crime.

Protectionism. This strategy has as its main objective protection of domestic business and industry, hence jobs, from foreign competition. It takes on many different forms including: (1) voluntary agreements with foreign countries to limit their exports, usually with a threat of imposing tariffs or taking other defensive measures; (2) temporary or permanent measures to protect infant industries or ones that are declining; (3) imposition of import duties where domestic prices are higher than those of imports; (4) use of trigger-price mechanisms; (5) establishment of restrictive content rules on products that are allowed to be sold (e.g., a specified percentage of parts must be produced domestically); (6) requiring government agencies to purchase domestic goods or services that are available; and (7) use of tariff and nontariff barriers.

There are many disadvantages to protectionism. Among other things it (1) artificially maintains higher prices of domestic goods; (2) has a spillover effect on the rest of the economy; (3) encourages foreign manufacturers to upgrade their products in order to maintain their earnings; (4) can be circumvented by exporting from nonrestricted countries or by changing products; (5) attracts restrictions onto the protected country's exports; (6) discourages development of domestic industry and workforce; and (7) promotes diversification rather than productivity improvements in protected industries.

Thus, protectionism is a double-edged sword: it can preserve jobs, but it increases the cost and decreases the quality of products and services available in the protected country.

Subsidies. Governments sometimes provide industries with temporary or long-run assistance in order to preserve the jobs they make available. Some governments have attempted to keep ailing industries alive by subsidizing demand for their products or services.

Products are purchased and stockpiled by governments in order to maintain a level of production that facilitates survival of the producers. Where demand is sufficient but markets drive prices so low as to make production unprofitable, governments sometimes provide price supports. This involves guaranteeing producers a minimum price for their products by committing the government to purchase some or all of the product at a preannounced price. This is what CONASUPO, the National Basic Commodity Agency of Mexico, does. Such subsidies raise prices to consumers unless these too are reduced by subsidies. This is also done by CONASUPO through its chain of retail stores, CONASUPERS.

Such subsidies do little if anything for proper allocation of resources. They seldom add to the wealth to be distributed, and often reduce it.

Nationalization. The ultimate form of government subsidy is nationalization. It provides long-run security to enterprises and their employees. However, if one examines recent conversions to government ownership of enterprises in England, Mexico, France, and Portugal, to mention but a few, it is apparent that their efficiency and profitability have almost always decreased. Many of them consume more wealth than they produce. But, since they produce something, they are generally considered to be preferable to welfare. However, like welfare, they have frequently been accused of reducing the will to work. They ordinarily maintain an exceptionally high level of employment, breeding make-work and discouraging increases in productivity. For example, the government-owned railroads in Mexico were so overloaded with employees in 1976 that their payrolls exceeded their revenues. In the same year PEMEX, the government-owned petroleum monopoly in Mexico, employed seven people for every job it had. This not only required a huge government subsidy, but it resulted in a higher price for its products than was being charged by profitable oil companies in the United States. And PEMEX still lost money.

Another reason government-owned companies are so frequently wealth consuming is that their managers are often selected for political rather than professional reasons, for connections rather than competence. Such ownership enlarges the field in which patronage can be practiced.

The combination of incompetent managers, the absence of an incentive to be wealth producing, and the lack of competition virtually assure wealth-consuming operations. There is no government that has been able to manage a nationalized industry as efficiently as has the private sector.

Work stabilization. In an increasing number of both more and less developed countries it has been made very difficultt if not impossible for employers to lay off or change work rules. This type of work stabilization converts the cost of labor into a relatively fixed cost and makes it necessary for managements of for-profit organizations to try to maximize their returns on this cost as well as their investments and assets. Without the ability to use employees flexibly, work stabilization increases the cost of production and often decreases its quality. In times of declining demand, work stabilization can accelerate corporate bankruptcy and thus become self-defeating. The principal argument against job tenure is that it protects incompetent employees and discourages individual efforts to increase productivity.

Enlarging government bureaucracy. When unemployment is high and especially when it is increasing, governments come under pressure to do more than protect existing jobs; they are expected to create new ones, to reduce unemployment.

Perhaps the easiest and most tempting way for governments to create employment is to enlarge themselves. Regardless of their ideologies, governments of countries at all stages of development find enlarging themselves to be attractive. It enhances their power and importance. Unfortunately, however, many of those employed in such expansions become engaged in make-work that obstructs those who have real work to do. It also tends to reduce the quality of service provided by government and increases society's overhead, thus abetting inflation.

Until governments can productively use those already employed by them, increasing the numbers they employ is likely to reduce the unemployment problem by increasing the underemployment problem. Underemployment contributes to neither quality of life nor the production of wealth. It does contribute to the distribution of wealth, but in a way that provides no opportunity for either individual or societal development.

In summary, the measures taken by governments to decrease unemployment have failed to have a significant impact on it or to stimulate economic growth. All the measures have the ability to redistribute a portion of the nation's wealth, but they fail to increase the amount of wealth to be distributed. In some cases they reduce it.

MALDISTRIBUTION OF WEALTH AS AN OBSTRUCTION TO DEVELOPMENT

In general, wealth is distributed less equitably in LDCs than in those that are more developed. An equitable distribution does not mean an equal distribution, but it does imply the elimination or maximum reduction of involuntary poverty. Poverty deprives people of an equal opportunity for survival and development. Equality of opportunity neither presupposes nor implies absolute economic equality. The amount of wealth that an individual acquires should, we believe, depend in part on his or her own efforts and values. For example, different individuals place different values on work and leisure, hence should be free to sacrifice one for the other. Furthermore, the imposition of complete equality of wealth would remove any incentive to increase one's own productivity and that of others. Even communist China recognizes this and offers financial incentives to workers and factories (Yongkang, 1982, pp. 20ff).

The more inequitably wealth is distributed, the more those who have it try to keep things as they are.

There is great subtlety in the way the affluent manage to maintain the stability of a less developed society despite an inequitable distribution of wealth and opportunity within it. They do so by consciously engaging in a conspicuous conflict with government. Unconsciously and inconspicuously, however, they cooperate with government in obstructing any change that can improve the distribution of wealth and opportunity. For example, the affluent in the private sector argue that economic, social, and environmental problems are the government's business and that the private sector should not be expected to take any responsibility for solving them. The business of business, they argue, is business, not social welfare or protection of the environment. The only social obligation they accept is compliance with the law, and the less law, the better. The private sector does not want interference from government but it does want to be protected by it against foreign competition, provided with the physical and social infrastructure it requires, and to be "bailed out" when it gets into financial difficulties that it cannot handle by itself.

They refuse to pay their fair share of taxes on the grounds that the government is wasteful. The government, by maintaining its inefficiency and ineffectiveness, assures preservation of this conspicuous conflict and the inconspicuous cooperation that together preserve the status quo. Therefore, the indifference and selfishness of the affluent and government's inefficiency and ineffectiveness must be overcome before wealth can be equitably distributed and poverty can be eliminated.

Echeverria, when president of Mexico, said that inequitable distribution of wealth among nations was the principal obstruction to world development and peace. He also said that the affluent nations would have to invest heavily in the development of poor nations if peace and justice are to prevail. We heartily agree with this. But what Echeverria said is equally true within nations, including Mexico.

Average family income in the Federal District (which houses the national government of Mexico) is more than eight times that of rural families in the state of Oaxaca. Fifteen percent of the families in Mexico receive about 50 percent of the income. No wonder one political scientist characterized Mexico as a country colonized by its Federal District.

It is clear . . . that whatever economic successes occurred in Mexico . . . between 1950 and 1977, they did not reach the poorest sector. The bottom tenth of the population was receiving only 2.43 percent of the national income in 1950, but the pitiful amount actually declined during the period of so-called stabilizing development and shared development. For these people there was no development at all. [Velasco, 1983, p. 179]

Mexico is by no means exceptional. In Latin America as a whole: . . . per capita income rose by 26% in the period 1960–1967 a figure which is certainly satisfactory. Only 10% of this growth, however, benefited those who were below a certain poverty line in 1960, while 60% of it was absorbed by the richest 20% of the population. Thus, in absolute terms the 40% of the population who were poor in 1960 increased their per capita income by only 20 dollars between then and 1970. [Iglesias, 1979, p. 1]

John Friedmann (1979) provides similar data for Asia. Nevertheless, because average income may increase, a government can easily convince itself that all the governed are benefitting.

No one wants others to be poor or deprived of opportunity, not even the affluent; but they seldom are willing to sacrifice any of their wealth or opportunity to make more available to others. Unfortunately, up to this point, no one has found a way of improving the lot of the poor without reducing the lot of the affluent in the short run. In the long run, however, both can benefit. For example, William Finnie (1970) showed that in the United States it costs the white majority a considerable amount of money to maintain discrimination against the blacks, and that if this amount were invested in the development of the black, both they and the whites would eventually benefit. The short run, however, is much too long for those who already have what they want.

In LDCs the affluent are not alone in resisting change; many of the poor also resist it. Usually without education, they are not equipped to cope with change. They are resigned to a familiar life style, however unpleasant it may be. This life style often obstructs their development.

When maldistribution of wealth is supported by law or custom, it is very difficult for a government to change it. A radical change in the law (e.g., land reform) often has no significant effect. It does not even fool those supposed to benefit from it. If unenforced, it is simply ignored; if it departs too much from custom, it is resisted as unnatural, foreign, or immoral. Religious institutions, which should assist in this matter, are notoriously reluctant to become involved. They are often among the prominent recipients of privilege and they often depend on the support of the rich and powerful, while preaching justice for the deprived.

Systems of taxation in many LDCs (not to mention the more developed) exempt the very poor, since the cost of collecting taxes from them would exceed returns, and penalize wage earners. Workers of all sorts bear the brunt of taxation because taxes are deducted from their pay, leaving them no way to escape the tax collector. The affluent, on the other hand, have means of getting favorable legislation and administrative rulings. Government is virtually impotent to deal with the wealthy who evade taxation.

Although the political power of government can be used to improve the distribution of wealth, in most Third World countries it is also the principal means by which maldistribution of wealth is perpetuated and increased.

The Maldistribution of Land

The feudal system in some LDCs is being disassembled by the redistribution of land. However, the cynical point out, this is occurring only because modern industrialization and international finance provide the wealthy with easier access to additional wealth than does landholding. Nevertheless, most agricultural output still comes from large farms owned by a few rich landowners. Where land has been redistributed, agricultural production has often been reduced. The farms resulting from land reform are usually too small to operate productively or profitably. Therefore, most land reform has produced massive migration to urban areas that cannot adequately support the migrants.

A reduction or insufficient increase of food production usually requires importing more food. This in turn increases the cost of food and results in imbalances in foreign trade. Such imbalances often lead to devaluation of currencies which further raises the cost of imported food and the supplies and equipment required to produce it domestically. In sum, land reform that is intended to improve the distribution of wealth often decreases the amount of wealth to be distributed and makes its distribution worse. On the other hand, land reform tends to preserve rural culture and the spiritual and sentimental values that derive from working the land.

An alternative to land reform, the formation of large industrial farms capable of employing modern agricultural technology accelerates the migration from rural to urban areas where most migrants join the underclass and live under miserable conditions. This exacerbates the maldistribution of wealth even more than land reform and destroys rural culture in the process. Those who remain in the rural areas and work on large industrial farms seldom earn more than subsistence wages.

Therefore, the development of an alternative to conventional land reform and formation of large industrial farms in the hands of a few is essential for national development. Such an alternative usually requires the conversion of land currently unsuitable for farming into land that is suitable and the reorganization of agricultural production and distribution on a national scale. We consider such an alternative later in this chapter.

ECONOMIC INSECURITY AS AN OBSTRUCTION TO DEVELOPMENT

Economic insecurity derives from fear of appropriation, loss, or devaluation of one's wealth or the reduction of one's capacity to earn. Such insecurity can be experienced by rich and poor alike, but its impact on the rich usually has more obstructive consequences for development.

The way the affluent try to protect their wealth depends on what they fear most. Fear of the loss of wealth acquired from business often derives from fear of effective domestic or foreign competition. The profitability of business in LDCs is often protected by various types of government intervention that reduce or remove competition. For example, before the overthrow of the last Shah of Iran, his government allowed privately owned domestic companies to set the prices of their products at a specified percentage above their costs and taxed competitive imports so much that they could be sold only at higher prices. This not only removed all incentive for cost reduction, but it also encouraged increases in costs since profit per unit rose as costs did.

Public or private organizations whose survival is independent of their performance seldom perform well. Protection against competition among them is almost always disadvantageous to consumers, particularly those who are poor.

Collusive price setting is commonplace among "competitors" in less LDCs. This, together with prohibition of, or severe restrictions on, competitive imports (as in the case of the brewing industry in Mexico) also keeps prices high.

Those who fear appropriation of their wealth by government usually export much of it for safe keeping. Efforts by most LDCs to preclude such a flow of capital have not been effective. There are few if any measures governments can take that the wealthy cannot evade.

Fear of the devaluation of currency often leads the wealthy to convert their savings into a more stable foreign currency. This enables them to benefit from devaluation. Their ability to do this is often enhanced by access to inside information about impending devaluations.

Inflation, of course, is a major contributor to reduction of the value of money. Therefore, if wealth is kept in the form of domestic money, inflation reduces its value. For this reason the wealthy often convert their money into objects or investments that tend to increase in value more than inflation decreases the value of money. Such investments usually require amounts of money and a degree of financial sophistication that only the affluent have. This practice, of course, increases the maldistribution of wealth.

The poor suffer most from inflation. Nevertheless, it is the middle class who object most because their stake in the existing economic system erodes most rapidly. Therefore, this class displays the strongest signs of incipient revolution in the face of high inflation.

Inflation enables governments to engage in deficit spending, paying back loans with less valuable money later. As long as they can borrow at a rate that is less than that of inflation, and they often can, they pay back less in the future than they borrow today. This is certainly no deterrence to wasteful and inflationary public spending.

ECONOMIC SCARCITY AS OPPORTUNITY FOR DEVELOPMENT

Scarcity of a resource becomes an opportunity when it leads to more effective use of that and other resources than would otherwise occur. Effective use of available resources can yield surpluses that can be exchanged for scarce resources.

Poverty can exist even when needed resources are available but are not accessible for lack of income. Therefore, we first consider what can be done about lack of income, then lack of material resources, and, finally, lack of the human resources required to convert available resources into usable products and services.

Scarcity of Income

Since employment can be the most productive way of providing income, increasing employment is the most effective way of reducing poverty. We have already considered a number of ways by which governments try to preserve and create jobs and saw that they seldom succeed, have too small an impact when they do, and are generally wealth-consuming rather than wealth-producing. Measures that do not suffer from these deficiences are available. We review some of them briefly here.

The service sector. Government itself is usually the principal or a major provider of services to the public. As we have already pointed out, these services are often provided at a cost that restricts their availability and accessibility. To the extent that they could be provided at a lower cost, more could be made available even with the number currently employed in providing them. In addition, employment of more people can often be justified when services are provided efficiently and at low cost.

Since most public services are provided by public and private monopolies that are permeated by bureaucracy, the debureaucratization is essential if their efficiency is to be increased. Recall that a bureaucracy is an organization that values its own survival more than efficient and effective performance of the function for which it was created. Therefore, their orientation must be changed from survival to providing effective service to others. This reorientation can be encouraged and facilitated in a number of ways.

E. S. Savas's (1982) comparisons of public and private provision of services "indicate that private provision is superior to public provision of these services" (p. 111). Therefore, private enterprises should be encouraged to bid against public agencies for the right to provide public services where only one can serve at a time.

Where government cannot turn over a complete service function to the private sector, it should reduce its role as much as possible by turning over as much as it can.

Whether a service is provided by a public or private agency, the consumer has an advantage when he can select from among competing sources and pay for the service he receives. Publicly provided service for which there are no direct charges stimulate misuse and abuse. Those who need a service but are not able to pay for it should be subsidized, rather than the providers, for example, by issuing vouchers as Christopher Jenks (1970) has suggested for education, or stamps for food as is done in the United States.

Vouchers and direct payment for services can have their desired effects on quality and cost of service only if there are alternative competitive sources of service. Competition between public agencies can be brought about by making their income depend entirely on the amount and quality of service they provide. Additionally, if public agencies have to compete with private agencies, they are further motivated to perform efficiently and effectively.

Where subsidies of public-service agencies cannot be avoided, these subsidies should be made proportional to the amount of service they provide and, if possible, to its quality.

Such measures as are suggested here can help create a wealth-producing service sector. To the extent they do so, more employment in this sector can be justified.

Denationalization. Nationalized industries are often wealth-consuming rather than wealth-producing for reasons we have already considered: patronage, protectionism, bureaucracy, monopoly, and corruption. To the extent that such enterprises can be made wealth producing, they can generate capital for investment in other wealth- and employment-producing activities. This has been accomplished in some cases by governments sharing ownership with private parties who assume responsibility for managing the enterprise. The efficiency of such enterprises can be further increased by making compensation of all employees, including managers, depend on the profitability of the enterprise.

Intersectoral collaboration. It is assumed that all means of increasing the income of the poor require at least short-run reduction of resources available to government, industry, or labor. Rarely has industry or labor been willing to incur these losses. Each sector believes that its loss is another's gain. Unilateral sacrifices are frequently not made for the benefit of the public.

But through collaboration of government, labor, and industry it is possible for each of them, as well as the poor, to gain. For example, in a country that with full employment would produce more than it could consume, export of the surplus would be necessary. This would require the ability to sell abroad at an attractive price despite additional distribution and marketing costs and import duties. This disadvantage can be overcome if government is willing to forego or reduce taxes on profits made through export, labor is willing to produce goods for export with either increased productivity or decreased wages, and corporations are willing to accept reduced profits on export sales. Under these conditions each would benefit: Government would benefit from a larger tax base created by increased employment and the increased political stability it yields; labor would benefit from more stable employment and the increased number of jobs; and corporations would enjoy increased profits even though they were obtained at a lower rate than would be obtained domestically. In addition, there would be considerable incentive to produce efficiently and market effectively. Such collaboration would differ significantly from the common practice of protectionism in which governments tax imports heavily to reduce their competiveness with domestically produced products.

By establishing trading companies and retail outlets for domestic products in foreign countries, markets can be developed for the outputs of artisans as well as large and small businesses.

Small businesses and self-employment. Governments can encourage self-employment by the creation and expansion of small businesses. Even in MDCs like the United States this is where most new jobs are created. In this connection, John Naisbitt (1982) wrote:

The entrepreneurs who are creating new businesses are also creating jobs for the rest of us. During a seven-year period ending in 1976, we added 9 million new workers to the labor force—a lot of people! How many of these were jobs in the *Fortune* 1,000 largest industrial concern? Zero. But 6 million were jobs in small businesses, most of which had been in existence for four years or less. [p. 16]

Governments can provide tax incentives and financial support to new small businesses and encourage large businesses to create local suppliers of the materials, goods, and services they require. Governments can facilitate this by providing training and assistance in operating small businesses, and assisting them in the domestic distribution and sale of their products by arranging for this to be done cooperatively. In many countries there is a tradition of buying and selling farm products cooperatively, but this has seldom been extended to artisans and small businesses.

Government can further encourage self-employment by setting up workshops in which tools, equipment, and facilities are available for use in making things for oneself or for sale. Instruction in their use can be provided, and these shops can lend or rent their equipment for external income-producing or quality-of-life–improving activities.

New social calculus. We have argued repeatedly that productive employment is the most effective means of simultaneous production and distribution of wealth. However, the existing social calculus considers employment only as a cost, therefore, and not surprisingly, tries to minimize it.

To remedy the situation we need a new framework, one that will use employment on both sides of the equation, input as well as output. We also need a performance criterion that in addition to efficient production of wealth explicitly considers its proper distribution as a social service to be adequately rewarded. Consider the following simple exchange system.

A productive unit consumes the scarce resources of its environment; in return it produces outputs (goods or services) that partially fulfill the needs of that environment. The assumption is that the unit will survive as long as the total value of the outputs produced is greater than or equal to the total value of the inputs it consumes. The pricing system determined by "dollar votes" is supposed to be a reliable and sufficient criterion for determining production and distribution priorities. This supposition might be tenable if dollar votes were more equitably distributed and end prices were not manipulated. However, factors such as price control or government protection make the actual cost of services much higher than perceived. In other words, inputs are purchased from the environment at a lower price and outputs (measured by the classical accounting method) are made to look more valuable than they really are.

The following scheme is a simplified version of an attempt to measure the actual costs and benefits of each major economic activity as perceived on the national level. The model registers the needs of those members who lack the dollar vote to register their needs. It also explicitly values the distribution of wealth (salaries paid) as social service.

For simplicity, let us limit inputs to the two categories of raw materials and human resources and the outputs to the two corresponding categories of finished goods produced and employment opportunity created (this assumes that distribution of wealth is a social service). Assigning a "scarcity ratio" to each set of inputs obtained from the environment, and a "need ratio" to each set of outputs (goods/services) yielded to the environment, we can compute the relative contribution of each major economic activity using the following table:

Suppose a certain productive unit produces bread with a contribution ratio of 2, and a low rate of return on investment of 8 percent (because of the weak purchasing power of the consuming class). On the other hand, suppose another unit produces yo-yos with a contribution ratio of 1, but the rate of return on investment of 18 percent. Then our incentive system ought to be able to change the relative rates of return on investment in favor of bread. An integrated and coordinated application of well-known tools such as differentiated loan structure,

Table 9.1
Calculating the Contribution Ratio for Each Economic Activity

INPUT CONSUMED	OUTPUT PRODUCED
RAW MATERIAL	GOODS PRODUCED

A: Quantity(A) x Price(A) x
   Scarcity Ratio(A) = VC(A)
	D: Quantity(D) x Price(D) x
	   Need Ratio(D) = VP(D)

B: Quantity(B) x Price(B) x
   Scarcity Ratio(B) = VC(B)
	E: Quantity(E) x Price(E) x
	   Need Ratio(E) = VP(E)

C: Quantity(C) x Price(C) x
   Scarcity Ratio(C) = VC(C)
	F: Quantity(F) x Price(F) x
	   Need Ratio(F) = VP(F)

HUMAN RESOURCES UTILIZED	EMPLOYMENT OPPORTUNITY CREATED

No.of Employees (I) x Training Cost/
   Productive yrs. x Scarcity Ratio=VC(I)
	No.of employees (I) x Salary paid
	   x Need ratio for employment=VP(I)

No.of Employees (II) x Training Cost/
   Productive yrs. x Scarcity Coeff.=VC(II)
	No. of employees (II) x Salary paid
	   x Need ratio for employment=VP(II)

No. of Employees (III) x Training Cost/
   Productive yrs. x Scarcity Ratio=VC(III)
	No. of employees (III) x Salary paid
	   x Need ratio for employment VP(III)

Total value consumed: TVC	Total value produced: TVP

TOTAL VALUE PRODUCED/TOTAL VALUE CONSUMED = Contribution Ratio

Category (I)	=	Highly Specialized
Category (II)	=	Skilled
Category (III)	=	Unskilled

differentiated interest rate structure, and differentiated tax structure will overcome the problem. Depending on the contribution ratios (computed from the previous table), a different loan/equity ratio, a different interest rate, and a different tax rate can be assigned to each economic activity. This, as illustrated in Table 9.2, will increase the rate of return on investment for bread to 18 percent and decrease that of yo-yos to 10 percent.

The advantage of such a scheme is that it will minimize the bureaucratic dangers associated with centralized planning while enhancing the strength of market economy by promoting a more equitable allocation and distribution system.

MALDISTRIBUTION OF WEALTH AS AN OPPORTUNITY FOR DEVELOPMENT

Taxation is the principal means by which governments acquire wealth for distribution. However, tax collection is often difficult and costly in LDCs. There is a need for a way of collecting taxes that is cost efficient and effective, does not demotivate individual productive and entrepreneurial efforts, does not motivate exportation of capital and capital-generating enterprises, and does not create insurmountable political opposition.

Taxes on income are difficult to collect and easy to evade in LDCs because their governments seldom have or can obtain the information required to enforce tax laws. As a result, income in the form of wages is normally taxed where it is paid, and consumption taxes are imposed on products considered to be luxuries, harmful, sinful, or that are imported. Such consumption taxes tend to be regressive, affecting those with lower income relatively more than those with high incomes. Therefore, they exacerbate the maldistribution of wealth.

Nevertheless, consumption-based taxes, which were proposed as early as 1651 by Thomas Hobbes in *Leviathan*, have an advantage over income-based taxes. John E. Chapoton, assistant treasury secretary for tax policy in the United States, said "A tax system based on consumed income, rather than on all income earned, would eliminate the bias against saving in the current tax system" (quoted in *Business Week*, June 13, 1983, p. 80). In addition, such taxes can be easier to collect and would not demotivate productive and entrepreneurial efforts. Therefore, the development of a nonregressive consumption-based tax system that does not generate insurmountable political opposition is a challenge and opportunity in LDCs.

Ideally, a consumption tax could be collected somewhat as follows.

1. All income would be deposited in the recipient's bank account. Everyone would be required to have a bank account. All bank accounts would be identified by the bank's and the recipient's identification numbers. Then, if a person had multiple bank accounts, the government could collate the records of each.

2. Money left in the bank, not withdrawn for use, would not be taxed, nor would the bank pay interest on it. This exemption from taxes would be worth more than interest payments currently are.

3. Taxes would be paid only on the money withdrawn from banks. Each withdrawal could be taxed at a rate proportional to the person's income. Adjustments could be made annually. The tax would be graduated with consumption and provide for exemptions, for example, for necessary work-related expenditures.

4. Bank loans would be interest-free, but the borrower would have to pay taxes on their use.

5. Bank income would derive from charges for each transaction.

6. Payments for goods and services would be made by either electronic funds transfer, checks, or nontransferable currency, like food stamps (in the United States), coupons, or vouchers obtained from banks that could only be deposited at a bank.

Since currency would not be transferable in this system, hoarding would serve no useful purpose.

Implementation of such a consumption-based tax system would be very dif-

Table 9.2
Changing Relative Rate of Return on Investment Based on Contribution Ratio

Product	Bread	Candy	Yoyo
Contribution Ratio	2	1.5	1
Current return on investment	8%	12%	18%
Initial equity	$1,000,000	$1,000,000	$1,000,000
Equity/loan ratio	1/4	1/2	1/1
Total loan	$4,000,000	$2,000,000	$1,000,000
Interest rate	5%	9%	16%
Cost of loan	$200,000	$180,000	$160,000
Total capital employed	$5,000,000	3,000,000	2,000,000
Income	$400,000	360,000	360,000
(Income-cost of loan)	$200,000	180,000	280,000
Tax coefficient	10%	25%	50%
Net Income after Taxes	$180,000	135,00	100,000
Final return on investment	18%	13.5%	10%

ficult in most LDCs. However, if such a system is adopted as an ultimate objective, the transition to it can be accomplished gradually, thereby minimizing disruptions.

Land

Money, of course, is only one form of wealth. Land is another. As we pointed out earlier, efforts to redistribute land more equitably by land reform often reduces the size of farms, making them uneconomical to operate, thus reducing agricultural output. Some countries have avoided this problem by keeping farms large and having them jointly owned and operated. The kibbutzim in Israel are an outstanding example.

In some cases individual families are additionally given small plots for their own use. Portions of the profits generated by the large cooperative farms are invested in their further development, in some cases into rural industrialization. This creates new jobs that absorb at least part of rural population growth.

Cooperative farming requires participative planning. Since rural development relies heavily on land use and since people living off the land are accustomed to running their own lives, participation is not something to which they take easily. Therefore, government has a critical role to play in encouraging and facilitating such cooperative efforts.

ECONOMIC INSECURITY AS AN OPPORTUNITY FOR DEVELOPMENT

Economic insecurity derives from fear of such things as inflation, devaluation of currency, insolvency of banks, appropriation of property by government without fair compensation, theft, and damage to or destruction of possessions by man or nature. Clearly, then, such fears are minimized when the economy is developing and the government is stable, provides good protection of property, and is not subject to external aggression.

Economic insecurity is a symptom of lack of economic progress. It is a sign of the need for economic development. It provides an opportunity for government to organize a crusade for economic development because people who are economically insecure are often willing to make sacrifices to attain security. Therefore, if a participatively prepared plan for economic development, one that people can believe in, is developed, they will invest their time and effort in its implementation.

An outstanding example of this can be found in the recent history of Jamestown, New York (Eldred, 1978, and Jamestown Labor-Management Committee, 1979), a small city that was deteriorating as industry and its young people deserted it for more attractive places. A collaboration, initiated by its mayor, between labor, management, and government led to a remarkable renaissance of the community. A similar effort is taking place in Sudbury, a small city in Northern Ontario (Starrs, 1979).

No plan is as believable as one developed participatively by the governed, not government. No government is as likely to be trusted as one that commits itself to the support of plans that are produced by the governed.

CONCLUSION

The efficient pursuit of short-run objectives, let alone ideals such as omni-competence, requires the use of resources—natural, man-made, and man himself. Economic development consists of increasing one's ability and desire to provide oneself and others with such resources. Society's responsibility for encouraging and facilitating this increase is vested in its economic institutions. Responsibility for providing the information, knowledge, and understanding required to operate these institutions effectively is vested in economists. The ability of economists to perform this function well has recently come into serious question, but they continue to be used extensively by those who manage society. The belief that economics has much less to offer by way of guidance for economic development than it claims forces one to turn to experience, informed judgment, and common sense for guidance until an economics worthy of being called a science is created.

Development is obstructed by poverty: a scarcity of economic resources that deprives people of those opportunities for survival that are biologically possible and for "thrival" that are psychologically and sociologically possible. Poverty may derive from a shortage of natural resources, an inability to convert what nature provides into resources, or the wasteful use of these resources, including human resources. Work is the activity by which resources are produced and distributed through society. Employment is an exchange of work for resources produced by others. It is the principal and only known productive way by which society can distribute wealth. Wealth is the difference between what is produced and what is consumed, hence is a potential for consumption. For these reasons full employment is a much sought economic ideal. It is best approximated when the opportunities for work are equitably distributed, when people are educated to create and engage in productive work, and when the sectors of an economy (government, management, and labor) collaborate in the conversion of economic conflict into economic competition and cooperation.

Employment must be productive for there to be resources to exchange for work. For work to be productive, both natural and human resources must be used efficiently and effectively. Even affluent societies have failed to do so as well as is known to be possible. Therefore, less affluent societies have an opportunity to avoid the inefficient and ineffective utilization of resources by more advanced countries and thus "catch up"—something that cannot be done by emulating them.

Even where enough resources are available for all, many may live in poverty because wealth is inequitably distributed. Some may have much more than they need or can even use, while others are deprived. This inequity exists both between and within nations. Other than appropriation and redistribution by government, taxation is the principal means by which society can redistribute wealth. However, the less developed a society, the more difficult it usually is for its government to collect the taxes due it, particularly from the most affluent. Tax laws based on those of advanced countries do not work well in less developed countries because they require information about individual and organizational income and expenditures that is not generally available. Therefore, the less advanced are confronted with a challenge to design tax laws they can enforce or systems of enforcing the laws they have and an opportunity to develop a system of taxation that does not arouse obstructive political opposition and produces an equitable distribution of wealth. We believe that such a system is more likely to be based on taxing consumption than income.

Economic insecurity derives from fear of loss of either those resources that people have or the ability to obtain those they need and want. This fear may be directed at nature, society, or man. It stimulates hoarding of wealth in ways that do not contribute to economic development, for example, exportation of capital. The insecure rich bring pressure on government to protect their wealth and increase their ability to obtain more at a cost to the less affluent. The less affluent who are insecure often seek radical changes of government. The political instability thus produced increases the sense of insecurity throughout society.

The unsettled and unsettling state of society produced by economic insecurity presents an opportunity because it stimulates the desire for change, and change is necessary for development. Insecure people are more willing to sacrifice some of what they have for increased security. This makes it possible for governments to take major economic development initiatives. But these initiatives will be supported only if they are believed in and government is trusted. The necessary assurances are best obtained when the initiatives taken are designed and planned participatively by all those who can be affected and care to participate and when government commits itself to support the plans they produce.

10

Ethics and Morality

Social ethics and morality are concerned with promoting cooperation and reducing conflict. Lasting reform normally begins with demands based on moral
arguments that are then converted into political programs and finally incorporated
into law or religion. Sometimes, in the rush to effect reform, laws are passed
before moral conversion has taken place, as has often been the case in the struggle
for human rights, particularly those of women and racial minorities. Laws that
do not have widespread moral support are at best slow to take effect and at worst
are ignored or perverted. Only a morality-based human-rights movement can
support political action that, if successful, culminates in legal reform. Thus,
morality can be a prime mover of development, but it can also be a major
obstruction to it.

Our concern here is with social morality, which we take to be the sum of the
means that a society adopts for the continuous reduction of conflict among
individuals and groups. For our purposes, law is taken as a form of morality.
Thus, to the extent that interpersonal or group behavior facilitates development,
as we use the term here, it is moral; and to the extent that it obstructs development,
it is immoral. If it has no effect on development, it is nonmoral. Hence, for us
the essence of morality is cooperation, that of immorality is conflict. This position
is consistent with our previously expressed assumption that the continuous pursuit
of omnicompetence requires the continuous reduction of conflict.

Cooperation then facilitates development; conflict obstructs it. Does this mean
that competition, widely viewed as a form of conflict, is necessarily obstructive?
Hardly. Still, it is necessary to examine the notion of competition in order to
see in what way it may further development.

We start with the conventional idea of competition as constrained conflict.
Constrained conflict sums up the difference between a prize fight and a street
brawl. Constraints are imposed on the first in the form of rules of permissible
behavior. A brawl, on the other hand, is, as we say, "unruly." Without rules

there is no competition. However, not all conflict according to rules is necessarily competition. War is an obvious example. We must go further.

Rules designed to govern human behavior serve many functions. The rules of war are very different from the rules of the road. War is total conflict; traffic rules are intended to abolish conflict. The rules of competition are still different, and their purpose discloses its essential nature. Competition assumes that the ultimate purpose of competitive effort is a socially approved goal. Fairness is an essential ingredient in this form of social effort. Hence, unfair competition is condemned, whereas it is said that all is fair in love and war.

In competition, conflict is made to serve as an efficient means to one or more ends that the competitors and others share. A useful example is a competitive game. In such games the recreation of the players or the entertainment of an audience are the shared objectives. However, if winning the game becomes more important than the common objective it serves, the rules may be broken, the social purpose of the contest forgotten, and the game degenerate into pure conflict. The social purpose of the game is obstructed. Development becomes regression.

In economic competition, competitors are in short-term conflict (perhaps we should now say "opposition") with respect to such things as income, earnings, and market share. Such opposition is supposed to serve consumers' interests by keeping prices low and quality high. It is also supposed to serve the long-term interests of the competitors by producing a stronger economy and a larger market within which they can operate. Such competition is moral because within it cooperation dominates conflict and endows opposition with social purpose. It can, however, easily convert to conflict when rules are broken and social purpose is subverted, as occurs, for example, when cheating is resorted to. Cheating, as we will see, derives from moral insecurity.

Cooperation and freedom (the absence of conflict) are the "resources" with which social moralists are concerned. Development is obstructed when they are scarce, maldistributed, or insecure. We turn now to a consideration of each of these states and to the opportunities as well as the obstructions they present.

MORAL SCARCITY

The absence of human rights that guarantee freedom is a scarcity of morality. Freedom is the right to do anything that does not preclude others or oneself from doing whatever they want except when they want to deprive others of their freedom. Thus, the legislation of human rights is intended to reduce or eliminate conflict, particularly between the state and the individual, but it does not make cooperation obligatory.

Among the rights traditionally dealt with are freedom of conscience, religion, speech, thought, opinion, and petition; fair procedures for those accused of a crime; the rights of private property, protection against public appropriation or use without just compensation, from ex post facto laws and arbitrary arrest;

freedom to assemble and associate peacefully; and the right to equality before the law.

This list has been and is being extended to include such things as the right to work; to choose one's work freely; to an adequate standard of living including health care and shelter; to education, knowledge, and inquiry; to a satisfying quality of life and life's environment; and to equal opportunity regardless of race, color, sex, language, religion, political or other opinion, national or social origin, property, birth, or other status. In addition, increasing attention is being given to the rights of minorities.

Recall that the normal sequence of steps to incorporation of moral principles into a culture is, first, moral debate, then political programs, and finally legislation. This sequence involves the conversion of functional (moral) demands into structural prescriptions (laws). Human rights are currently an international (as well as a national) issue being debated with more political than moral slogans. Therefore, they are being met by reluctant nations with counterslogans of opposite political intent; for example, "freedom from external pressure or constraints," "freedom to work out our own destiny without outside interference," and "we are not yet ready for human rights." It should be borne in mind that freedom does not include freedom to deprive others of their freedom.

Most of the more developed nations reached their current level of development by war, colonial exploitation, exploitation of the poor, and destruction of the natural environment. Such activities were once widely approved and thought to be essential for development, but the climate of opinion has changed significantly. It is now generally believed that countries with poor human-rights practices cannot develop easily or rapidly. This is a considerable turnabout.

The attempt to incorporate functional (moral) demands into the structure of the law, as in the Declaration of Human Rights, is an expression of the desire to guarantee freedom. The implication of this for development planners is that, while freedom cannot be planned, rights can be if collaboration with political and legal planners can be obtained. Therefore, this is one area in which the natural propensity of development planners for structural change might perhaps be indulged.

Freedom and Opportunity

A development process that permeates a society requires freedom of access to opportunity; opportunity to inquire, question, learn, and know; opportunity to pursue ideals and to derive satisfaction from their pursuit; and opportunity to work with others in planning for the future, in enterprises and in civic endeavors.

A changing and developing society needs to increase its stock of knowledge to cope with the changes that are occurring. It needs to diffuse knowledge so that its members develop their abilities to participate and increase their capacity to innovate and pursue their goals. As they learn from study or experience, individuals and groups also require freedom to participate in formal and informal networks of communication through which knowledge rather than rumor is transmitted.

If there are no safeguards to protect intellectual exploration, the capacity of a society to learn, even from its own experience, may be destroyed. If scholars live in a climate of fear and suspicion, subject to unknown informers (who are often personally biased) and to arbitrary penalities for statements or opinions thought to be critical of government or its dogmas, their productivity is greatly decreased.

Advance in knowledge is not only made by scholars working alone, but by exchange of information, knowledge, understanding, and methodology with other scholars through meetings and publications of professional associations and even more effectively through informal networks of individuals with common interests. If these contacts and exchanges are hindered by actual or feared government repression, learning is severely curtailed.

In most autocratic countries the social and behavioral sciences have not developed precisely because scholars dare not produce and publish results seen to be contrary to government dogma by the government. As a result, scholarship in those areas stagnates.

Freedom and Government

Human rights seem to suffer most where a current government is invested with a symbolic identity with its nation. Where this is the case, continuity of the current administration and preservation of its power becomes the primary social objective. This condition breeds political "overkill," excesses in individual repression. On a contrary note, in the United States, Richard Nixon could be removed from the presidency without a major upheaval because there the president is not confused symbolically with the nation. He is a leader, administrator, and hired hand. The people are the state.

Freedom from Religion

Up to this point we have considered human rights largely in the context of protection of individual freedom from interference by the state. But the state is not the only institution against which individuals need protection; organized religion is another. Suppression of human rights by religious organizations is commonplace even in communities that consider themselves to be purely secular. The situation is even worse in communities in which religious organizations are so strong that they co-opt some, if not all of, the right to govern, as in contemporary Iran. Although most bills and declarations of human rights guarantee freedom *of* religion, few, if any, protect freedom *from* it.

Many organized religions dictate what their followers can and cannot do in personal areas that have no significant effect on others; for example, what they can eat or wear, who they can marry, and so on. There is no harm in such injunctions if they are accepted voluntarily, but they are frequently imposed (or efforts are made to impose them) on nonbelievers as well as believers. Examples can be found in efforts of the Catholic church to have states legislate against abortion, divorce, and cremation.

In Iran, the organized religion has gone even further. It has imbedded its version of the holy book, the Koran, into the nation's constitution, which is actually only designed to "propagate the faith." Much of what has been done is immoral in the sense in which we use the term here because it diminishes all forms of individual freedom and reverses the trend in Iran toward equality of the sexes and freedom of inquiry.

Throughout history organized religions have opposed inquiries into the validity of their dogmas and suppressed findings that contradicted them, even where natural phenomena were involved—for example, support by the Catholic church of the geocentric theory against Galileo. Organized religions have punished infractions of proscriptions of this type with death, imprisonment, and ostracism where they have had the power to do so.

Organized religions pretend to an infallibility that precludes the need to consider alternatives. They imbue their followers with a sense of self-righteousness that removes ethics and morality from the domain of choice. This, combined with the missionary zeal many of them propagate, provides a rationale for imposing their will on others and depriving them of freedom. It is worth keeping in mind the fact that more people have been killed and oppressed in the name of God than in the name of the devil.

Few social institutions are as dedicated to self-preservation as organized religions. Because devotion and adherence to them tend to diminish with learning and development, they try to suppress these but, to avoid criticism, in very subtle ways. For example, by preaching the greater importance of life after death they breed tolerance of and resignation to exploitation in life before death. They collaborate with oppressive governments that protect them. They oppose oppression only if they are its target.

Where organized religion has had its own freedom suppressed it has become an active proponent of civil rights; for example, in Iran under the Shah or in Poland. But such involvement has seldom been motivated by moral principles; it has been stimulated more by institutional self-preservation than preservation of its individual members' freedom.

Organized religions are among the most divisive forces in the world today. They divide humanity into "we" and "they" and minimally provide a rationale for discriminating against "them," maximally for engaging "them" in a holy war.

The most effective means of protecting individual freedom against religious suppression is by complete separation of church and state. This is easier said than done; for example, in the United States where such separation is supposed to be complete, religious groups continuously try to impose their will on others through legislation.

Separation of church from state is not enough. The church must be precluded from political activity. This is possible as Mexico has so effectively demonstrated despite the fact that it is a very religious country dominated religiously by the Catholic church. The Mexican clergy and nuns are not permitted to wear religious habits in public nor to deliver sermons on political issues. Moreover, the church is not allowed to own any property. As a result, the church has virtually no political power.

MALDISTRIBUTION OF MORALITY

Wherever individual freedom and opportunity are not equally available to all members of a society, there is a maldistribution of morality that obstructs development. Maldistributions of morality are based on discrimination which, in turn, is based on prejudice. Prejudice derives from a wide variety of distinctions; for example, color, sex, language, religion, political or other opinion, national or social origin, property, occupation, and physical deformities. Where discrimination is based on hereditary characteristics or ones determined by conditions of birth, the result is a caste system, the best known example of which is Hindu society. Caste is a structural conversion of functional discrimination, slavery being its most intense form.

The function of caste is to legitimate exploitation of those of lower class by those of higher. This is a form of conflict; it deprives the exploited of freedom and opportunity, hence obstructs their development. It similarly handicaps the exploiters but this is usually not as apparent, particularly to the exploiters. They almost always see an end to their exploitation as an end to their freedom and opportunity—this despite the fact that historically it has been uprisings of the exploited that have most frequently disenfranchised the exploiters.

Discrimination is present to some degree in almost every society, but it varies in character and intensity. In South Africa it is intense against the blacks, in Saudi Arabia against women, in the United States against communists, in the Soviet Union against capitalists, in Northern Ireland against Catholics, and in Eire against Protestants. In some cases those discriminated against are in the majority (e.g., South Africa); in others, the minority.

Where discrimination is based on hereditary or visible physical characteristics such as race or sex, it is usually rationalized by claims that those discriminated against are intrinsically inferior as, for example, in intelligence or some other important mental capacity. Pseudo-science is often used to support such claims, which develop an immunity to any objective evidence to the contrary.

For example, in one large American corporation some of the senior executives were concerned over the fact that although almost half of its employees were black and less than one percent of the managers were. They feared government charges of unequal opportunities for promotion. Therefore, they wanted to initiate an educational and training program for blacks that, they said, would "increase their upward mobility." The university-based research group that was retained to design the program began with a study of the educational differences between black and white employees in the same types of jobs. This group found that blacks averaged more education of equal quality than the whites in the same types of jobs. Therefore, they concluded that the problem was not the educational deficiencies of the blacks, but the prejudice of their white supervisors. An educational program for their supervisors was proposed. Both the results and the recommendation were summarily rejected by corporate management. It went ahead with the program it wanted, using company resources. Several years later the black employees of the company brought suit against it for discriminatory employment practices, won in court, and were awarded a very large financial return for the damages they had suffered.

Where discrimination is based on such acquired characteristics as political opinion, it is usually defended by the argument that those discriminated against are a potential danger to the status quo. Such discrimination forces its victims either to conceal their characteristics and "go underground," or to organize into overt opposition, often violent, to the powers that be.

In its extreme form, discrimination produces civil and uncivil wars such as are current in Northern Ireland, many parts of Africa, the Middle East, and Latin America. The cost of such confrontations includes retarded development and destruction of human and natural resources. It should be apparent that discrimination is a social luxury that only an affluent society can afford, and it can do so only in the short run. Discrimination is, in effect, a type of conspicuous consumption of human resources—a waste of the most valuable resource available to man: mankind itself. But perhaps a greater importance is its revelation of man's cruelty to man, and the sadistic satisfaction some get out of the suffering they impose on others. Freedom and opportunity are renewable resources of infinite supply; their availability to some does not require that others be deprived of them. To believe otherwise is, perhaps, the most self-destructive doctrine that mankind can entertain.

MORAL INSECURITY

Recall that competition can be moral when the cooperation within it dominates the conflict also within it, and endows it with a social purpose. As we observed, however, competition easily degenerates into conflict when rules are broken and its social purpose is subverted. This occurs when cheating takes place. Cheating derives from a fear of the loss of opportunity—"If I don't get what I want now, I may never get another chance to do so."

Cheating and Corruption

Cheating is so pervasive in economic intercourse that the famous cynic Ambrose Bierce was led to formulate a single categorical imperative for business morality: "Never steal; cheat."

The tolerance and acceptance of cheating as a social norm is of course a serious obstruction to development. It seems to grow rather than diminish with technological and economic development (as that term is customarily used). It is easy, therefore, to be cynical about cheating. Its practice is widespread and its inevitable concomitant, lying, is apparently universal. But it is well to remember that between evenly matched opponents, lying and cheating pass into a relatively innocuous game in which neither party can seriously harm the other. Hence, these practices affect mainly the weak, the poor, the disadvantaged, the innocent, and the upright. That is to say, lying and cheating constitute a serious obstruction not only to economic development, but to the whole moral fabric of society. It is well to remember that although the cynical will say that cheating is so deeply a part of human nature—imbedded in its genetic structure, so to speak—that all attempts to control it must necessarily be in vain. This can be only part of the story. Biological investigators find apparently altruistic behavior in even the lowest forms of living creatures. It seems fairly obvious that if its altruistic component had not prevailed over contrary forms of competitive self-seeking behavior, the human race would surely not have survived in the universal struggle for existence.

Ordinary economic cheating passes easily into one of its more serious forms of social degeneracy—corruption. The unavowed and indeed scarely recognized outcome of corruption is the total subversion of law and order—anarchy. For while corruption may begin among private individuals and organizations, it quickly infiltrates government. When it becomes necessary to bribe public officials to obtain what they are under a legal obligation to provide freely, or what they may not be legally obligated to provide but will do so at a price, corruption stands forth in all its ugly unfairness for all to see. Such corruption makes public resources and services accessible only to the affluent who can afford to pay for them, thus further exacerbating the maldistribution of wealth.

Trust and Confidence

The expectation by one party that another will cheat tends to encourage the other to do so. Mistrust (for example, of students by professors) encourages behavior that justifies it. It is, in effect, a self-fulfilling prophesy. Cooperation cannot flourish in an atmosphere of mistrust and, therefore, neither can development.

Mistrust generally derives from the failure to fulfill explicit or implicit promises. Because of a long history of broken promises, the Mexican peasant, for example, is said to mistrust three things, which, in increasing order, are the federal government, the local political boss (cacique), and his neighbor. Even where such mistrust is unjustified, it obviously is a significant obstruction to development. Therefore, the replacement of mistrust by trust is essential to development. The best way to create trust is by helping others without being asked to do so or by making oneself available to help others in doing whatever they want to do.

Trust is a fragile thing, easy to destroy and hard to build, especially where suspicion and rumor run rampant. Rumor is a black market in beliefs about institutions, people, and events which must exist where open communication is not available to provide the information upon which people determine their activities and relationships. Rumor seizes real or fancied instances of repression, unfairness, or cruelty—or avarice or corruption in officials—and inflates them into images of institutionalized attitudes and practices, particularly on the part of the powerful, whether or not such attitudes and practices exist in reality. If the practices are so widespread as to be institutionalized, rumor exaggerates them and reinforces the perception of them as evil and dangerous. For example, estimates or reports of the numbers being executed in Iran vary greatly. But if people *believe* that a very large number of their countrymen are being executed without fair trial and without due process of impartial law, the climate of confidence in government necessary for effective public participation in national development is greatly damaged. One thinks, "Why bother to try! It's safer not to; so I'll take care of myself." The resonance of many fears may produce a kind of societal paranoia with respect to those holding political or economic power.

A predisposition toward mistrust of others and of government may be present when it is commonplace for politicians to intentionally communicate to the public in such a manner that the meanings of words or statements are ambiguous, thus concealing the intentions or the knowledge of the speaker. The informal communication of misinformation in conversation or rumor may be reinforced by the formal communication of misinformation or partial truths in official propaganda. These conditions may not only alienate a population, but may also breed mistrust and misunderstanding among the elite in government itself. Those responsible for the development of policy and the administration of programs are deprived of the information they require about programs and activities in sectors other than their own, and will not receive an upward flow of facts and their interpretation from the people and opinion groups in the nonelite population and in regions outside the capital. Decentralized channels of communication from regional representatives of government may not transmit information or opinion that may be thought to be adverse to government or even fancied to be "subversive." Thus, fear produces poor communication and poor communication inhibits innovation and action both in and out of government and discourages personal and social development.

All governments employ surveillance and police power. In moderation and within a legal system this is necessary to assure impartial protection of individual rights. Sometimes, however, governments come to believe that to preserve their power they must increase their use of force, or other more subtle forms of compulsion, to prevent the mobilization of antigovernment forces and actions. Every government must preserve order; but it should use means that are not perceived by the governed as unduly repressive, arbitrary, unfair, cruel, or enforced without due process of law and with a widespread network of secret informers. Means so perceived inhibit communication, immobilize decision and action, and retard or prevent development in both the governmental and non-governmental parts of the society.

THE MORALITY OF PLANNING

There are many who raise moral objections to planning in general and to development planning in particular because they are carried out in a paternalistic mode. Planners and politicians usually decide what is good for others and how to bring it about. Doing so raises questions about the morality of planning. Those engaged in it naturally assume that their activity is moral; that they are doing good to and for others. Nevertheless, among the others there is often a strong and widespread opinion that all government planning is immoral because it reduces the freedom of individuals to choose for themselves, and it increases the power of government to do so for them. It is just such an argument that has prevented the government of the United States from engaging in national economic planning.

There are many who believe that individual and collective decisions should be made instinctively and intuitively because instinct and intuition operate better than reason. Moreover, they argue, planning should be a matter for individuals, not societies. They contend that social planning that does not arise spontaneously and ''naturally'' reduces individual freedom. Some go further and argue that planning cannot bring about development; only revolutions or counterrevolutions can do so. Others think planning can be safely entrusted only to the authorized guardians of people's salvation, the authorities of the church. In sum, many are hostile to planning as a secular professional activity, and, while there is some professional rivalry involved in this condemnation, its main ingredient is moral sentiment. It thus constitutes a formidable obstruction to planning, if not development.

The argument that it is immoral for professional planners to prepare plans that are imposed on others is one that we accept. In Part II we reconceptualized planning as a participative activity rather than one restricted to an elite. The role of the professional planner is substantially changed in the concept of planning that we developed.

The argument that the fate and future of man should be left in the hands of God or those who speak for Him with authority is another matter.

ORGANIZED RELIGION AND PLANNING

The opposition of organized religions to secular planning is often direct and powerful. Indeed, it can be so powerful that planners are forced to treat it as the primary obstacle to the exercise of their trade. Worse still, in some communities in which religious organizations are very strong, they may oppose not only planning but any change, hence development itself. Therefore, how can modern secular development planners meet the constraints of determined religious obstruction?

Where the concern of established churches in public affairs is not predominantly political, as in many more developed countries, the secular planner may well obtain their cooperation, especially where the churches themselves participate in the planning process.

The situation in many less developed countries is quite different. Although their religious organizations usually see themselves as progressive, peaceful, subservient, and universal, they are in fact conservative, war-like, autonomous, and exclusionary. Therefore, the secular planner, especially in communities in which the churches compete with secular government, must take the churches as political organizations and use the learning gained from dealing with political obstructions in other contexts.

Contrary to popular belief, large religious establishments are seldom monolithic. Fundamental doctrinal agreement conceals disagreements that are also fundamental in character. Where this condition pertains it is good to remember that from the late Middle Ages on, the history of Western religion is largely one of division and sectarianism, as in Protestantism, and of unavowed but massive political accommodation both within and outside of the church, as in the case of Roman Catholicism. This means that secular development does in fact proceed inexorably. To put this matter more cautiously: Secular life changes and the established churches split or sooner or later accommodate these changes.

Religious reform is currently the order of the day, even in Moslem countries. Obstruction may thus turn into opportunity. The main danger to secular development planning from this situation is involvement in it. For example, the current strong evangelical movement wants dedicated partisans, and the ecumenical movement wants consolidation of religious power. In either case the planner may find it difficult to maintain a secular stance. This becomes critical in the case of participative planning because the churches are disposed to participate only on their own terms. Nevertheless, where possible, it is better to do battle with the churches within the planning process, despite their inherent conservatism, than to have them as enemies on the outside.

The opportunity that is provided by opposition from churches to development planning is obtained by raising for social consideration the separation of church and state. Whatever the outcome of the debate that follows, it is likely to produce a better definition of the limits of the churches' encroachment into affairs of state. The more precise the definition, the more planners can determine just how, and with respect to what, they must interact with churches.

CONCLUSION

The presence of immorality almost always provides an opportunity for moral reform because it is seldom defended as such; that is, although practiced, it is rarely preached. On the other hand, at least some, and usually a great deal, of what is preached is not practiced. Attempts are usually made to conceal or disguise immoral behavior. Therefore, it is almost always accompanied by hypocrisy or self-deception. Moral hypocrisy and self-deception are widespread, particularly among governments. What government, for example, acknowledges the corruption within it or admits to its suspension of morality in the treatment of its enemies? Herein lies the opportunity for change.

The greater the deviations between what a government preaches and what it practices, the easier it is to identify the deviations. Their exposure to the public almost always produces pressure for moral reform. On the other hand, where a government's hypocrisy is conscious and blatant, its exposure is likely to be met with a strong defense, if not offense, and reluctance to change. But hypocrisy can seldom be preserved more than temporarily against a continuing attack. The mounting and maintenance of such an attack requires courage. The risks are often great. But without courage among development planners, their activity is a hollow ritual; it is the whimper with which development ends rather than the bang that starts the race toward it.

11

Aesthetics

The neglect of aesthetics in both more and less developed countries occurs because its relevance to development is not well understood, hence a low priority is usually assigned to it. To depreciate aesthetics is to fail to appreciate the interconnectedness and mutually reinforcing character of each of the five essential aspects of development: the scientific and technological, the economic, the moral, the political, and, of course, the aesthetic.

We reject the notion of "priorities" in development planning as a matter of principle. They deny the critical interdependencies of the different aspects of development. It is not surprising, therefore, that they are the chief weapon of static bureaucracies. Priorities preclude consideration of newly emerging issues in rapidly changing environments. They restrict the domains in which solutions to problems are sought and the way problems are formulated.

There are no such things as scientific, technological, economic, moral, aesthetic, or political problems. There are only problems each of which has scientific, technological, economic, moral, aesthetic, and political aspects. To focus on any one or subset of these and ignore the others is to reduce the likelihood of formulating the right problem and finding the right solution to whatever problem is formulated.

To neglect or depreciate aesthetics is to obstruct development in a very serious way. Aesthetic considerations are commonly forced to yield to other types. They are treated as luxuries, frosting on the cake of life, rather than as essential ingredients of the cake itself. As a result, the current public clamor for enhancement of quality of life in the more developed countries of the West is an embarrassment to many of their politicians who treat it as blackmail by political extremists, if not subversives. A few politicians endorse the idea of such enhancement but fewer do anything about it. Those who do put their political careers at stake.

Enhancement of the quality of life should be a primary objective of development planning, and quality of life is largely (but not exclusively) a matter of aesthetics. Because of the widespread lack of understanding of the role of aesthetics in society, there is very little understanding of its relationship to either quality of life or development. To some they appear to be unrelated. After all, they argue, there are many less developed countries. If anything, they continue, there seems to be an inverse relationship between aesthetics and development. Even though the more developed countries devote more resources to the production and distribution of art and entertainment, they seem to have incorporated less art and more entertainment into everyday living than have less developed countries. The informal arts and related crafts seem to be healthier and play a larger role in less developed countries.

Even if this is true, it does not imply that socially pervasive aesthetic sensitivity obstructs development, but rather that the conventional concept of development as fundamentally economic in character has no aesthetic component. As long as development is thought of as something that is measured by standard of living rather than quality of life, it includes no essential role for aesthetics. (This suggests that some of the more developed countries may be less developed, in our sense of the notion, than they suppose; and that some of the less developed countries may be more developed than they suppose.) When planners focus on quality of life, there is no way they can avoid or neglect aesthetics because quality of life depends on the satisfaction derived from what people do independently of what they do it for and from making progress toward ideals, and these are aesthetic satisfactions.

The "resources" made available by aesthetic activities can be identified simply as inspiration and enjoyment (fun). These, it will be recalled, are the products of creative and recreative activities, respectively. Beauty inspires, and play and entertainment yield fun. Now we consider the scarcity, maldistribution, and insecurity of these "resources" as both obstructions to and opportunities for development.

AESTHETIC SCARCITY

Ugliness is the absence of beauty; it discourages the pursuit of ideals. Boredom is the absence of excitement; it discourages activity. Those who live in poverty and squalor suffer from a scarcity of beauty and fun.

They derive neither inspiration nor satisfaction from their everyday activities. Nevertheless, there are many affluent people in both more and less developed countries who believe that the poor and ignorant occupants of squalid environments are in some sense happier and more contented than the affluent are. This is romantic nonsense that the affluent have fabricated to rationalize their affluence. For example, black slaves in pre–Civil War United States were imagined by many advantaged whites to be contented and carefree. It took the book, *Uncle Tom's Cabin*, to reveal the truth.

Of course the poor and underprivileged are not continually sullen or sad. They sometimes find pleasure and display their satisfactions in an uninhibited way. But this does not mean that they find life easy or pleasurable. Even soldiers living under the worst of combat conditions joke and grasp as much fun as they can, but this hardly indicates a satisfaction with their lot. It reveals that desperation and misery can only be made bearable by the introduction of humor.

The affluent's tolerance of and insensitivity to the ugliness and squalor in which the poor live and the resignation of the poor to such a life are major obstructions to development. The affluent isolate themselves and shut out the ugliness and squalor that surround the poor. They hid behind walls and cluster in compounds from which the impoverished are excluded. When the affluent leave their sanctuaries, they travel on media and by modes from which most of the ugliness and squalor are hidden. By segregating themselves, they segregate the poor, thereby keeping them both out of sight and out of mind. (This led one wit to observe that they are blind idiots.)

On the other hand, the poor who live miserably in ugliness often accept their lot fatalistically, with resignation, and abandon responsibility for and hope of improving themselves. For them the pursuit of ideals is an abstraction that has no reality. Often aided and abetted by religion they accept misery in life as the price they must pay for an infinitely extended sojourn in paradise after death. To accept, let alone extol, suffering in this way is to obstruct development. On the other hand, to treat the qualityless life of others as something for which one has no responsibility is also to obstruct development.

Beauty generates aspirations for ideals and commitment to their pursuit; ugliness destroys them. Yet ugliness can often be replaced by beauty with little or no cost. With labor, care, and aesthetic sensitivity, which often abound in less developed communities, even a slum can be converted into an attractive and enjoyable place to live. People who can make commonplace objects—baskets, plates, stools, toys, boxes, and so on—into works of art can certainly make either a cave or hovel into one also. Poverty is not the mother of ugliness; hopelessness is. To give others hope is to give them the opportunity to make of life itself a thing of beauty.

Numerous disadvantaged communities and neighborhoods in both more and less developed countries have managed to initiate development processes that have significantly improved their quality of life. Reference has already been made to one such example: In the 1960s Mantua, a black urban ghetto (considered by many to be the worst) in Philadelphia, under the inspiring indigenous leadership of Herman Wrice, began to pull itself up from despair by its own bootstraps. Pride in the neighborhood returned and some human dignity was recaptured. A large number of similar efforts have been reported from around the world. Critical to those that have been successful is the fact that the external personnel who have been involved have not directed the efforts; they simply made themselves available to the communities for their use as they saw fit.

Such programs are an alternative to the despair that permeates so many disadvantaged communities. With modest encouragement and support from government, they can multiply and thrive. Unless something of this type is initiated, the occupants, who have little satisfying or inspiring activity with which to occupy their time, turn to such self-destructive activities as the use of alcohol and drugs, and such socially and environmentally destructive activities as covering buildings and vehicles with graffiti, crime, and rioting. Interviews recently conducted among the young rioters in both Northern Ireland and England revealed that their destructive and criminal activities had been stimulated by boredom and despair. They lashed out resentfully to destroy some of the fruits of development that they had never tasted.

As we have said, no matter how poor a community is, it can be made into a work of art. Cities can be things of beauty. We do not know for sure what properties of a thing make it beautiful, but we are not wholly ignorant in this regard either. St. Thomas suggested three properties that a work of art must have. Freely translated, these are wholeness or integrity, harmony or congruence, and radiance.

Since few communities are works of arts, most must be wanting in one or more of these respects. Consider how.

A collection of elements constitutes a whole if each element provides something that is necessary for the whole to perform its function, and if, collectively, they do all that is necessary for the functioning of the whole. Therefore, the parts of a whole are individually necessary and collectively sufficient for performing the function that defines the whole. For example, if the back of a chair is removed, it is no longer a chair because the function of a chair is to provide a backrest as well as a place to sit. If a whole contains a unnecessary part, that part is thought of as an appendage, a separate thing; for example, a cushion lying on a chair is not a part of the chair. An appendage is not an integral part of the whole. To integrate elements is to make a whole of them. (One cannot sit on a leg of a chair.) If the parts of a whole are separated so they no longer interact, the whole is disintegrated, and the parts are segregated.

If wholeness is required for beauty, a segregated community cannot be beautiful. In fact, a segregated community is a contradiction in terms; it is not a community but an aggregation. A neighborhood created by segregation may be a community in itself, but a city that consists of segregated communities is not a community itself. There is no "co" or "com," no togetherness, in it. Therefore, to assert that segregation is ugly is not a mere figure of speech. It is an aesthetic judgment. Segregation is an aesthetic, as well as a moral, obstruction to development.

Now consider harmony or congruence. Parts of a whole operate in harmony if each part contributes to the effective functioning of at least some other parts and does not detract from the functioning of any. For example, if two people are trying to move something, they work harmoniously if they work cooperatively. If either makes it harder for the other to do what he is trying to do, there is disharmony. Therefore, if the removal of any part of a whole enables other parts to perform their subfunctions more effectively, there is a lack of harmony in the whole.

To the extent that removal of a part of a community can improve its functioning, the community is disharmonious, hence lacks beauty. This is why slums make a city ugly.

Since it is a function of an aesthetic object to inspire, any part or property of it that detracts from its ability to do so is an obstruction to development. Dirt and filth are such detractors. They are ugly. Cleanliness is not sufficient for a beautiful city, but it is necessary. One blemish can keep an otherwise beautiful work of art from being inspiring. Graffiti is just such a blemish.

Crime is a social disharmony. The criminal and his victim are not working together. Cooperation is necessary for social harmony. Therefore, cooperation is not only good, it may be beautiful, as when we see two children in harmonious play. Thus, when we say that conflict or war is ugly, it too is not a mere figure of speech; it is an aesthetic judgment.

Finally, there is radiance. Of the three aesthetic requirements cited by St. Thomas, this is the most difficult to elucidate, but we must try.

A radiant thing is one which, we say, sings, glows, sparkles, soars, is vibrant, alive, and so on. What are we trying to communicate when we say such things? First, it is clear we are referring to what the radiant thing does to us—it affects us. Second, it says something about how we are affected by it. Clearly, we are in some sense uplifted, not depressed, by it. It makes us feel good. But more than this, it activates or motivates us; it makes us want to do something. It destroys fatalism and indifference. Even more, it seems to us, it makes us outgoing and want to do something that will enhance the quality of life of others just as the radiant thing enhances ours.

Therefore, a radiant community is one that makes those in it want to enhance the quality of life of others, to share their joys and good feelings. It is a community of friends. The essence of friendship is the desire to share what one has with others. But it is the joy of sharing voluntarily, without instigation, obligation, or compulsion. Therefore, those who are unwilling to share freely, who hoard their sources of satisfaction, are not merely immoral; they are, in a literal sense, ugly characters. The essential property of an artist is his desire to share what brings him satisfaction with others and to inspire them. The lack of such desires in a society is an aesthetic obstruction to development.

Recall that there are two aspects to aesthetics: the recreative and the creative. The function of the recreative is cathartic, to produce satisfaction with what we do. It is clear, however, that if we had no creative or stimulating art to produce desire for something better, progress and development would be more difficult. It is not surprising, therefore, that in developed countries that are quite satisfied with themselves, more time and effort are spent on the recreative arts than on those that are creative. They provide more entertainment than stimulation. Such an imbalance reflects a dominantly conservative mood—a desire to retain the quality of life already attained. In such societies there is a greater concern about losing what they have than about improving.

For these reasons, the communication media of developed countries are saturated with soporific entertainment. They carry very little that stimulates the pursuit of ideals. Unfortunately, much of the entertainment in less developed countries is imported from the more developed, particularly television programs and motion pictures. Therefore, less developed populations are bombarded with cathartics that may keep their discontent within manageable bounds, but they also reduce the likelihood of development. The imbalance between recreation and stimulation, therefore, is a major obstruction to development.

Entertainment, of course, is an antidote to boredom. Boredom obstructs development. It may do more: It may induce the unemployed to deface or destroy some of the fruits of development as they have done recently in Northern Ireland and England. But boredom is by no means reserved for those who are unemployed; it is liberally distributed among the employed as well.

The Scarcity of Quality in Work Life

Dissatisfaction with quality of work life has spread widely across more developed countries. It emerges out of boredom, among other things, and results in alienation from work. Whereas the alienation of the unemployed receives little attention from governments, the alienation of the employed from work receives a great deal of attention by governments and employers because it hits them where they are sensitive: It reduces productivity and thus obstructs economic growth.

In the factories that have emerged out of the industrial revolution, large numbers of people perform simple, dull, repetitive tasks. They often do so in an uncomfortable and unattractive environment in which they are subject to offensive and often irrational supervision and discipline, and they are poorly compensated to boot. When and where those so employed are poorly educated, hence expect little from life, and have no source of income other than such employment, they accept their lot with resignation that in time becomes despair. With more education and access to communication media that makes them aware of better working conditions in other places, resentment grows and the quantity and quality of their output decreases. Absenteeism, lateness, accidents, attrition, insubordination, and even sabotage become commonplace.

In the more developed countries where all this has been going on for some time, alienation from work has been further stimulated by the emergence of the "welfare state" which provides income to those who are not employed even if by their own choice.

Measures to counteract alienation from work began shortly after World War II. The experience with these measures in developed countries can provide less developed countries with an opportunity to prevent the problem from arising in their futures.

It is not our intention to provide a scholarly history of the steps taken to improve quality of work life in the West, but to identify the seminal ideas that spur this continuing effort. There are six such ideas: work structuring, job rotation, job enlargement or enrichment, autonomous work groups, and community councils. We consider each in turn.

Work structuring. In this process management turns over to the workers all decisions that do not directly affect what work they do and how they do it. Therefore, the workers collectively are given control of their work environment and supporting facilities. For example, they determine what kind of food is served in the lunch room, what is published in the company newspaper, the location and design of locker rooms and recreational facilities, and so on.

This relinquishment of managerial control results in increased productivity and worker satisfaction for a while, but eventually the novelty wears off and most changes the workers want have been made. Then productivity and job satisfaction level off and, in some cases, return to their initial state. Therefore, it becomes clear that continued maintenance, if not an increase, in productivity requires that something be done about work itself.

Job rotation. To reduce the boredom of repeating a simple task, workers are given the opportunity to rotate among different tasks. This relieves boredom, but not for long. If each of the tasks between which a worker moves is boring, it takes him longer to become bored with the set, but bored he becomes sooner or later. This suggests that the individual tasks themselves require redesign to make them more challenging and interesting.

Job enlargement or enrichment. Here a fundamental change is made: Work is redesigned to fit people better. Previously, work was designed to fit machines, and people were fitted to those tasks that machines either could not do or could not do economically. Through job enrichment tasks are made as large and complex as workers can be expected to perform well. In some cases individual workers produce or assemble a complete product or a large subassembly. Such redesign of work requires an integrated look at the technical, psychological, and social aspects of work. These different aspects are no longer treated separately. Their integrated treatment is known as socio-technical systems design.

Since even larger tasks become boring if repeated many times, it is natural to combine job rotation and job enrichment.

Autonomous work groups. The concept of work is further enlarged when the individual is replaced by a group as the basic work unit. These groups are given as complex a task as feasible and are left free to organize themselves to do it. They can structure the work and rotate responsibilities as they see fit. In many cases they select their own leader or rotate leadership among group members. In some cases the groups are allowed to negotiate the exchange of tasks or personnel with other groups. Autonomous work groups are given almost complete control over the means they employ. Only the outputs expected of them are passed down from a higher authority.

Industrial democracy: participative management. An important extension of the preceding sequence of ideas is made when workers are given an opportunity to participate in the selection of organizational and group ends and the policies under which they work. In some cases they participate in the selection of their immediate superior and in the formulation of corporate strategy.

Community councils. One further synthesizing idea has been introduced in Jamestown, New York, where a council consisting of representatives of government, employers, and employees consider all issues that affect the future of the community and its ability to provide satisfying work to its members.

This evolution of the work process, still very much in its infancy, has been accompanied by a number of other "humanizing" measures; for example, the introduction of career planning with the employer providing financial support of the education required to attain objectives set in these plans; choice of benefit "packages" from among elements arranged in a cafeteria-like way; and flextime, that is, flexible working hours.

Reports of the effects of such types of change as have been briefly identified here have been almost uniformly favorable, both from the employees' and employers' points of view.

Although most of this effort has taken place in more developed countries, it has great significance for those that are less developed. Because they are generally in the earlier stages of industrialization, they can avoid the errors in work design that more developed countries have made and are now trying to correct. By incorporating consideration of quality of work life into the development of their industries, less developed countries can bypass a quality of work life that produces alienation from work and declining productivity and move directly to one that the more developed countries are only beginning to realize. LDCs can thus gain an economic advantage that can only be obtained by the dedicated pursuit of aesthetic objectives.

MALDISTRIBUTION OF AESTHETICS

Most urban areas in both more and less developed countries are segregated rather than integrated, in the sense of these terms used above. Neighborhoods and sections of metropolitan areas tend to be homogeneous with respect to at least the economic characteristics of their inhabitants and often to their race, national origin, and sometimes religion. Because the poor and the affluent tend to live in separated enclaves, their urban environments tend to be very different, particularly from an aesthetic point of view. The poor often occupy densely populated slums and the wealthy, less densely populated attractive neighborhoods. The qualities of life these environments provide differ significantly. The beauty of urban neighborhoods is usually proportional to the economic status of their inhabitants, and so is the availability of and access to artistic, cultural, and recreational facilities.

To be sure, television and radio make it possible technologically to bring at least some of the arts and great deal of entertainment to every household. However, many urban households do not have electricity available or cannot afford television. Moreover, as we have already observed, these media tend to be saturated with soporific entertainment rather than content that can inspire. Most of the recreation they provide is passive: It provides no opportunity for participation. Nor can radio and television transmit many of the arts effectively; for example, painting and sculpture. The inspiration to be derived from natural beauty is not to be derived from images on a television screen. Radio, of course, is even more restricted.

In principle it is easy to provide everyone in urban areas with equal access to and availability of artistic and recreational opportunities. To do so requires an integrated city, one in which each neighborhood is as heterogeneous economically and socially as the city is as a whole. Each part of such a city would be a representative sample, a cross section, of the whole. Availability of and access to all public services and facilities would be unrelated to economic and social characteristics of its inhabitants. It would have additional advantages. The affluent living in each neighborhood would be unlikely to allow it to deteriorate into one that is ugly and without recreational facilities. Moreover, they would be likely to be more sensitive than they currently are to the plight of the less fortunate and be more inclined to help them improve their lot. Despair is less likely to thrive in heterogeneous neighborhoods than in homogeneous enclaves.

AESTHETIC INSECURITY

Those who have an acceptable if not satisfying quality of life and who find it insecure usually react by attempting to isolate themselves from their environment by encapsulating themselves. They build walls or fences around their homes or join together with others to build "protected" enclaves to which others are denied access. In effect, they withdraw from society to the extent possible and thus make little or no contribution to the development of others. Moreover, since people who seek separation from their surrounding environment are precisely the ones who are most likely to possess works of art and to live in beautiful settings, these are made inaccessible to all but a few in their inner circles. The same is true of such recreational facilities as they can build privately; for example, tennis courts and swimming pools.

Most recreational facilities and many works of art are publicly owned and are housed in public facilities. To the extent that public administrators feel that the recreational and cultural facilities and their contents will be abused or misused, they are centralized so that access to them can be controlled and they can be policed. Centralization requires most people to use transportation to get to these facilities. This is clearly discriminatory against the poor because of its cost and inconvenience. Ideally, works of art, the performing arts, recreational facilities, and recreational performances (e.g., athletic games) should be widely dispersed so that all have easy access to at least some of them.

To a large extent insecurity has immobilized and isolated the arts and recreation. The wandering minstrels of medieval times now travel by jet and perform in forbidding palaces or arenas. Travelling art shows are confined to fortress museums where they can be closely guarded. Little street art remains. What there is of it is more likely to be found in expensive neighborhoods. Only affluent parts of a city can afford local art and recreational centers. There are few if any places to play in the slums and even fewer in which to find inspiration.

CONCLUSION

Less developed countries have a tremendous aesthetic opportunity in that they can avoid an error of dissection made in the development process of most advanced countries. More developed countries have separated work, play, and learning both in concept and practice. Workplaces were so conceived as to exclude opportunities for play and learning. Schools were developed so as to exclude opportunities for doing something useful (work) or playing, at least while learning. And places for play were constructed so as to exclude the possibility of useful work or learning; for example, sports arenas, country clubs, and resort areas. Because of these exclusionary designs the quality of work life in these countries has suffered. It has resulted in a pervasive alienation from work that has only recently begun to receive the attention it deserves. Schools have been suffering from a similar malaise, one that is reflected in increasing drop-out rates, irregularity of attendance, and the decreasing quality of the education received. Functional illiteracy is on the increase in a number of developed countries.

Work and learning were conceived as activities to which a person should bring either his muscle or mind, but not both—and certainly not his heart. Education was directed at producing the kind of people who would fit into mechanistically conceived jobs. Work was not designed to fit people as human beings but as machines. Witness the orientation and content of the fields of work study and industrial engineering.

At best, quality of life was considered only in connection with leisure time, after-work and after-school hours. The need to bring it into consideration in the design of every human activity is only now beginning to be recognized in developed countries; for example, in the emerging quality-of-work-life movement. But it will take a long time to undo the segregation of work, play, and learning. The institutions and processes in which such segregation is imbedded must be changed. Less developed countries, in which these institutions and processes are not fully "developed," have an opportunity to avoid these difficulties by taking a holistic approach to the design of every social institution and process, integrating opportunities for work, play, and learning in every activity, whatever its principal function. They can bring scientific, technological, economic, ethical, moral, and aesthetic considerations to bear on every part of the whole that we call life and thereby make living itself an art form.

12

Politics

Politics has to do with the distribution of power in society between those who govern and the governed and among those who govern and the governed.

As an expression of their instinctive desire to live with others, people form such social groups as families, clans, tribes, and communities. Similarly motivated, social groups come together to form societies. Social groups and societies define themselves, hence give themselves an identity, by adopting principles of inclusion and exclusion; some individuals and groups in, the rest out. When, in addition, a society claims a territory for its exclusive use and selects some of its members to manage its collective affairs—to govern it—it becomes a state.

The ways by which a government is selected, organized, and works is a matter of politics, and politics is a matter of power, of who has control over whom. The practices of a government with respect to power—in possible contrast to its proclamations—can be partially characterized along two scales having to do with ends and means. One of these scales has to do with who selects the ends to be served by government and the other with who selects the means.

Any organization, including governments and governmental agencies and institutions, can be characterized by its position on these two scales, hence in the "space" they define. (See Figure 12.1.) The position of a society in this "space" defines its prevailing political philosophy.

The division of power between a government and the governed is the structure of a state. It can differ significantly from the structure of the government. For example, the government of a democratic state can be organized autocratically and conversely. The highest governmental authority may have complete control over others in government yet be completely controlled by those outside it who elected him. On the other hand, an autocratic governing body can itself be organized democratically.

Mechanistically conceived societies are usually ends and means autocratic. Organismically conceived societies are generally ends autocratic and means dem-

Figure 12.1
Types of Political Philosophy

		One Person → **Everyone**
M E A N S — **E V E R Y O N E**	ENDS AUTOCRATIC MEANS DEMOCRATIC e.g., some autonomous work groups, guerilla army units, and political parties	ENDS AND MEANS DEMOCRATIC ABSOLUTE DEMOCRACY e.g., some cooperatives, professional societies, and social clubs
S E L E C T I O N — **O N E P E R S O N**	ENDS AND MEANS AUTOCRATIC ABSOLUTE AUTOCRACY e.g., some prisons, and military units	ENDS DEMOCRATIC MEANS AUTOCRATIC e.g., some health, education, and welfare organizations

Ends Selection

ocratic. The ends of the whole take precedence over those of the parts. Societies conceived as social systems are ends democratic and may be either means autocratic or means democratic. In such societies means autocracy is generally restricted to those types of choices for which expertise or access to restricted information is thought to be necessary.

The distinction between autocracy and democracy has to do with the extent to which those who are governed participate in selecting society's ends and means. When a government restricts or constrains such choices it is variety-decreasing or monistic; to the extent that it increases the variety of ends and means available for individual choice, it is pluralistic. It may, of course, be monistic with respect to either ends or means and pluralistic with respect to the other.

To the extent that individuals can make their own choices and have equal ranges of choice (i.e., equal opportunity and access to social goods and services), their society is pluralistic. The more pluralistic a society, the more autonomous each of its members is. Nevertheless, even in a completely pluralistic society some socially imposed constraints are necessary if conflict and anarchy are to be avoided: Individuals must be precluded from doing anything that deprives others of choice.

Most prisons, armies, and totalitarian societies are monistic. In such societies the kind of clothing, work, and housing available, the schooling one can receive, the religion one can practice, the occupation one can pursue, and much more may be determined by an authority or severely constrained by an authority. Monism requires conformity to standards, hence discourages creativity; pluralism permits, if not promotes, nonconformity, and hence encourages creativity.

A society may be monistic in some respects and pluralistic in others. For example, Mexico permits any choice of religion but essentially precludes all but one political party. The United States assigns children to public schools but imposes no restrictions on the colleges to which high school graduates can apply.

It is commonly argued that democratic pluralism cannot work in a society where most of its members are less than well developed. They are said to be unprepared or not ready for it. This argument, of course, is used to support autocratic monism for at least the short run. The short run has a tendency to become long, as was the case in Portugal under Salazar.

Experience and experiment are universally regarded as the best teachers. The more choice there is, the more varied the experience and the more learning and motivation take place. One obviously learns and is motivated more by what one chooses to do than what others decide one should do. Therefore, pluralism and democracy are more conducive to development than monism and autocracy.

Autocratic monism may reduce the likelihood of costly errors, but one learns more from one's own errors than from the right decision made by others. To deprive people of the opportunity to make their own mistakes is to reduce their opportunity to develop.

The limit of pluralism is not anarchy if the moral principal previously discussed is applied: that one should not act so as to reduce the likelihood of any other person doing what he or she wants. The effective prohibition of such acts requires a set of laws, judgment as to when they have been violated, and punishment for their violation. These requirements can only be met by an organized society, not one that is anarchic.

We have argued that society should encourage and facilitate the development of its members. If this argument is accepted, then it is the responsibility of government, which is the management of society, to see to it that this function is carried out efficiently and effectively.

Development planning is a societal activity that cannot be carried out without the involvement of government; hence it is necessarily involved in politics. Unless planners are sustained by government, they cannot even begin to work. However, without some political control from the governed, planners tend to become political autocrats and their plans utopian.

Development planning is always confronted with political obstructions and opportunities, and always has implicit or explicit political aims. There is no such thing as politically neutral or apolitical development planning. One cannot engage in such planning without "being in politics."

Politics arises in answer to problems generated by social life. The process of living together entails sacrifice of individual interest, desires, greeds, illusions. The political state arises to handle this condition of conflict of all against all, and the political practitioner makes a living out of such conflict.

Politics has been defined as the art of the possible. Perhaps it would be better if it were defined as the art of the impossible, since no important political proposal ever seems to survive intact. Compromise and its handmaiden, hypocrisy, are inevitably involved in political actions.

Nevertheless, development planning must come to terms with political reality. At times popular enthusiasm can prevail against political opposition because popular enthusiasm is itself political. If it marshals sufficient countervailing force then obviously it can prevail over political opposition. Either way, with political approval or against it, the planner is in politics.

The involvement of planners in politics and with government follows from their preoccupation with bringing the future of social life under more or less conscious control. The implementation of plans requires the ability to control the collective behavior of those who form the society planned for. Power is the ability to control or influence the behavior of others.

There are two types of power: power to and power over. Power to is the ability to get others to do voluntarily what one wants. Power over is the ability to punish those who either do not do what one wants or do what one does not want. Power over may, of course, be used to force others to do what one wants, but this is not power to because the compliance thus obtained is not voluntary. One may have either type of power without the other, or both. For example, an elected leader of an association may have power to but not power over. On the other hand, a ruler may have power over without power to.

The essence of power to is the ability to lead, to influence. The essence of power over is the ability to enforce, to coerce. In an ideally moral state in which everyone cooperates with everyone else, only power to would be required. However, in a real state where conflict abounds, power over is also necessary. As a society approaches the ideally moral state, coercive power should wither because the need for it would diminish. Therefore, the amount of coercive power that the government of a state requires is a measure of its distance from an ideally moral state.

Authority is coercive power sanctioned by law. It can grow or diminish, depending on how it is used. It can become a virtually irresistible force. It can also be divided into forces that oppose each other and thus become impotent. The opposition of approximately equal powers can produce social paralysis. However, two strong powers in paralyzing opposition often can be overcome by even a weak countervailing power that is concentrated on that opposition.

The greatest obstructions to the exercise of power for social good lie within a society, not external to it, as many in government who have power over but not power to would have us believe. If the power to obstruct is great, it is only because the political power it opposes is also great. Otherwise, powerful obstructions would be pointless. Turned about, the power behind such obstructions can become a power capable of contributing significantly to a society's development.

Power, then, is the "resource" with which politics is concerned. Therefore, we turn now to a consideration of its scarcity, maldistribution, and insecurity as obstructions and opportunities for development.

SCARCITY OF POWER

Scarcity of power in a society means an inability of its government to implement its policies, to get anything done, and, most of all, to maintain law and order. Anarchy reigns and chaos and confusion pervade where there is a complete lack of power. Such a condition is currently approximated in Iran, Northern Ireland, and Lebanon, among others. In each of these cases the government lacks sufficient public support to generate the power required to coerce, let alone influence. This obviously does not imply an absence of violence and bloodshed; it does imply the inability of force to produce law and order because there are two or more forces of approximately equal strength that oppose each other. The consequence is a state of civil war that not only precludes development but produces retrogression.

Obviously, a government that cannot maintain law and order cannot sustain and implement development planning. But it is not only the inability to induce or enforce law and the order it is intended to create that obstructs development and development planning; less obviously, law itself may do so. In effect, the overabundance of power, as well as its scarcity, can be obstructive.

Law is a means for coercing human action through political institutions. This is true for both public (e.g., state) and private (e.g., corporate) law. Government is the executive arm of the law in both cases, since law effectuates political decision through government. It often does so regardless of its effects on society. The law considered independently of its effects is considered structurally rather than functionally.

The structure of law coerces. Its function, however, is justice: the ethical resolution of human conflict through political structures. From the time of ancient Greece until today, those for whom the structure of the law is paramount have been in disagreement with those for whom the justice of its disposition has been more important. Legal theorists have studied deeply both the forms of the law independent of its effects and its effects with a disregard of legal form.

Historically, Roman and common law have alternated periods of strict law (structure, form, amorality) and periods of equity (dissolution and disregard for form and insistence upon "justice in the individual case"). In no other discipline has the dialectical opposition of structure and function so nearly contributed the entire learning and the whole practice of the subject.

In the public realm, law is the final arbiter in the clash of political opinion. Proponents of particular political actions try first to make their position consonant with the principle of justice. Then they endeavor to embed it in legal structure. The layman has an apparently unshakable conviction that once embodied in legal form (its structure), a matter that at first had been only the object of conflicting opinion is now settled as law. They disregard what is apparent to those who look for it: that settled law also serves conflicting opinion. Its function is not to end dispute—this is utopian—but to resolve it again and again, however often it arises.

Planners are not exempt from the general temptation to believe that a plan receives its highest fulfillment when and if it is enacted into law. Nothing could be further from the truth. Legal enactment of a plan is the end of planning and the beginning of the political process of enforcement. This process can be a mixed bag of legal threat, bureaucratic sabotage, and general public indifference. Then, often too late, the planner discovers that the law can be an obstruction to development, whereas previously he had thought of legal obstructions as those enactments already on the books and settled modes of legal delay and contention.

Development planners should resist as strenuously as possible the premature crystallization of plans into settled law. Once plans become law they immediately lose their dynamism and become the property of a bureaucracy. They cease to develop despite the fact that the law of the plan may actually prescribe development. In fact, settled law is what the term implies: settled. It puts an end to continuous participation and adaptation in the planning process.

What can planners do when the law is against them? The simple-minded but appropriate answer is: ''See a lawyer.'' The planner's tendency to put off consultation with lawyers until trouble arises is not different from that of the ordinary citizen, and the results are no better. Our suggestion can best be put boldly: Bring the lawyers into planning from the beginning. Experienced planners know this. The problem is how to do it.

The beginning of wisdom for the development planner is the recognition that the lawyer too is a planner, in fact a rival planner with different professional training, different outlook, different aims. The problem then is how to convert a rival into a collaborator. The prescriptions for success in this venture at cooperation are equally well known. They are time, patience, respect, and at least a little mutual admiration. What makes the effort feasible at all is the fact that both sides frequently can agree on common objectives.

The nature and quality of a system of law and justice has a (if not the most) profound effect on development. If this system is believed by the people to be fair, impartial, consistent, and just, then confidence grows. If they believe themselves to be subject to arbitrary search and seizure, detention, or other punishment without fair trial, the spying of possibly prejudiced informers or secret police, or a lack of continuity and consistency in justice, confidence is shaken and alienation and withdrawal follow.

Only law and government with sufficient power can guarantee freedom of expression, organization, and assembly that does not explicitly advocate the overthrow of the government by force or that does not in fact constitute *lese majeste*. These are necessary for development, hence should be encouraged.

Therefore, development planners who work in a power vacuum in which government is paralyzed must direct their efforts at having this vacuum filled. They must plan for the creation of effective and just law and a government with sufficient power to enforce it. Without these, decisions, let alone plans, cannot be implemented. With them, human beings can aggregate their individual abilities and work wonders far surpassing the sum of their separate potentialities.

MALDISTRIBUTION OF POWER

Power is maldistributed when some members of a society have more than they need, and others less. This occurs when power is concentrated in the hands of a few while the many who are subject to it remain virtually powerless. There is, of course, the need for some concentration of power in government, but no more than those governed should collectively have over government. An authority who is not subject to the collective control of those controlled rules rather than governs. To govern is to execute and administer the collective will of the governed. To rule is to execute and administer the will of the ruler even when it conflicts with the collective will of the governed.

In a strongly centralized government the power structure is like a pyramid. Authority flows down from the top spreading throughout the entire organization. On the other hand, responsibility flows from the bottom to the top. Therefore, the one at the top has authority over and responsibility for everything. The great source of strength of such an organization is the immense base upon which it rests. It reaches all the way down and encompasses even the lowest and most numerous elements of the governmental and communal power structure. Nevertheless, such a government can be quite unstable because of its susceptibility to coalitions of countervailing power in the hands of the echelons near the top, to coups and other types of "palace revolution."

The structural weaknesses of a strongly centralized government are both vertical and horizontal. On the vertical dimension, since authority and responsibility flow directly between the top and the bottom, there is inadequate communication between the separate lines; hence they lack cohesion. Interactions of units at the same level are discouraged in order to consolidate the power of the superior to whom they report. Orders tend to be narrowly transmitted and interpreted and lack reinforcement from adjacent sectors or units. Responsibility is constantly segmented bureaucratically, making coordination difficult to obtain. The obstructive character of such an organization of government to development is captured in the notion of paternalism.

Paternalism

Paternalism is "a practice of treating or governing people in a fatherly manner, especially by providing for their needs without giving them responsibility."* The instability of paternalism derives from the fact that children eventually grow up and want to "take over" from the father. If the system works at all successfully, it does so only in small groups of immature people who, when they mature, can go off on their own. When expanded to the body politic in which there are many mature "children" who have no place to go off to, paternalism fosters internecine and implacable enmities.

The highest virtue in a paternalistic government is personal loyalty and obedience to the "father," regardless of the best interests of the governed and even of the father himself who, like all human beings, is often wrong. Nevertheless, disloyalty and disobedience are normally treated as crimes on whose perpetrators the coercive power of the "father" is brought to bear.

Because of the concentration of power at the top of a paternalistic structure, virtually anyone with authority can revoke or revise any decision made at a lower level. Therefore, all decisions made below the top are regarded as tentative and provisional and are subject to long delays. Their implementation is held up until final approval is reached from the top. A decision not ultimately validated may entail serious consequences on the one who executes it before final approval. Therefore, such structures are characterized by extensive red tape and bureaucratic formalism.

A paternalistic bureaucracy provides those charged with responsibility with a convenient way of avoiding it. By seeking approval from above, they absolve themselves of responsibility for their actions. For this reason it is generally difficult to determine who is responsible for a decision. The inability to do so makes it almost impossible to evaluate the performance of individual decision makers. A victim of poor service or policies of a paternalistic government can seldom get to the source of his difficulty. However, if he has influence he can usually get something done about his complaint. (Who one knows is often more important than what one knows.) Such an adjustment does not result in generally improved service because it applies only in the single case. Less influential victims of government bureaucracy continue to suffer without recourse.

Even routine decisions and services require large amounts of time unless someone higher up the line asks for them. Working time is allocated on a rank-based priority system, which, as we have already noted, raises havoc with schedules and appointments.

---

*The American Heritage Dictionary of the English Language, paperback edition, Dell Publishing Co., New York, 1970.

The pyramidal system pushes so much responsibility to the top that conscientious high-ranking officials are overloaded with work. They frequently outwork any of their subordinates. Contrary to the idea that this sets a good example for subordinates, it encourages them not to take responsibility and to push decisions as far up the line as possible. The highest official has the most to do. Instead of this being perceived as poor management and a consequence of the inability to delegate, it is often taken as a mark of self-sacrifice (which indeed it is). However, far greater results would be obtainable if the highest officials could learn to put others to work. Needless to say, even the highest official cannot delegate if his subordinates do not accept responsibility for implementation.

In most public or private organizations that are run in the paternalistic mode, there is neither organizational democracy nor participative management. Little if any pressure is applied for participation from below. Even student radicalism tends to be temporary; it is largely confined to the short period of schooling, after which the graduates rapidly take their places among the conforming elite.

However, it is easy to forget that a paternalistic culture is usually conservative, not reactionary. Witness the case of the extremely conservative Japanese culture. It succeeded in what might be called a total modernization wholly under the form of paternalism. A single generation sufficed for the "sons" to displace the "fathers" with well-known spectacular results.

Paternalism can easily and swiftly change to pluralism as environmental turbulence increases. To view such turbulence as an unmixed evil is to miss many opportunities that it presents for development.

Genuine participation moving from the bottom upward is the antidote to paternalism. Indeed, it is an obvious fact of psychic life that fathers want their children to succeed. Therefore, when the "children" are perceived as the whole younger generation and not merely as one's biological descendants, the impulse to paternalism emerges as a beneficial force in the development of a country. The type of development planning we proposed in Part II relies heavily on this natural altruistic sentiment.

Patronage

Paternalism and patronage are two sides of the same coin, the coin being maldistribution of power. In a paternalistic power structure the head makes an incredibly large number of appointments, not only to important posts, but to many far down in the lower echelons. Even where the officials are appointed or elected locally, only those who receive endorsement from above can hope to be appointed or elected. If elected contrary to the will of those higher up, the new official will be unable to perform his function effectively.

Where patronage prevails, officials are selected more because of who they know (their connections) than what they know (their competence). Therefore, their general level of competence tends to be lower than it is in less patronistic systems. Even where heads of agencies and other high officials are selected because of their qualifications for the job, they usually feel it wise to support their superiors since even the suspicion of disloyalty can unseat an official, however good his performance has been. Appointees at even lower levels tend to be concerned with what those higher up think of them rather than with what they themselves think.

Patronage is generally considered to be an unmitigated obstruction to social progress. Here again, this view overlooks the strengths in such a system and the reasons for its existence and continuance. The roots of patronage lie in family loyalties, friendships, long associations, and shared aspirations. Patronized officials know the others with whom they deal and in general place a higher value on known loyalty than unknown competence. Patronage, however, creates informal networks through which social objectives can be achieved.

The implacable foe of patronage is the expert, the professional, the new intellectual elite. Turbulent conditions give the latter their opportunity and they often succeed in invading paternalistic organizations, bringing with them the weaknesses associated with impersonal and individualistic competence, rivalry in competitive expertise, short-sighted insistence on radical change in the interest of their own field of competence. When not restrained by a holistic approach to organization and reorganization, such a loose confederation of experts can rapidly wreck a stable paternalistic organization by turning it into a battlefield of competing interests, as was the case in Iran under the Shah.

The correct response to such a threat lies in a comprehensive, integrated approach to development in which all stakeholders have their say, including the paternalistic managers of the existing system. This assures that their long experience and institutional loyalties are taken into account. These are the strengths that efficiency experts are at times all too willing to sacrifice.

The Military

The military in paternalistic power structures tends to identify itself with the head of state and the head tends to identify himself with the military. The temptation of the head to encourage this identification often becomes overwhelming since a paternalistic power structure depends critically on the ability to impose punishment. If the military arm is absorbed into the political structure, the result is often unfortunate: The civilian sector becomes military and no true division between them is possible. The military is thus degraded to a political tool. But as Napoleon Bonaparte said, "You can do anything with bayonets except sit on them." The military may exert power, but it cannot rule.

The military attempts to justify itself by exaggerating the danger of foreign invasion. It tends to demand increased equipment, facilities, and money. It seldom makes a realistic appraisal of the defense needs of the country, taking into account especially the morale and fighting potential of the bulk of the population that it customarily treats paternalistically. Students of military affairs constantly warn the military against identification with the government and the confusion of their proper role in defending the country with the responsibilities of civilian rule. Astute military leaders avoid, where possible, the dangers of civilian involvement although they often find themselves used by civil leaders for purposes having nothing to do with their proper function.

The military can participate in a country's development even in the sense of the term used here. Almost every country in the world is afflicted by a proliferation of arms and armament. The expense of this unproductive activity is often great enough to practically bankrupt some countries and it constitutes a heavy burden on almost all. There is a cause-and-effect relationship between the paranoidal fear that countries feel for one another and the growth of their military arms, the aggrandizement of military expenses, and the interference of the military in every sector of the national life. Strangely enough, the military, who are trained for destruction, are finding themselves either voluntarily or involuntarily drawn into the actual governance of the civil affairs of the country, a task for which they are not trained.

Nevertheless, in a few countries the military actually plays a helpful role in promoting national development. They have certain logistical skills in organizing the movement of people, in planning strategic and tactical moves in defense of the country, and in innovative technological improvement. In addition, the military has a stake in an improved economy and, assuming that its primary function is defense, in the development and growth of the nation and its resources.

Long experience indicates that civilian control over military affairs is virtually necessary if the nation is to prosper. What is not recognized by many reformers is that the military, given its proper role of national defense, is a necessary stakeholder in the participative aspects of national planning. Civilian national planners hesitate to include the military in their plans, except of course for those in totalitarian societies where there is little use in trying to separate military from civilian affairs.

A clear distinction should be made between the regularly constituted military establishment in a country and its secret police. By the very nature of its secrecy, it is hard to imagine a progressive role in national development for a secret police force. Even if it is deemed necessary, it is at best a necessary evil.

Diffusion of Power

Not all governments of less developed countries are paternalistic. In some, power and authority are widely dispersed, resulting in a large number of social forces no one of which can control the society. Therefore, unless some of these are willing to cooperate, government is virtually impossible. In such situations, differences that cannot be bridged usually incapacitate. Although no one group can carry out its social program without the support of others, one group may be able to prevent any coalition of other groups from carrying out a program negotiated among them.

The so-called middle class is increasingly playing such a role in countries with widely dispersed power. This is a strange phenomenon for the middle class has heretofore recognized itself, if it recognized itself as a class at all, as representative of all the people, the backbone of the nation, so to speak. Revolution was incompatible with this self-image. The upper class were merely the rich, the idle, the overpaid custodians of tradition and ritual. The poor were those who were not yet or who would never be normal ordinary members of society.

In the past the middle class could only "revolt" against itself. Increasingly, however, it now sees itself as oppressed by either concentrated or diffused power in the hands of others. As it does so it more often resorts to violence. Middle-class progressive intellectual elites are banding together either with reactionary elements in society, whether secular or religious, or with leftist coalitions to overthrow existing governments. Here the modest pleas of development planners to the quarreling factions to set aside their differences and to plan for the common good are simply brushed aside as partisan maneuvers or as utopian nonsense. Groups committed to the use of force, whether liberal or reactionary, left or right, are necessarily antagonistic to any planning effort that requires a modicum of peaceful agreement or at least a willingness to try to reach agreement. The revolutionaries mean to seize power first and then impose their own planning on the country. Therefore, it seems that peaceful planners and proponents of the use of force can never get together.

All planning assumes conflict of interests. This, however, is very different from conflict in the quest for power. Since most planning seeks to reconcile conflicting interests it must have the support of authority. If authority exists, planning can proceed. Otherwise not. This is very different from conflicts in power which can only be resolved by countervailing power. How the planners should seek to obtain the necessary authority to enable them to start the planning process is a professional matter depending on the particular circumstances of time and place. No general conditions exist for bringing about authorized planning and no general principles govern its exercise. Needless to say, some central authority must organize public opinion before planning for societal development can get under way.

INSECURITY OF POWER

To be effective, power has to be justified and accepted by those who are subject to it. Insecurity of power arises from the fear of losing its legitimacy.

In most of the industrialized Western cultures, the process of legitimization is explicit and primarily embedded in the concept of "due process of law." So strong is the commitment to this that the courts in these societies prefer to set known criminals free "on technicalities" rather than deviate from due process.

In this type of society insecure authorities tend to become more bureaucratic. Their typical response to perceived threats to their power is to tighten controls to ensure conformity and close adherence to the rules, even to the detriment of the organizations' objectives.

By contrast, in most of the nonindustrialized countries, especially in complex Eastern cultures, the concept of legitimacy is much more ambiguous and implicit. Due to historic misuse of legal processes there is general mistrust of due process, which is also considered inefficient and time consuming. There is more concern with the ends to be achieved than with the appropriate means to be followed. Since there is no guarantee that due process will lead to desired outcomes, in general it is avoided and only given lip service.

In the absence of an explicit mechanism for legitimization, the insecure power holders try to personify the legitimacy in themselves. To do so, they have to portray themselves as supernatural beings. They must be perceived as infallible: having perfect knowledge; total control over resources; embodying the culture's value system; being charismatic and forceful. Such authority is personal and nontransferable. Any sign of weakness threatens the image of perfection on which the legitimacy of the power holder is based. Since the leader is portrayed as the authority in all realms of activity, no criticism of any kind can be tolerated. It would be viewed as an attack not only on the legitimacy of the leader, but on the system as a whole. Critics are accused of being disloyal to the leader and their country as well. Ironically, such a power base is highly vulnerable. To control all dissent is not easy. It is a task to which the government must devote most of its attention and resources. In particular the flow of all information into and within the country has to be controlled.

The more insecure the government, the more it tends to overprotect itself by means of a subservient press, which reinforces the illusion of infallibility. This becomes counterproductive because an increasingly cynical public dismisses all the reports as propaganda.

Where the press is controlled, there is little or no public discussion of major structural or strategic issues and no post mortems on failures. Consequently, there is practically no feedback control over government policies and practices. Mistakes are quickly and effectively buried and nothing is learned from them. After all, there is nothing left for those who believe in their omniscience to learn.

The response of a government that senses extreme insecurity often goes beyond the suppression of public opinion; it involves control of even the most private thinking. The mechanisms employed for this purpose are the secret police and private informers. They make for the most severe type of oppression, hence are the most obstructive to development.

The amount of time, effort, and resources consumed in suppression of deviating opinions and beliefs can be large enough to reduce significantly the time, effort, and resources available for investment in development. More critically, this confines learning to what is already known and accepted. Without unrestricted exploration of ideas, even education stultifies development.

The tragedy of this type of society is doubled when it considers itself to be in the Western political camp. In order to be accepted by its Western industrialized friends, it has to conform to the Western concept of legitimacy and demonstrate its respect for due process. This is usually done by a caricaturistic imitation of representative democracy with an emphasis on bureaucratic orientation. Superimposition of bureaucracy, which has lost its effectiveness even where it was originally conceived, with the existing system of personified legitimacy leads to corruption, inefficiency, and further resistance to change. Under these conditions, only an authority who gets his influence from association with the leader can produce some results. Therefore, individuals seek out and support these influential patrons and reward them in exchange for their valuable support. This allows corruption to spread throughout the system, ultimately to become a justifiable way of life. Identification of the corruption and inefficiency with the leader, who, after all, claims to symbolize the whole nation, constitutes a fatal blow to his legitimacy.

Leaders of Islamic nations face another formidable constraint. For some radical elements there, antimodernization or anti-Westernization has become the most radical posture to assume. It would be a mistake to underestimate the force of this type of "radical conservatism" among the contemporary elite of these societies. Obviously this was the mistake made by the recent Shah of Iran.

In Iran we saw radical elements organize on both the right and the left and join forces in an attack against a leader who had lost his legitimacy because of the perceived corruption of his government and his close identification with the West.

All this is not to suggest that democracy is a lost cause in these cultures. On the contrary, it is to emphasize that institutionalization of democracy requires a serious and integrated planning process for the creation of a system of participative democracy along the lines we suggested in Part II.

The ultimate source of a government's impotency is the lack of public support. This can be overcome by making the public responsible for development planning and development itself. This would not remove the government from the planning or development process, but would give it the critical roles of coordinating the multiple efforts entailed and generating and distributing the resources required. It is precisely such a planning process that we describe in detail in Chapter 6.

To be sure, a democratic participative planning process would reduce a government's power over, but it would more than compensate for this by significantly increasing its power to. Power should be perceived as a means to development; development should not be perceived as a means to power of anything less than society as a whole.

The most powerful government possible is one in which every member is both governor and governed, where responsibility for managing society is shared by all, where government is taken to be an instrument of the governed, and the governed are not taken to be instruments of government. This is most closely approximated in a society that is organized "lowerarchically" rather than hierarchically. A "lowerarchical" organization is one in which ultimate power lies at the bottom and is distributed upward, not the other way around as is almost universally the case in contemporary societies.

A lowerarchy is a participative democracy. All existing democratic national governments are representative democracies, and these are hierarchical. Lowerarchical government emphasizes responsibility rather than authority and service rather than control. The secure government derives its security from efficient performance of socially needed or desired functions and the popular support this engenders. Therefore, the opportunity that governmental bureaucratic insecurity presents is that of debureaucratizing in a way that increases its popular support.

Debureaucratization of government and its agencies, and the increase of popular support, can be accomplished by giving them a "consumer orientation" and requiring them to compete efficiently against alternative sources of the services they provide.

An insecure government imposes its will on the governed. The more it does so, the less support it receives and the more insecure it becomes. Therefore, to the extent that a government serves well the interests of the governed, it can attain security. This requires a government to place the evaluation of the services it provides in the hands and minds of those it serves. This can be done by making the survival and size of governmental service agencies depend on their ability to satisfy those they serve. A voucher system, such as that described earlier in the discussion of education, does just this. Such a system places government resources directly in the hands of the governed. They can use them to "pay for" government services. The income of the service agencies then derives directly from those served in return for service rendered. This, combined with the availability of alternative sources of a service, assures responsiveness, efficiency, and effectiveness of a service agency.

In a lowerarchy the governed are self-governing to the extent that they desire and they control any governmental units they create. The governed are the ultimate source of power and resources, available for collective use at any level.

The basic unit of government would be small enough to be governed by all its adult members. Therefore, the basic units should contain no more than about 100 adults, for example, a cityblock or small village. Such a unit would have the ability to do whatever it wants, providing this has no effect on any other unit. Anything that can affect another unit would have to be approved by a higher-level coordinating unit, the lowest one reporting to all the units affected.

Each basic unit would elect a leader from among its members. The leaders of about ten contiguous basic units would form the next more aggregated unit of government. These once-removed units are accountable and responsible to their constituent basic units. Leaders of the once-removed units in turn form twice-removed units, which are responsible to their constituent once-removed units. This process continues until a national unit is formed.

The leaders of every derivative unit are expected to participate in meetings of its constituent units. Therefore, all leaders of derivative units, except the leader of the all-encompassing unit, participate in the unit at the next level of aggregation. Then all unit leaders except those of the basic and once-removed units would interact directly with five levels: two more removed, two less removed, and their own. Such interaction would facilitate horizontal coordination and vertical integration of the actions of different units.

Using about 100 adults per basic unit and 10 as a factor of aggregation, the number of people represented in units at each level of aggregation might be as follows:

Unit Degree of Removal	Adult Population Represented
1	100
2	1,000
3	10,000
4	100,000
5	1,000,000
6	10,000,000
7	100,000,000
8	1,000,000,000

These numbers are not fixed. Several considerations would affect the actual number and size of units.

Finally, it is important to note that there is no more effective way of converting a subversive minority into a majority than by oppressing the majority and taking punitive measures against the minority. If a government converts its insecurity into win-win cooperation with the governed, it can gain the support of the majority and contain any threat of insurrection by a minority.

In general, the amount of security one can obtain in a win-lose conflict situation is never as great as it is in one that is win-win cooperative. This is also apparent, for example, when one considers the continual insecurity of both management and labor in situations in which collective bargaining is used to divide power among them. In such situations the focus is on "power over." In the type of cooperative interactions that occur between management and labor where there is participative democracy, power is shared. Here the focus is on power to, not power over. A win-lose negotiation that involves power over can reduce the power to of both parties. On the other hand, in win-win collaboration the power to of both parties is increased.

CONCLUSION

The world is currently witnessing a titanic struggle between two basically antagonistic types of political structure. These are what have been called "democratic capitalistic parliamentarianism" and "communistic bureaucratic statism." The most commonly used examples are the United States and the Soviet

Union. The political structures of these nations are so firmly set that only a major revolution could upset them. However, there is a large number of national, social, and cultural groupings in the Third World that seek an alternative political structure. Whereas the superpowers strive to maintain structure in tact and vary political functions in conformity with their structures, much of the Third World has rejected these two structures as being capable of carrying what are perceived as the necessary functions of political states. Therefore, their energy is directed at finding adequate new political forms. To date their success has been minimal.

Although in political life as elsewhere one should expect structure and function to be inseparable correlatives, it does appear that people instinctively feel that structure must precede function as a necessary prerequisite to settled political life. It is also true that people are much more willing to kill one another over structural matters than functional ones. This means that functional political changes are really the stuff of ordinary political life. It also means that development finds its best opportunities in functionalism rather than structuralism, despite planners' disposition to structural, rather than functional, changes.

We think it easier to change function within a fixed structure than to change structure within a fixed function. We find it most difficult to conceive of political systems in which both structure and function are subjected to political change. Yet this is precisely what is urgently needed. Experience has shown that there is no perfect political structure, no perfect form of government. Therefore, we must learn how to design structures that adapt and learn and, therefore, can modify themselves continually and peacefully without loss of identity.

Development planning, if it is to be effective, must treat both the political structure and functioning of society as variable. There is no way this can be done without involvement in the political process. Such involvement by planners may invoke political disapproval. If it does, then it is the first obstruction that development planners must face.

Let us see briefly what consequences this perspective entails for national development planning in a world experiencing massive political upheaval. Both capitalistic parliamentarianism and totalitarian bureaucratic statism are in such internal disarray that they fail dismally to act as models for either the multitude of newly emerging nations or older conservative regimes attempting to modernize. Nevertheless, the superpowers are perfectly willing to impose their own political structures on the heterogeneous mass of world's peoples, however incongruous the results.

The very idea of the political structure known as the "nation" is itself under attack. Internationalistic movements are being presented as remedies to the ills of the political structural form of the nation. But these movements are not structures at all. They are aggregations of functions attached to no basic political structure. Indeed, they disavow the need for structure and substitute vague, diffuse entities of freely associating political members possessing no political authority and assuming no political responsibility.

Ethnic groups aspiring to independent political status are at the opposite pole of utopian internationalism. These adopt or aspire to the developed political structures of the "advanced" nations, without the necessary material base or political experience to get them under way. The usual result is some form of indigenous or foreign-supported dictatorship.

This is the present state of the world's governments. It makes the prospects for development planning seem grim. One can hardly speak of political obstruction when political impossibility seems the more appropriate way to describe the situation. What then are the prospects for national development planning in this state of the world's affairs?

Strangely enough, all the political parties, superpowers, newly emerging nations, conservative theocracies, and ethnic pressure groups agree in proclaiming that their purpose is the development of their people. This is also the objective of the professional national development planner. Moreover, all political entities proclaim themselves as true champions of democratic ideals; that is, ideals of government, in Abraham Lincoln's phrase, of the people, by the people, and for the people, if not now, then in the foreseeable future. We must bear constantly in mind that all political ideals that once competed for supremacy have been swept away by the overriding determination of the world's people to govern themselves, if they only knew how. The end of government that they all accept is self-development, not development imposed from without, in whatever way the "outside" may be conceived.

It is because of this general conviction of the great mass of the people of the world that development must be and remain in their own hands, that the massive obstruction of current political chaos could turn into an equally massive opportunity. It is this political possibility, more than anything else, that makes our program for participative planning feasible. Were it not for the basic desire of people everywhere to change not only the functions of government but its very structure, our program for fully participative planning would be just another ideology; that is to say, an attempt to draw practical conclusions from the mere logic of a dominant idea.

13

On Getting Started

It is very difficult to start anything new in the social domain. In fact, it often seems impossible. The type of interactive development planning we have proposed is not an exception; to many it must appear to be "more than impossible." Recall, however, that we characterized planning as "the art of the impossible," of converting the apparently impossible not only into the possible, but into the actual. Therefore, interactive development planning can itself be brought about through planning. It cannot be expected to start spontaneously.

Parmenides, the ancient Greek philosopher, argued rationalistically (and convincingly, to many) that all change is an illusion. To respond with the assertion that experience refutes his doctrine is not to refute it but to formulate a paradox, one that arises out of a conflict between his reasoning and our experience. On the other hand, since things certainly appear to change, those who believe they don't are obliged to explain how such a universal illusion comes about.

The planner, perhaps better than most, knows the futility of looking for such things as absolutely "fresh starts," "clear breaks," and "virgin territories." Such imagined possibilities are available only to utopians. Plans, it seems, are designed to interrupt or intervene in a process that, quite contrary to the position taken by Parmenides, not only is capable of change, but is quite incapable of remaining unchanged. Therefore, the philosophic mentor of planners seems to be, not Parmenides, but Heraclitus.

Heraclitus argued that change is continuous, unavoidable, and pervasive. "One cannot step into the same river twice." Indeed, the river from which one withdraws one's foot is not the same as the one into which it was put. Nor is the person who puts his foot into the river the same as the one who withdraws it. Nothing stays the same.

Does the Heraclitean view of reality as continuous flux improve the planner's lot? If everything is already changing, what does it mean to change, then? How does one change change? Moreover, if one could do so, would not the effect of what one does also change, thus making the effort futile? Is not the function of planning to bring about an improvement that will persist?

The answers to these questions appear to lie in the fact that planners try to change the direction of change, not the fact of change. But if everything is constantly changing, the direction of change must be as well. Then how can one change a direction that is constantly changing and make it stick?

The horns of the Parmenidean-Heraclitean dilemma that appear to face planners can, we believe, be escaped with the assistance of aesthetics—a new perspective, a new resolve, or a new mood of either heroic determination to succeed in the pursuit of something desirable or utter abandonment of hope. When a mood changes we can agree with Parmenides that (as yet) there has been no objective change and with Heraclitus that "everything" has changed. Objectively, nothing has changed; subjectively, everything has. An objective change clearly can produce a subjective change, and one that is subjective can produce one that is objective. If the latter were not the case, planning would be futile.

If we now say that a planner is a change agent, or better still a change artist, we reveal an aspect of his role that is too easily forgotten in this age that thinks of all important change as either technological, economic, or political. By saying that planners are change artists we intend to direct attention to a type of power that is neither technological, economic, nor political—not even religious, though it is closer to this. This type of power is aesthetic. If a planner can help people see that by changing their mood—the way they feel about and see things—they can change "everything," then a true start can be made despite Parmenides' philosophic assurance that change is impossible and starting is meaningless and Heraclitus' assurance that change cannot be stopped. Such a start can be made not by stopping change but by stopping its meaninglessness. In the words of James Joyce in *Finnegans Wake*, nothing has changed, "only is order othered." To "other order" is to redesign it.

Every design is a redesign because most of what a planner deals with are human artifacts, all of which have been designed, however unconsciously. The prefix "re" fortunately has a double meaning: It means "back" as in return, retreat, and resign, but also "again" as in rearrange, redo, and redesign.

We can now see the sense in which even a reactive planner can be said to be a redesigner: He tries to redesign the present to make it conform to his image of the past. Thus, he attempts to deny change, to redesign a Heraclitean world into one that is Parmenidean.

The inactive antiplanner does not believe he is redesigning anything, but he is. He is trying to redesign a Heraclitean world into one that is Parmenidean, but he differs from the reactivist with regard to the point of time at which he wants to stop change.

The preactive planner seems to us to be pure Heraclitean. He takes change to be continuous, unavoidable, and pervasive. His efforts are directed at redesigning the entity planned for so that it can benefit maximally from changes it cannot control.

The interactive planner tries to redesign both the system planned for and its environment, to stop some things and start others, to order change, and give it direction toward ideals. But mostly he tries to redesign those intended to be affected by a plan by involving them in planning and its implementation. Development is the implementation of a redesign of people into effective ideal seekers. It is in this sense that the interactive planner is a change artist.

The work of a change artist begins with bringing about a change in mood so that people see that what is desirable may indeed be possible. This start-up of planning is as much a part of it as is implementation.

The moods of people change frequently. Being based on emotions, they seem to exemplify Heraclitean change. But herein lies the planner's opportunity. He may not be able to create a mood but he can grasp the opportunity presented when a mood of apathy or despair changes and attempt to redirect that change toward a disposition to make things better, toward development. When a nation's or a community's mood begins to change, the planner can come forward with his offer to help people plan a future that is nearer to their hearts' desires. He must inspire them, not with the desire for a better future—for to desire at all is to desire a better future—but with a conviction that one is possible. He can do this if he is equipped with an inspiring concept of planning.

Is it really the planner's task to inspire? In the face of widespread popular turmoil perhaps it is wise to admit that people currently need little stirring up. Witness the spontaneous arousal of the entire population of Iran that resulted in nothing but chaos. However, we are not saying that the planner's function is to inspire change, but to inspire the planning of change.

Conventional reactive and preactive planning and inactive antiplanning, because of repeated failures, have lost their ability to move people to a conviction that a better future is possible. They fail because, among other reasons, they put the future of a people in the hands of "others." It must be put into the hands of those whose future it is.

Unless a planner has authority he will have no more effect than the many well-wishers with ideas for the improvement of humanity. A planner must have authority, but not political power. If the source of a planner's authority is political and his aim is power, he is a politician, not a planner. In our view, the quest for power disqualifies anyone as a professional planner. The only power he should seek is for the people whose development is the objective of planning. A planner's authority should be grounded, like that of any professional, on professional criteria only.

A significant part of a planner's authority must rest upon professional expertise; it legitimizes his offer to help people plan, but this is not enough. Nor is it enough to be authenticated by being a part of an official governmental entity with manifest resources and assigned responsibility for planning. This, at best, makes it something in which people may place their trust and confidence, but they only do so if the enterprise gets under way with fair prospects of accomplishing something worthwhile. It must be evident that the enterprise is about to get under way because someone in authority has said that it will, and this announcement is believed. In addition, there must be a prevailing belief that it has good prospects for success, otherwise countervailing interests will quickly relegate it to the graveyard of forgotten political promises.

Skepticism, if not cynicism, with respect to planning is best overcome by satisfying two conditions: first, by enabling people to plan for themselves with the assistance of professional planners, not enabling others to plan for them; and second, by providing those planning for themselves with the authority and resources required to implement a significant portion of those parts of their plans that have no effect on others. These are conditions that we have designed into the interactive planning process.

The confluence of all the requirements for starting large-scale development planning is what we have called a crusade. We have also said that the startup of planning is as much a part of planning as is its implementation. Is it possible to plan a crusade? How can it be done? Are not crusades necessarily spontaneous? Can spontaneity be planned?

These relevant and difficult questions embody well-known dilemmas that obstruct national development. Dilemmas, however, are subjective in our minds— not objective in our environments. They are constraints not imposed by nature, but by ourselves on ourselves by the way we think.

Now let us consider how spontaneity can be planned. Aesthetics provides an answer by means of drama. Greek tragedy was the most meticulously planned art form imaginable. All of its formal and substantive requirements were known in detail by its spectators. Yet it consistently aroused spontaneous feelings of surprised pity and horror. According to Aristotle, such feelings, discharged by drama, became prelude to political action.

Therefore, we suggest that governmental planning be dramatized, that the business of government should be to create drama. Without it, obviously needed development programs either do not get under way or, if they do, have no significant effect. Drama involves the viewer emotionally as well as cognitively; it affects how he feels and what he thinks. It can change his point of view, his mood, his convictions about what is possible and what is not. The response to it is spontaneous and can be planned.

Can an unplanned crusade ever be successful? History shows that most of them end in disaster precisely because they were not planned. Once an "enemy" had been overcome, there was a lack of plans for successive steps. Anarchy or autocracy usually followed. Therefore, victory often turned out to be worse than defeat, as many Iranians now will confirm.

Successful social transformations are possible with serious planning that dramatizes the ordinary and makes it inspiring. Drama can create optimism, hope, and commitment. It can transform the dull repetitious course of human events into something exciting. Then and only then can the development planner become what he normally conceives himself to be: an expert on ways of bringing about changes of direction. Spontaneity can be converted into directed pursuit of ideals.

A political leader or a government, reinforced by good planners, can make all this happen. Together they can inspire and facilitate peoples' self-mobilization into development planning. They can provide the resources and assistance required to make it succeed.

In order to inspire others, those who govern must themselves be inspired. This is the planners' task.

Starting must start with planners.

Bibliography

Ackoff, Russell L. *Creating the Corporate Future*. New York: John Wiley & Sons, 1981.

———. *The Art of Problem Solving*. New York: John Wiley & Sons, 1978.

———. *Redesigning the Future*. New York: John Wiley & Sons, 1974.

Ackoff, Russell L., and Fred E. Emery. *On Purposeful Systems*. Chicago: Aldine Atherton Inc., 1972.

Ackoff, Russell L., Jamshid Gharajedaghi, and Elsa Vergara Finnel. *A Guide to Controlling Your Corporate Future*. New York: John Wiley & Sons, 1984.

Allport, G. W., and H. S. Odbert. "Trait-Names: A Psychological Study." Psychological Monographs, no. 211. Princeton, N.J. and Albany, N.Y.: Psychological Review, 1936.

Balakrishnan, T. R., and G. D. Camp. *Family Planning and Old Age Security in India*. Calcutta: India Institute of Management, 1965.

Beer, Stafford. *Brain of the Firm*, 2d ed. New York: John Wiley & Sons, 1982.

Berger, Peter M. *Pyramids of Sacrifice*. New York: Anchor Books, 1976.

Bergh, T., et. al. "Growth and Development: The Norwegian Experience, 1930–1980." *IFDA Dossier*, no. 19, September-December, 1980, pp. 43–57.

Berkeley, G. A. *The Works of George Berkeley*. Ed. G. Sampson. London: George Bell & Sons, 1897.

Boulding, Kenneth E. *Ecodynamics*. Beverly Hills, Calif.: Sage Publications, 1978.

———. *Kenneth Boulding: Collected Papers*. Ed. Larry Singell. Boulder: Colorado Associated University Press, 1975.

———. *Beyond Economics*. Ann Arbor: University of Michigan Press, 1970.

———. *The Image*. Ann Arbor: University of Michigan Press, 1956.

Brimelow, P. "What to Do About America's Schools." *Fortune*, September, 1983, pp. 60–67.

Churchman, C. West. *The Systems Approach and Its Enemies*. New York: Basic Books, 1979.

———. *The Design of Inquiring Systems*. New York: Basic Books, 1971.

———. *The Systems Approach*. New York: Delacorte Press, 1968.

————. "On Large Models of Systems." Internal Working Paper, no. 39. Space Science Laboratory. University of California, Berkeley, 1966.

Crowther, J. G., and R. Whiddington. *Science at War*. London: Her Majesty's Stationery Office, 1947.

Eldred, John C. "Labor Management Committee Improves the Quality of Working Life." *New Directions for Education and Work*, no. 3, 1978, pp. 81–87.

Elull, Jacques. *The Technological Society*. New York: Vintage Books, 1967.

Emery, M., and F. Emery. "Searching for New Directions in New Ways for New Times." In J. W. Sutherland, ed., *Management Handbook for Public Administrators*. New York: Van Nostrand, 1978.

Emshoff, J. R., and Ian I. Mitroff. "Improving the Effectiveness of Corporate Planning." *Business Horizons* (October 1977), pp. 49–60.

Finnie, William. "Toward a Systems Analysis of Racial Equality." Ph.D. dissertation in operations research. University of Pennsylvania, 1970.

Freire, Paulo. *Education for Critical Consciousness*. New York: Continuum, 1973.

————. *Pedagogy of the Oppressed*. New York: Continuum, 1970.

Friedmann, John. "Surviving in Rural Asia." *IFDA Dossier*, no. 9 (July 1979), pp. 9–15.

Friendenberg, Edgar Z. "How to Survive in Your Native Land." Book review in the *New York Times Book Review*, April 11, 1971, p. 19.

Gharajedaghi, Jamshid. *Towards a Systems Theory of Organization*. Seaside, Calif.: Intersystems Publications, 1985.

————. "Social Dynamics: Dichotomy or Dialectic." *Human Systems Management*, vol. 4 (1983).

Gordon, William. *Synectics*. New York: Harper and Row, 1962.

————. "On Being Explicit about the Creative Process." *Journal of Creative Behavior*, no. 6 (1972), pp. 295–300.

Gross, Lisa. "Bargained Birthright?" *Forbes* (June 6, 1983), pp. 46–50.

Henderson, Hazel. *Creating Alternative Futures: The End of Economics*. New York: Berkeley Windover Books, 1978.

Henry, Jules. *Culture against Man*. New York: Random House, 1963.

Iglesias, Enrique. "Broadening the Social Impact of Growth." *IFDA Dossier*, no. 10 (August 1979), pp. 1–13.

Illich, Ivan. *Tools for Conviviability*. New York: Harper & Row, 1973.

————. *Deschooling Society*. New York: Harrow Books, 1972.

Jamestown Labor-Management Committee, "Improving the Quality of Work Life." in *Jobs Through Economic Development*, Washington, D.C.: U.S. Department of Commerce, January 1979.

Jencks, Christopher. "Giving Parents Money for Schooling: Education Vouchers." *Phi Delta Kappan* (September 1970), pp. 49–52.

Kobayashi, S. *Creative Management*. New York: American Management Association, 1971.

Laing, Ronald. *The Politics of Experience*. New York: Ballantine Books, 1967.

Long, Frank. "Technology Planning in Third World Countries: Undue Economism." *IFDA Dossier*, no. 10 (August 1979), pp. 10–12.

Mason, Richard O. "A Dialectical Approach to Strategic Planning." *Management Science*, vol. 15, no. 8 (April 1969), pp. B403-B414.

McRobie, George. *Small Is Possible*. New York: Harper & Row, 1981.

Meadows, D. H. et al. *The Limits to Growth*. New York: Signet, 1972.

Mehta, Prayag. "Participation of Rural Poor in Rural Development." *IFDA Dossier*, no. 9 (July 1979), pp. 1–8.

Morehouse, Ward. "Technology and Equity in Black Holes." *IFDA Dossier*, no. 29 (May-June 1982), pp. 71–73.

Naisbitt, John. *Megatrends: Ten New Directions Transforming Our Lives*. New York: Warner Books, 1982.

Nicholson, Simon, and R. Lorenzo. "The Political Implications of Child Participation: Steps toward a Participatory Society." *IFDA Dossier*, no. 22 (March-April 1981), pp. 65–70.

Noller, R. B., and S. J. Parnes. "Applied Creativity: The Creative Studies Project. Part III—The Curriculum." *Journal of Creative Behavior*, vol. 6 (1972), pp. 275–294.

————. "Applied Creativity: The Creative Studies Project. Part IV—Personality Findings and Conclusions." *Journal of Creative Behavior*, vol. 7 (1973), pp. 15–36.

Noller, R. B., S. J. Parnes, and H. M. Biondi. *Creative Action Book*. New York: Scribner's, 1976.

Ortega y Gasset, Jose. *Mission of the University*. New York: Northon, 1966.

Osborn, A. F. *Applied Imagination*. New York: Scribner's, 1963.

Ozbekhan, Hasan. "The Future of Paris: A System Study in Strategic Urban Planning." *Philosophical Transactions of the Royal Society*, A287. London: Royal Society for Philosophy, 1977, pp. 523–544.

Parnes, S. J., and R. B. Noller. "Applied Creativity: The Creative Studies Project. Part I—The Development." *Journal of Creative Behavior*, vol. 6, (1972), pp. 11–22.

Paz, Octavio. *The Other Pyramid*. New York: Grove Press, 1972.

Pear, Robert. "Vouchers, Emerging as a Theme, Provoke Debate." *The New York Times* (February 8, 1983). p. A15.

Preiswerk, Roy. "Self-Reliance in Unexpected Places." *IFDA Dossier*, no. 30 (July-August 1982), pp. 3–15.

Reitman, W. R. *Cognition and Thought: On Information Processing Approach*. New York: John Wiley and Sons, 1964.

Sagasti, F., and R. L. Ackoff. "Possible and Likely Futures in Urban Transportation." *Socio-Economic Planning*, no. 5 (1971), pp. 413–428.

Savas, E. S. *Privatizing the Public Sector: How to Shrink Government*. Chatham, N.J.: Chatham House, 1982.

Schon, Donald. *Beyond the Stable State*. New York: Random House, 1971.

Silberman, Charles. *Crisis in Classrooms*. New York: Random House, 1970.

————. *On the Contented Life*. New York: Henry Holt, 1936.

Singer, Edgar A., Jr. *In Search of a Way of Life*. New York: Columbia University Press, 1948.

Snow, C. P. *The Two Cultures: A Second Look*. New York: Mentor Books, 1964.

Starrs, Cathy. "Development Alternatives—Some Examples." *IFDA Dossier*, no. 12 (October 1979), pp. 28–42.

Thurow, L. *The Zero-Sum Society: Distribution and the Possibilities for Economic Change*. New York: Penguin Books, 1981.

Velasco, Jesus-Agustin. *Impact of Mexican Oil Policy on Economic and Political Development*. Lexington, Mass.: Lexington Books, 1983.

Wald, George. "A Generation in Search of a Future." *The Boston Globe*, March 8, 1969, p. 27.

Ward, B. *The Lopsided World*. New York: Northon, 1968.

Ward, Barbara, and R. Dubos. *Only One Earth*. Middlesex, England: Pelican Books, 1972.

Williams, T. A. "The Search Conference in Active Adaptive Planning." *The Journal of Applied Behavioral Science*, no. 15 (1979), pp. 470–483.

Yongkang, Zhon. "Developing a Responsibility System in Industry." *China Reconstruction*, vol. 31, no. 9 (September 1982), pp. 20–26.

Index

About the Authors

JAMSHID GHARAJEDAGHI is President of Interact, The Institute for Interactive Management in Philadelphia and former Adjunct Professor of Social Systems Sciences and Director of the Busch Center, The Wharton School, University of Pennsylvania. *Toward a Systems Theory of Organization* and *A Guide for Controlling Your Corporation's Future* are two of his most recent books. He has published numerous articles in both English and Persian.

RUSSELL L. ACKOFF is Chairman of the Board of Interact and Emeritus Professor of Management Sciences at the Wharton School.